THE BATTLEFIELDS OF IMPHAL

In 1944, the British Fourteenth Army and the Japanese Fifteenth Army clashed around the town of Imphal, Manipur, in North East India, in what has since been described as one of the greatest battles of the Second World War. Over 200,000 soldiers from several nations fought in the hills and valley of Manipur on the India–Burma (Myanmar) frontier.

This book is the first systematic mapping of the main scenes of the fighting in the critical Battle of Imphal. It connects the present with the past and links what exists today in Manipur with what happened there in 1944. The events were transformative for this little-known place and connected it with the wider world in an unparalleled way. By drawing on oral testimonies, written accounts and archival material, this book revisits the old battlefields and tells the untold story of a place and people that were perhaps the most affected by the Second World War in India. The volume will be of great interest to scholars and researchers of military history, especially the Second World War, defence and strategic studies, area studies and North East India.

Hemant Singh Katoch is an independent scholar based in New Delhi. His research has focused on the Battles of Imphal and Kohima of 1944, and he has designed and conducted battlefield tours around them, the first of their kind in India. He conceived of the original idea to commemorate the 70th anniversary of the Battle of Imphal and helped organise a series of remembrance events in 2014. In the past he has worked for a Swiss foundation in Geneva, the United Nations in Timor-Leste, and the International Committee of the Red Cross in the Democratic Republic of Congo. He was an Honorary Visiting Fellow at the Centre for North East Studies and Policy Research at Jamia Millia Islamia in 2013 and is a donor member of the Indian National Trust for Art and Cultural Heritage.

THE BATTLEFIELDS OF IMPHAL

The Second World War and North East India

Hemant Singh Katoch

Routledge
Taylor & Francis Group

LONDON AND NEW YORK

First published 2016
by Routledge
2 Park Square, Milton Park, Abingdon, Oxon OX14 4RN

and by Routledge
711 Third Avenue, New York, NY 10017

Routledge is an imprint of the Taylor & Francis Group, an informa business

British Library Cataloguing in Publication Data
A catalogue record for this book is available from the British Library

Library of Congress Cataloging-in-Publication Data
A catalog record has been requested for this book

ISBN: 978-1-138-19334-5 (hbk)
ISBN: 978-1-315-63943-7 (ebk)

Typeset in Bembo
by Apex CoVantage, LLC

To my parents, Arjun and Dinky Katoch,
for always being there for me

CONTENTS

List of illustrations   viii
Foreword   x
Preface   xii
Acknowledgements   xv
Maps   xviii

Introduction: a truly forgotten tale   1

1   North East India: the canvas to the Second World War   4

2   Manipur: on the front lines   12

3   Imphal 1944: the Fourteenth and Fifteenth Armies clash   48

4   The battlefields: hub and spokes   57

5   Battlefield tourism: ideas for the future   157

Conclusion: the 'greatest' battle   167

Appendix   173
Bibliography   176
Index   179

ILLUSTRATIONS

Figures

4.1	Slim Cottage, Imphal	59
4.2	Imphal Indian Army War Cemetery	59
4.3	Imphal War Cemetery	60
4.4	Khurai Chingangbam Mandap in Imphal, the site of an aerial bombing on 20 April 1943	61
4.5	The Tiddim Road near Bishenpur	63
4.6	Red Hill (Point 2926) or Maibam Lotpaching	66
4.7	Japanese War Memorial, Maibam Lotpaching	67
4.8	India Peace Memorial	68
4.9	The Ningthoukhong turel	74
4.10	Site of the Torbung Roadblock, with Point 3404 in the background	78
4.11	Indian National Army (INA) Memorial Complex, Moirang	81
4.12	Looking on to Loktak Lake from the Silchar Track	87
4.13	Point 5846 or Laimaton	88
4.14	Looking south from Point 5846 towards Wooded Ridge/Mori, Wireless Hill/Antenna, Dome and the western hills	89
4.15	The Silchar Track near the old British position of Roadhead	91
4.16	Distant view of the old Palel Airfield from Kakching Garden	99
4.17	The Shenam Saddle and the Tamu–Palel Road. View from Recce Hill of Gibraltar/Hill 5185 and Malta/Yajima Hill	102
4.18	Scraggy/Ito Hill straight ahead and Nippon Hill/Maejima Hill on the right	105
4.19	Trenches on Recce Hill	113
4.20	The paddy fields that were once the Kangla Airfield along the Ukhrul Road	117

4.21 The battlefield of Kameng   119
4.22 Old Finch's Corner   121
4.23 Looking on to what was the main British defensive
position at Shangshak in March 1944   122
4.24 Shangshak War Memorial   126
4.25 View over the eastern side of Ukhrul town. The bare
peak in the distance is Point 7378   128
4.26 The sprawling Nungshigum/Hill 3833 in the distance   131
4.27 Runaway Hill   132
4.28 The Mapao-Molvom Range in the far distance   135
4.29 Imphal Main or Koirengei Airfield   142
4.30 Kanglatongbi War Memorial   147
4.31 The Imphal–Kohima Road between Kanglatongbi and
Saparmeina   148
4.32 The present-day site of the old Milestone 109 on the
Imphal–Kohima Road where the British 2nd Division
and 5th Indian Division met on 22 June 1944   148
4.33 Remains of old bridge on the Imphal–Kohima Road
near Kangpokpi   152

Maps

1 North East India   xviii
2 The Battle of Imphal   xix

FOREWORD

The battlefields around Imphal are surprisingly beautiful. The steep hills, gleaming paddy fields and bustling villages have recovered from the five months of death, devastation and heroism that played out upon them in 1944 when two powerful imperial forces clashed in Manipur.

In June 2014, during the 70th anniversary commemorations of the battle, I spent four extraordinary days with my friend Hemant Singh Katoch as he showed me round the six main 'spokes' of the Battle of Imphal. We walked across paddy fields, clambered up steep narrow hills and stared out at distant mountain ranges as Hemant recounted in intricate and moving detail how platoons and companies wrestled with one another in some of the most difficult fighting conditions ever experienced.

Growing up, I had heard accounts of this great battle from my grandfather, Bill Slim, who commanded the Fourteenth Army, from my father who often accompanied him as a young soldier and from many hundreds of British veterans of the Fourteenth Army whom I used to meet at annual commemorations in England. In my twenties, as an inevitable rite of passage, I read my grandfather's account of the campaign, *Defeat into Victory*, which gives honest and strategic insight into the campaign: British defeat in Burma in 1942, preparations for retaliation, the Battle of Imphal and the reconquest of Burma. None of these accounts would prepare me for the intimate experience of walking the ground itself where individual young men fought, died and survived for weeks on end.

Hemant Singh Katoch is the pioneer of battlefield tours around Imphal. Working painstakingly alone he has read, researched and walked miles of country to piece together historical chronology with current landscape in an exceptional endeavour to understand what happened where, when and to whom. Working with many others in Imphal and Manipur, Hemant has contributed to the great revival of historical interest in Manipur's experience of the Second World War. He shares the compassion that so many leading figures in Manipur's commemorative movement feel for the soldiers and airmen on both sides of this armed conflict.

This wonderful book is the culmination of all Hemant's efforts. It is, quite simply, the best battlefield guide that I have ever read. Hemant's sources are excellent and varied. His guide is full of vital detail delivered with simple clarity. The text deftly uses the words of soldiers, historians and battle logs to describe the hour-by-hour fighting of particular battles. Its pages conjure up the bravery of particular individuals in particular places and give a real sense of extreme battle conditions that were often hand-to-hand and face-to-face.

Hemant is an expert guide who tells you just enough so that you can imagine the rest for yourself. His analysis rightly gives equal treatment to the plans and experience of British Imperial Forces, Japanese Imperial Forces and the small Indian National Army of Netaji Subhash Chandra Bose which fought alongside the Japanese. Hemant also has a gifted sense of the topography that was so central in this battle and is still so essential to understand the battle's many twists and turns. Hemant also gives important space to the civilian experience of war. This is rare and valuable in a battlefield guide.

This book is a unique, intricate and moving guide to the terrible fighting that took place around Imphal in 1944. Guided so expertly and compassionately by Hemant, we re-enter the battle space to feel it a little for ourselves, to understand its logic and to empathise with the individuals who fought so heroically on both sides. This book is the perfect book to take with you as you walk around the battle sites. It is also very powerful as an intimate history of the battle if one is reading thousands of miles away from the hills and fields of Manipur.

In a very timely and important way, this book is a powerful tribute to the many soldiers – Indian, Gurkha, Japanese and British – who took part in the gruesome struggles described so well in the pages that follow. It speaks to their memory and means that they are not forgotten but remembered anew in the landscape on which they fought.

This book is also a great tribute to Hemant Katoch himself. It is a testament to all the work he has done and all the facts he has uncovered. His guide will be a valuable companion to thousands of people – Indian, Gurkha, British, Japanese, American, Canadian, African, Chinese, Australian and New Zealanders – who want to understand what happened years ago to members of their family and to thousands of other people who found themselves in Manipur in 1944 fighting for Imphal.

Dr Hugo Slim
Senior Research Fellow
Oxford Institute for Ethics, Law and Armed Conflict
Department of Politics and International Relations,
University of Oxford
(Grandson of Field Marshal Viscount Slim)
August 2015

PREFACE

I must admit that I knew little about the Battle of Imphal until 2009. Visiting Manipur for the first time that February for a friend's wedding, I was quite taken in by this stunningly beautiful place tucked away in a corner of India. Until then I had only been aware of Manipur and Imphal, its capital city, because of two friends from high school who came from there and, like many Indians, from news coverage of its insurgency. After my first visit, I became more curious about the place and started to read up on it. It was then that I stumbled upon information about a great battle that had taken place around Imphal during the Second World War.

The initial references to the Battle of Imphal and Manipur's Second World War experience came in passing and were a bit vague. It was because I was looking in the wrong place. Any texts on Manipur and North East India perhaps naturally focus on the politics, insurgencies and peace accords since Indian independence; the Second World War is always mentioned in the background section, if at all, as part of the lead up to the outbreak of fighting in the region after 1947. It was when I directed my attention more explicitly to books on the Burma Campaign that the Battle of Imphal of 1944 came into much sharper focus. I was amazed at what I came across. In descriptions of the battle, together with the one at Kohima, the words 'dramatic' and 'greatest' showed up regularly. The more I read about it, the more I realised what a significant battle it had been. I was especially struck by how the Battle of Imphal's apparent importance as mentioned in those books contrasted with ignorance about it in India. The seeds of an idea were planted.

Those seeds took some time to germinate. I was working with a Swiss organisation in Geneva at the time. At the end of 2010, I was accepted for a year-long field assignment with the International Committee of the Red Cross (ICRC) which saw me move, a couple of months later, to the Democratic Republic of Congo. I was conscious that the 70th anniversary of the Battle of Imphal would be in 2014. I had been abroad for almost a decade and a half and longed to be back home in India. My fascination with Manipur and the Battle of Imphal had only grown since my first visit there. I therefore decided that after my stint with the ICRC, I would move to Manipur and work to promote the 70th anniversary of the Battle of Imphal. And that is precisely what I did. On my return from the Congo, I met with officials at the Indian National Trust for Art and Cultural Heritage (INTACH) in New Delhi, of which I was a donor member, and they agreed to informally associate me with the organisation for such an initiative. Later, the Centre for North East Studies and Policy Research at Jamia Millia Islamia in New Delhi also agreed to recognise me as an Honorary Visiting Fellow for a year.

I set off for Imphal on 1 May 2012, armed with nothing but a vague – yet determined – idea to promote the Battle of Imphal and its 70th anniversary in 2014. Over the course of the next two years, I advocated the cause of marking the 70th anniversary, both in private and publicly. A logo was commissioned, a website on the Battle of Imphal launched, a first brochure on the battle developed, and a new battlefield map produced.

My efforts got a major boost with the unexpected naming of the combined battle at Imphal and Kohima as 'Britain's Greatest Battle' by United Kingdom's National Army Museum in April 2013. Almost overnight, the idea of marking 70 years since the Battle of Imphal got more traction – and takers. Two Manipur-based organisations, the Manipur Tourism Forum, of which I became a member for a year, and the Second World War Imphal Campaign Foundation, adopted the cause. The two, together with support from the government of Manipur, pulled off a very successful commemoration from March to June 2014. The commemorative events saw the participation of some veterans and their families and of diplomats from the countries who had fought in Manipur during the Second World War. This included Japan, the United Kingdom, the United States and Australia. These events were well covered in the national and international media, especially in Japan. The Battle of Imphal had now become more widely known than ever before.

What occupied me most during my time in Manipur, however, were its battlefields. I was eager to match the locations I was reading about in war accounts, where some truly intense fighting took place some 70 years ago, with what I was seeing around me. After designing an illustrative map of the Battle of Imphal, I set out to find those very sites, with intriguing names in British military memoirs like 'Scraggy', 'Point 5846' and 'Red Hill'. I was also motivated by the firm belief that Manipur needed proper battlefield tours around the events of 1944. What had passed for tours until then were perfunctory visits to the two Second World War Cemeteries in Imphal impeccably maintained by the UK-based Commonwealth War

Graves Commission or the Japanese-constructed India Peace Memorial outside Imphal or the Indian National Army (INA) Museum in Moirang. While these venues were undoubtedly of immense value and would always be on the agenda of visitors to Manipur, I felt that tours were needed that wove into their narrative the Battle of Imphal and the many locations where it had been so intensely fought.

Over a two-year period I read as many accounts of the Battle of Imphal as I could and set about identifying the locations they mentioned. I designed eight Second World War battlefield tours across Manipur, the first of their kind in India, including four that covered different geographical areas (around Imphal, the Tiddim Road, the Shenam Saddle and the village of Shangshak), two that were thematic (on the INA and the actions in Manipur where the Victoria Cross was awarded) and two treks (to Nungshigum/Hill 3833 and Point 5846). From April 2013 to November 2014 I conducted over 80 battlefield tours around Manipur and Nagaland; the latter focused on the Battle of Kohima.

This book is a result of my efforts to map the battlefields around Imphal. I hope it encourages others to make their own journeys to Manipur. Indeed, as New Delhi eases access to North East India and neighbouring Burma (Myanmar) opens up, it is hoped that more and more people will be able to visit Imphal and appreciate for themselves the stories Manipur's striking landscapes tell about the Second World War.

ACKNOWLEDGEMENTS

The idea for such a book came from and was pushed by several: from Squadron Leader Rana T.S. Chhina (Retd.) at the Centre for Armed Forces Historical Research at the United Services Institute in New Delhi, who first mooted a guide to the Imphal battlefields in mid-2012; to Prof. Irene Salam at the History Department in Manipur University, who said a book must result from my research; to Harry Fecitt, who further encouraged the idea after taking my tours around Manipur in early 2013; to Gardiner Harris of the *New York Times* in mid-2014, who made the point that a book could potentially reach many more people over time than individual tours. Quite appropriately, it was left to Dr Hugo Slim, the grandson of none other than Field Marshal Viscount William J. Slim, who commanded the British Fourteenth Army to victory at Imphal and Kohima in 1944, to make the final case for this book after taking my tours. He said, *en gros*, that I should put on paper what I say while taking people on tour and that relating the present-day sites to the past would be the value added of such an endeavour. I have tried to do just that here. To all of these people, I extend my thanks.

In Manipur, I am very grateful to many, for far too many things: to Dr Dhabali Thangjam and the members of the Manipur Tourism Forum for allowing me to join them for a year, and for throwing their full might into organising the 70th anniversary of the Battle of Imphal in 2014. Without them, such a commemoration would never have been possible. I thank Robin Wahengbam, for converting my first, rough sketch of the Battle of Imphal map into a beautiful, digital image, and Harjeet Sinam and his entire team at Kok Sam Lai Solutions for their excellent subsequent work on the map, Battle of Imphal website and tour brochures; especially Bishwajeet Hemam, for his wonderful aesthetic sense and his endless patience.

I thank Maku and Chungsek, for making the mapping of the Shenam Saddle battlefields such a fun experience; Dr L. Surjit Singh and his team at the Manipur Mountaineering and Trekking Association, especially Thangboi and Boi, for repeatedly organising the Lamdan-Point 5846 trek for me; Zyrus and the entire Arthur family in New Delhi and Imphal, for their help and support in ways innumerable, but especially for showing me their stunning village, Shangshak; and Vunga Uncle and Shanti Aunty, for their assistance in Churachandpur and for just being their lovely selves.

I thank Yaiphaba Kangjam, for investing himself so fully into battlefield tourism, for helping with the interviews of survivors of the war and for carrying forward the baton of the Battle of Imphal Tours (www.battleofimphal.com); Bobo and his father, Uncle Newton, for enthusiastically driving my groups of battlefield tourists and me around Manipur and Nagaland for over two years; Babloo Loitongbam for always being ready to lend a patient ear; Pradip Phanjoubam, for making the exploration of Scraggy so thoroughly enjoyable; and Ranjit Moirangthem for the terrific photos.

I thank Somi Roy at Imasi: The M.K. Binodini Devi Foundation for letting me quote from M.K. Binodini Devi's brilliant essay; Chitra Ahanthem for showing me the temple at Khurai and Awon Luithui for introducing me to N. Luikham in Ukhrul. I am grateful to everyone in Manipur who recounted their stories of the war to Yaiphaba Kangjam and I; they keep alive precious memories of the war.

I thank Sachidanand Singh (Momo) and Naoba Thangjam, for all their help and for running such fantastic hotels in Imphal under the Classic brand; R.K. Imo and his family, especially Aunty, Bhabhi and my dear friend Momocha, for being like my own family in Manipur – and for feeding me for months at end; and Esha Roy, for her indispensable advice and support on all matters in Imphal.

In New Delhi, I would like to thank Mrs C.T. Misra and Nerupama Modwel for allowing me to associate myself with INTACH for my work in Manipur. The same goes for Prof. Sanjoy Hazarika at the Centre for North East Studies and Policy Research at Jamia Millia Islamia. Squadron Leader Rana T.S. Chhina (Retd.) was kind enough to allow me access to the United Services Institute library. Mr Narender Yadav of the Ministry of Defence, History Division, in RK Puram and his staff were extremely helpful in letting me spend hours poring through the war diaries at their archives.

In the United Kingdom, I would like to thank Robert Lyman for his support. From the time I had the idea to go to Manipur when I was still in Geneva to his suggestion to develop a proper map of the Battle of Imphal as a first objective to spreading the word about the tours and my work, Rob has been nothing but helpful throughout. Dr Preeti Singh's prodding on the book and guidance on publishing was invaluable. I am grateful to Prof. Kaushik Roy at Jadavpur University for his suggestions on improving the manuscript; it is vastly better for it, despite its present shortcomings. At Routledge, a vote of thanks to Aakash Chakrabarty for being so patient and understanding. Finally, I would like to thank my family for being supportive throughout and for letting me just do my thing - in particular, my uncle, Rajan Katoch, and brother, Charit, for their feedback on earlier drafts of the manuscript; my grandfather, Baba, who is sadly no more, but whose critical feedback on an earlier text helped shape this book; my father, for reading and re-reading the manuscript and for never letting up on the need for a book on the Battle of Imphal; and my mother, who is a wellspring of love and care, and makes all this possible.

MAPS

1 North East India

Source: Prepared by the author

Note: This map is for representation purposes. The international boundaries, denominations and other information shown here do not imply any judgement on Routledge or the author concerning the legal status of any territory or the endorsement or acceptance of such information. For present boundaries and other details, see Survey of India maps.

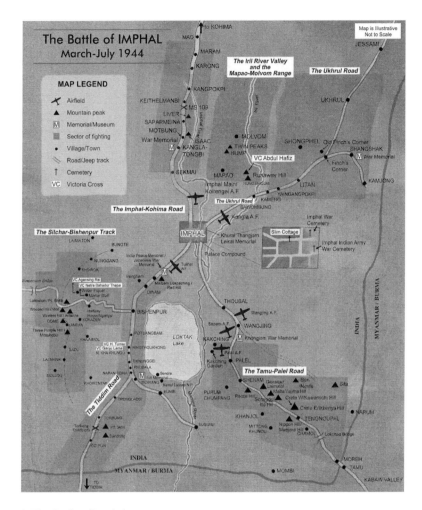

2 The Battle of Imphal

Source: Prepared by the author

Note: This is a historical map. The international boundaries, denominations and other information shown here do not imply any judgement on Routledge or the author concerning the legal status of any territory or the endorsement or acceptance of such information. For present boundaries and other details, see Survey of India maps.

INTRODUCTION

A truly forgotten tale

Manipur and Imphal are not names that the world at large is familiar with, nor ones that many fellow Indians can locate on a map. Perhaps this is understandable. Manipur is a small state with under three million people and one that is easily overlooked in a large, sub-continental nation whose population is now approaching 1.3 billion. It does not help either that Manipur is in North East India, on the country's eastern frontier with Burma (Myanmar), one that rarely gets the kind of sustained attention its western border with Pakistan enjoys.

For most Indians today, Manipur and Imphal are places usually associated with unrest and insurgency and, occasionally, sports and culture. Anyone outside India was, until very recently, unable to visit Manipur, thanks to the need for special permits from the Ministry of Home Affairs that were difficult to come by. Not that they were encouraged to either by Western governments which continue to have travel advisories against visiting Imphal and its environs. And so for Indians and foreign nationals alike, Manipur for the most part has slipped off the map. Ironically, among the limited few abroad – especially in the United Kingdom – who have heard of Imphal in the context of the Second World War, many think it is in Burma, and not India.

India and the Second World War. There is perhaps no other country in the world that is as ambivalent, at best, and uncaring, at worst, about its own role in the Second World War. This is remarkable, especially if one considers the oft-quoted fact that at the outset of the war in 1939, the Indian Army[1] consisted of some 200,000 men; by the time the war ended in 1945, that number had gone up to over two million. It was the largest volunteer army the world had ever seen. Indian soldiers fought alongside the Allies in many of the campaigns – Italy, North Africa, Burma, Malaya. For that matter, they also fought alongside the Japanese, as part of the Indian National Army (INA).

1

Not only did India send its sons, and in the case of the INA's Rani Jhansi Regiment, its daughters, to fight in the Second World War but, with the Battles of Imphal and Kohima of 1944, the war came home to India too. Yet none of this seems to resonate among the wider public or Indian officialdom. With the exception of the present-day Indian Army, which studies the different campaigns of the war or remembers particular battle honours, and a couple of recent books, India's role in the Second World War is still largely forgotten.

Of course, forgotten is also how the British Fourteenth Army and, at times, the Second World War's Burma Campaign are often described. This description was perhaps more apt for a time when the Fourteenth Army's exploits in Burma were not so well known nor appreciated. With the passage of time and the number of books being written about it, however, there may be lesser cause to do so. The exception is the Battle of Imphal of 1944. To the extent that the twin battles of Imphal and Kohima – considered the turning point of the Burma Campaign – have been written about, the lion's share of the attention has gone to the Battle of Kohima. Even there it is the dramatic Siege of Kohima, with its heroic defence by some 1,500 combatants against a force of some 15,000 Japanese for a fortnight, which emerges as the main focus of interest. Simultaneous events around Imphal in Manipur, some 85 miles (137 km) away, have rarely received the same kind of treatment. The last book solely focused on the overall Battle of Imphal was Geoffrey Evans and Antony Brett-James's *Imphal: A Flower on Lofty Heights*; it was first published over half a century ago in 1962.

This book seeks to address the three issues outlined earlier. It is about a time when the Second World War touched India in a very real way. For here was an instance when some of the bitterest fighting the world had ever seen took place on Indian soil. The war was no longer something whose progress in faraway lands was being followed in the daily papers; it now struck much closer home, and how. Furthermore, the Battle of Imphal was very much an Indian affair. It had Indian troops fighting on both sides: those that made up the majority of the Fourteenth Army for the British and those in INA units alongside the Japanese.

This book is also about that point during the Burma Campaign when, some say, however speculatively, the very future of India hung in the balance – the Battle of Imphal, a battle involving the British Fourteenth Army and the Japanese Fifteenth Army that is now seen as one of the greatest of the Second World War. Indeed, it was at Imphal (and Kohima) that the Japanese march across Asia and their invasion of India was finally halted. This saw not just their offensive into India repulsed but ultimately reversed, with the Allies subsequently driving the Japanese out of Burma. Imphal–Kohima was a disaster for the Japanese, who suffered their largest defeat on land ever. The numbers vary, but some estimate that around 30,000 Japanese soldiers died in 1944; British-Indian[2] casualties are put at 16,000, including dead and injured. It is the battlefields around Imphal and the people whose lives were upended by the Second World War, however, that lie at the heart of this book. And what makes this a unique volume. For the first time, a systematic effort has been made to revisit and map the main scenes of the fighting in Manipur related to the Battle of Imphal. The emphasis is on connecting the present with the past; linking what exists today in Manipur with what happened there in 1944. A surprising finding is that while some of the old battlefields have changed from what they once were, others remain remarkably untouched some 70 years on.

One would do well to remember that many of the places covered here were not just points on the map that were fought and strategised over by the British and the Japanese. They were the homes of the people of Manipur, who suddenly found themselves caught up in the Second World War. For this land and its people, the war years form an extraordinary chapter of their history. A chapter that connects this little-known place on the India–Burma frontier with the wider world like no other, and one that transformed it. For from early 1942, when the Japanese took over neighbouring Burma, to 1945, when the British reconquered that country, Manipur was at the front lines of the war. Drawing on oral and written accounts, this book then is an attempt to tell at least part of the Second World War story of Manipur. Without understanding what Manipur and its people went through from 1942 to 1945, India's own, broader, narrative of the Second World War will remain incomplete.

In terms of structure, the book starts by putting the Battle of Imphal in context by looking at events in North East India and the region that lead up to 1944. It then focuses on the Battle of Imphal and the Second World War from an oft-forgotten viewpoint: that of the people of Manipur. There is a brief *coup d'oeil* at the Fourteenth and Fifteenth Armies and the overall battle, before moving on to the second main focus: the battlefields around Manipur. These are the routes leading to Imphal on or around which the fighting took place, starting with the Tiddim Road heading south to the Imphal–Kohima Road heading north. Before concluding, the penultimate chapter considers ideas to promote battlefield tourism in Manipur and the region.

Notes

1 This refers generically to the Indian Army that was under the overall command of the British until Indian independence in 1947.

2 The term 'British-Indian' is used throughout the text to refer to the mix of units – British, Indian, Gurkha – that made up the British Fourteenth Army that fought at Imphal and Kohima in 1944.

1

NORTH EAST INDIA

The canvas to the Second World War

The retreat from Burma

After attacking Pearl Harbour in December 1941, the Japanese moved swiftly across South East Asia, capturing huge swathes of territory. European colonial territories in the region fell like dominoes, and the British were particularly badly hit. In the first quarter of 1942, Malaya fell and, to the shock and dismay of the Allies, so did 'Fortress' Singapore. Burma was next on the radar of the Japanese as it was from here – via the fabled Burma Road – that Allied supplies were being sent overland to Chiang Kai-shek's forces in China. The Japanese had been locked in war with the Chinese since 1937, and shutting down the Burma Road was high on their list of priorities in the region.

The British were routed in Burma in 1942. The colonial administration was utterly ill prepared for war, and senior civilian officials in Rangoon escaped the swiftly advancing Japanese by the skin of their teeth. The (British-led) Burma Army was chased, outflanked and attacked by its opponent along the length of the country. It retreated 900 miles (nearly 1,500 km) northwards over a period of four months, a withdrawal that only ended once it crossed the Chindwin River and entered Moreh in Manipur from Tamu. It was the longest retreat in British military history.

Humiliating as the retreat of the military may have been, it paled in comparison to the disaster that befell hundreds of thousands of Indians in Burma as they fled. Described as the largest mass migration in history until then, it is estimated that some 600,000 people fled from Burma to India in 1942.[1] The majority of these were labourers, coolies and dockyard workers who had migrated from India to work under British-ruled Burma over the decades. Their concentration in the labour force, coupled with the economic dominance of Indian merchants and traders in the country, had caused deep resentment among the Burmese. This resentment had boiled over into anti-Indian riots in the 1930s, and so the

Indians were especially fearful of what might happen to them once the British rulers left. They voted with their feet in 1942. The exodus was an unmitigated disaster, and tens of thousands are said to have lost their lives in the desperate and chaotic scramble to reach India. Once the sea routes were cut off, Manipur and Assam were the main entry points into India over land for many of those fleeing Burma.

Fortunately for the British, the Japanese stopped their advance east of the Chindwin River in mid-1942. Nothing would have been able to stop them if they had pressed into India at the time. Mirroring their counterparts in Burma, the British in India were also woefully unprepared to resist a Japanese offensive. To the extent that an Axis power was ever even expected to attack New Delhi, the assumed route – by Germany, for example – was one that every other invader of India had taken since time immemorial: from the north-west, via Afghanistan. No one had really thought it could be the Japanese who would approach India from the east and that too at such speed.

But the Japanese did not press on beyond the Chindwin River in mid-1942. They had already overreached and had enough newly acquired territory to consolidate their hold over. They had succeeded in their main objective in Burma: to cut off the Burma Road as a supply route into China. They also had more to worry about in the Pacific with the Americans and their navy than to bother with the British who had hastily retreated into India. More practically, the monsoon rains had set in, which made the mountainous border between India and Burma, treacherous and difficult terrain at the best of times, a seemingly insurmountable barrier to cross.

This last point is significant. Through 1942 and the first half of 1943, the view that the high, jungle-clad hills[2] on the border would not allow a large-scale movement of forces across into India prevailed among the Japanese. This would come to be looked at afresh only later in 1943 after the British, under Orde Wingate, mounted the first Chindit expedition. Until then, however, the two sides settled in and began to consider their next moves, the Japanese in Burma and the British and the Americans across the border in what has since come to be known as North East India.

The North East in focus

North East India today consists of seven states: Arunachal Pradesh, Assam, Manipur, Meghalaya, Mizoram, Nagaland and Tripura. More recently, Sikkim has also begun to be counted as part of the region. During the Second World War, there was only the composite province of Assam, whose hilly parts had not yet been sliced off to form different entities, and the princely states of Tripura and Manipur. To the extent that there was any

NORTH EAST INDIA

infrastructure in the region at all, it was geared to support the main British economic interests, such as tea and oil.

Good roads were few and far between. To get from Delhi or Calcutta
to the region, there was a single, rickety railway line; there was no railway
bridge over the Brahmaputra River, so passengers and cargo had to cross
the river by ferry. The railway line resumed on the eastern bank of the
river, and its main branch passed via Dimapur – also known as 'Manipur
Road' as it was the railway head for Manipur – at the base of the Naga
Hills and continued on to the tea gardens around Dibrugarh and the coal
mines of Ledo in the far east of Assam.

This infrastructure, or its lack thereof, was to come under severe strain –
and into sharp focus – once the Japanese arrived in Burma in 1942, and
the Allies began to plot their return to that country soon thereafter. It
became clear to the Allies that this region was crucial to any push back
against the Japanese next door. It was also likely to be the route of a
future Japanese attack on India. Dealing with either required a dramatic
improvement in the North East's infrastructure.

Some would say that the Americans and the British probably did not
agree on much else about the way forward. For the Americans, their main
aim for Burma was to restore the supply line to Chiang Kai-shek's forces in
China, lost by the cutting off of the Burma Road. In the immediate future,
they felt that this could be done by constructing a network of airfields
around Dibrugarh in eastern Assam from where supplies could be flown
over the Himalayas to Kunming in China's Yunnan province. This became
known as the 'Hump' route (with the Himalayas being the 'Hump') and
involved some of the most dangerous flying conditions in the world.

The Americans also started work on a land-based option. This was
what later became famous as the Stilwell Road (or Ledo Road), named
after the top American commander in the region they called China–
Burma–India. General Stilwell believed that a road could be carved
through the extreme terrain of northern Burma to connect up with a
part of the old Burma Road. Stilwell and the Americans believed that all
Allied resources, including any military moves on the ground into Burma,
should be devoted to further this objective in the north. Washington was
not particularly interested in retaking Rangoon or, for that matter, helping the British regain control of any of their lost colonial possessions in
South East Asia.

For the British, northern Burma was not the primary concern. Rather,
it was more about how Rangoon could be retaken, by attacking over land
or via amphibious assault. Support for and the prospects of an overland
invasion of Burma dipped ever lower as time went on. The cause was not
helped by the failure by March 1943 of a British offensive launched at
the end of the previous year in Burma's western coastal belt known as

the Arakan (today called Rakhine State). British prime minister Winston Churchill, to the extent that he saw it useful to recover Burma at all (he would much rather go for Singapore and beyond), favoured an amphibious route, but this was not feasible due to the lack of sufficient numbers of landing craft.

Whatever may have been Allied differences on how best to tackle the Japanese in Burma, they recognised the strategic importance of North East India to this theatre of war. Any push back into Burma – or Japanese attack on India – would come this way. This was therefore a period of great transformation for the region. Indeed, the Second World War (from 1942 to 1945) gave the region the greatest burst of infrastructure activity in such a short period it has ever seen. Airfields were built, roads were constructed or upgraded and the capacity of the sole railway supply route expanded. The infrastructure built or improved upon in the North East during the Second World War continues to hold the region in good stead to this day. Airports are the best example: whether it is Dimapur or Mohanbari in Dibrugarh or Kumbhirgram in Silchar or Tulihal in Imphal, most of the present-day airports in North East India were constructed between 1942 and 1944. On their part, as 1943 progressed, the Japanese would soon start to pay particular attention to Imphal, the capital of Manipur.

Manipur

During the Second World War, Manipur was one of only two princely states in the North East. The other was what is today known as Tripura, for which Agartala is the capital. They were both ruled by Maharajas but were under British sovereignty. To Manipur's east and south-east lay Burma; on all other sides it was surrounded by what was then Assam. This included the Naga Hills to the north, which is today the state of Nagaland, with Kohima as its capital. To the south-west were the Lushai Hills, which is now Mizoram, with Aizawl as its capital. The town of Silchar lay beyond the high hills to the west of Imphal.

Manipur is spread out over an area of around 22,000 square kilometres in the eastern corner of India. At the heart of Manipur is a small, oval-shaped valley – the Imphal Valley – which makes up some ten percent of its area. The Imphal Valley is at an altitude of some 2,600 feet above sea level (approximately 790 metres). The city of Imphal is at its northern end, while the Loktak Lake takes up a large part of its southern half. Hills cover the rest of the state. The majority ethnic group in Manipur is the Meiteis, who are predominantly Hindu; some Meiteis are also followers of Sanamahism, the indigenous religion that predates Hinduism. The rest of the population consists mainly of Christian tribes, of which the Nagas and Kukis are the largest, as well as Muslims.

The fertile Imphal Valley has always been the most densely populated part of Manipur. A majority of the state's population lives there, including almost all of the Meiteis. The Nagas and Kukis, for the most part, live in the surrounding hills. Compared to the rest of India, Manipur and Imphal have always been thinly peopled. In 1941, the population of the state stood at just over 512,000 people.[3] Of this, some 343,000 lived in the Imphal Valley, while over 168,000 lived in the hills.[4] The population of Imphal was around 110,000. Following the tumultuous events of 1942, it was to Imphal that thousands of soldiers in the form of the Indian Army's 4 Corps were despatched in 1943 to prepare for an eventual return to Burma. The choice of Imphal and Manipur boiled down to geography. As then General Slim clearly explained:

> The Imphal plain, some forty by twenty miles in extent, is the only considerable oasis of flat ground in the great sweep of mountains between India and Burma. It lies roughly equidistant from the Brahmaputra Valley and the plains of Central Burma, a natural halfway house and staging place for any great military movement in either direction between India and Burma.[5]

Operation Longcloth: the Chindits

Importantly, it was from Imphal that the British major general Orde Wingate launched his first Chindit expedition, Operation Longcloth, in February 1943. The town served as the expedition's base and as Wingate's headquarters at the time. The expedition involved sending some 3,000 men in long-range penetration groups deep into Japanese-held Burma, with the objective of disrupting their communication and supply lines. The efficacy and military impact of the Chindits and their two expeditions (the second was in 1944) are the subject of much controversy and bitterness to this day. There are two things that most military historians agree on about the consequences of Operation Longcloth, however. One was that its publicity as a success undeniably and crucially raised British morale in a theatre of war that had seen nothing but defeat until then, most recently with the first Arakan operation.

Second, and what was entirely unforeseen, was its impact on Japanese thinking on the feasibility of attacking India from Burma in strength. Or to put it more bluntly, Operation Longcloth helped precipitate the great battles of Imphal and Kohima of 1944. It did so by influencing the thought process of the Japanese general Mutaguchi Renya in Burma who, until then, had believed the terrain of the India–Burma frontier to not be conducive to the launch of large-scale military offensives. The sheer audacity of Operation Longcloth and the fact that it could be carried out by several thousand men convinced Mutaguchi that the same could very well be done by the Japanese and, in his view, with much greater success. Once of the opinion that this was possible, the ambitious and powerful general went about systematically persuading his superiors of the merits of such an offensive.

Mutaguchi's arguments were helped by an apprehension among the Japanese that Operation Longcloth could soon be followed up by a broader Allied offensive into central Burma along the same route. This had to be prevented, if possible. His views also chimed well with those being put forth by Subhash Chandra Bose. The man who is known to most Indians today by the honorific 'Netaji' arrived in Asia from Germany in early May 1943. Within a few months, he had taken over the reins of the Indian National Army (INA) that had been originally formed from thousands of Indian prisoners of war of the Indian Army captured by the Japanese in 1942. As the Japanese military leadership considered an offensive into India, Bose offered the INA's support and active participation in such a move. He argued that the INA, made up of Indians of all faiths and with its aim of militarily liberating the homeland from British rule, would be welcomed by ordinary Indians on its 'March to Delhi', once it had broken through across the border into India from Burma, that is. He thus strove – and succeeded – to have his INA men be involved as an independent military unit in any Japanese operation into India. Mutaguchi's persistence also paid off, and Tokyo gave the approval for a strike on India, centred on capturing Imphal.

The Japanese Imperial General Headquarters (IGHQ) issued Army Directive No. 1776 on 7 January 1944, which stated:

> In order to defend Burma the Commander-in-Chief, Southern Army, may occupy and secure the vital areas of north-eastern India, in the vicinity of Imphal, by defeating the enemy in that area at an opportune time.[6]

In line with the IGHQ directive, Southern Army issued the following order to Burma Area Army, under which came Mutaguchi's Fifteenth Army: 'To destroy the enemy at Imphal and establish strong defensive positions covering Kohima and Imphal before the coming of the rainy season.'[7]

These remarks by a Japanese soldier from the book *Forgotten Voices of Burma* capture well the logic behind the Imphal offensive at the time:

> Wingate's Chindit first expedition changed Japanese thinking. We thought that the north Burma jungles were a defence against

British advance into Burma. We now realised that they could be traversed by both sides.

We had no intention of advancing into India, just occupy Imphal and Kohima to further the defence of Burma. But Chandra Bose and Mutaguchi wanted to invade India after occupying Imphal. There was a serious anti-British movement in India, so it was hoped that the INA would operate in Bengal to assist the rising.[8]

The IGHQ directive, Southern Army directive and the preceding quote all highlight that the Japanese offensive in 1944 was conceived of and authorised as being for the defence of Burma. Indeed, the Japanese military leadership wanted the Fifteenth Army to carry out a pre-emptive strike on Imphal, thereby blocking the best route between India and Burma – via Manipur. 'Pre-emptive' is the operative word here as they saw the utility of such an action as essentially preventing an Allied invasion into central Burma down that route through the Imphal Valley. They saw the scope of their offensive into North East India, named U Go, as being limited to the capture of Imphal (and Kohima) and as the best way to defend their interests in Burma. On their part, by early 1944 the British were indeed looking to push into Burma from Imphal, but this was planned to be a limited offensive in support of the Americans' efforts in northern Burma.

It was Mutaguchi Renya, the commander of the Japanese Fifteenth Army, who had grander plans in mind, including aiming for Dimapur and the railway line to Ledo. But why only stop at Dimapur? With luck, he believed he could push on further into India with the INA who, in turn, proclaimed Delhi to be their ultimate objective. And so, unlike his superiors, Mutaguchi saw U Go's aim as being far beyond the mere capture of Imphal; indeed, at its loftiest and most aspirational best, it could be about shaking the very foundations of British rule in India. The stage was set at Imphal and Manipur for what has since become known as one of the greatest battles of the Second World War.

Notes

1 Christopher Bayly and Tim Harper, *Forgotten Armies*, London: Penguin, 2004, p. 167.
2 In line with its popular usage in Manipur, the word 'hills' is used to describe the mountains and hills in the state.
3 E. F. Lydall, *Administration Report for the Manipur State for the Year 1943–44*, Imphal: State Printing Press, 1945, Manipur State Archives, Imphal, p. 1.
4 Ibid.
5 William J. Slim, *Defeat into Victory*, London: Cassels, 1956, pp. 330–31.

6 *Burma Operations Record: 15th Army Operations in Imphal Area and Withdrawal to Northern Burma*, Headquarters, United States Army, Japan, Revised Edition, 1957, p. 78.

7 Ibid.

8 Julian Thompson, *Forgotten Voices of Burma*, London: Ebury Press, 2009, pp. 252–54.

2

MANIPUR

On the front lines

Ningthoukhong, Tengnoupal, Shangshak and Saparmeina. These then villages and their environs, along with many other places across Manipur, became the sites of fierce battles between the British-Indian and Japanese forces in 1944. For the top military commanders of the two sides, these were points on military maps over which they strategised; for their soldiers on the ground, these were battlefields where they sparred under the most trying conditions. But these were also the homes of the people of Manipur. Indeed, an oft-overlooked point in most military accounts and memoirs is the experience of the people of Manipur, both of the Battle of Imphal in particular and of the Second World War in general.

And yet Manipur and its capital Imphal lie at the heart of India's experience of the Second World War. One can arguably make the case that Manipur is the part of India that was most affected by the war. This is no coincidence. It all came down to geography. As an earlier quote by General Slim in Chapter 1 noted, any large force aiming to move between India and Burma needed to pass through the Imphal Valley. This was true in 1944, and it remains the case 70 years on – Imphal was then and is today the main gateway between India and Burma, between South and South East Asia. Indeed, whether in 1944 or in 2014, the best and most easily navigable route through the mountainous border between India and Burma remains the one through the Imphal Valley. It is why the Japanese threw the bulk of their forces at Imphal in 1944; it is why when India and South East Asia talk of a Trans-Asian Highway and Trans-Asian Railway connecting them today, all of the planned routes pass through Imphal.

Three of the roads leading to Imphal that became Second World War battlefields are also associated with another significant event in the history of Manipur: the Khongjom or Anglo-Manipuri War of 1891. In 1944, it was the Japanese who used these, including the Silchar–Bishenpur Track, the Imphal–Kohima Road and the Tamu–Palel Road, to try and reach Imphal. They had to do so because of geographical constraints – these were the only routes that allowed passage through the hills surrounding the Imphal Valley. In 1891, for the same reason, it was the British who used the said three routes to get to Imphal. Only this time, it was to battle the Manipur State forces.[1]

The British had become embroiled in a dispute related to succession to the Manipur throne. The issue eventually snowballed and five British officials were killed in Imphal in the last week of March 1891, following which war was declared on Manipur State. The British sent three columns of troops to attack Imphal – via the Silchar–Bishenpur Track, the Imphal–Kohima Road and the Tamu–Palel Road. Unlike the Japanese in 1944, however, the British succeeded in taking Imphal, after defeating the Manipur State forces in the last week of April 1891. This has become known as the Anglo-Manipuri War or the Khongjom War.

Khongjom is a village in the Imphal Valley on the south-eastern route out of Imphal towards Palel and Tamu. It was where the main battle between the British and Manipur State forces took place. Interestingly, it was for his actions during the Khongjom War at a village called Athokpam near the town of Thoubal that Lieutenant J.W. Grant of the 12th Madras Infantry was later awarded the Victoria Cross. The Victoria Cross is the highest British military award for bravery. Manipur came under British sovereignty after 1891; it was not annexed but recognised as a princely state.

The Second World War hits Manipur

Manipur became a quiet corner of the Raj under the British after 1891, with relatively few links to the outside world. The prospect of the Second World War ever affecting this part of India's eastern frontier seemed remote. It all changed in 1942 as the Japanese swept through South East Asia and captured Burma, practically reaching the doorstep of Manipur, on the other side of the Chindwin River. Manipur's location as a land gateway between India and Burma immediately came into sharp and urgent focus. Soon enough, Imphal began to feel the consequences of these dramatic developments in the Second World War.

The first was the arrival of desperate refugees in their tens of thousands from Burma. Some 190,000 refugees streamed into Imphal in the first half of 1942, and a large camp was set up for them around what later became Imphal Main or Koirengei Airfield. Many refugees were fed by the then maharaja Bodhachandra Singh and maharani Iswari Devi of Manipur.[1] Conditions at the camp were terrible: they overflowed and thousands of those who had come to Manipur after a long and arduous march out of Burma were diseased, exhausted and starved. Their ordeal was not yet over, however, as they sought to continue on to beyond the Brahmaputra River in Assam.[2] The railway station at Dimapur was a key destination for many, while some went via Bishenpur (also known as Bishnupur) towards Silchar. Many died as they marched on, while others perished where they waited due to epidemics.[3]

The other arrivals in Manipur from Burma at this time were the remnants of the Burma Army, which, as noted earlier, had just completed the longest retreat in British military history. Much to their resentment, they were afforded a less-than-warm welcome by their fellow soldiers in Imphal; reflective of the overall state of affairs on the eastern frontier at the time, no preparations had been made for their arrival. The American general 'Vinegar Joe' Stilwell also made his way from Burma into Imphal via Ukhrul around this time (May 1942), as did some 5,000 Chinese soldiers.[4]

Aerial bombing of Imphal

For the people of Manipur, apart from the distressing scenes of the refugee influx from Burma, by far the most significant event of that year was the first bombing of Imphal in May 1942. There were two Japanese air raids on Imphal that month, on 10 and 16 May. The first targeted the Assam Rifles area (present-day Kangla Fort), while the second hit the British Residency (present-day Raj Bhawan), the main Bazar area and the jail.[5]

After the first raid, the centre of Imphal emptied of its residents, who fled to the safety of the outlying villages. More important, 'The civil administration of the State ceased to function . . . the State departments, the doctors, the clerical staff and the menials all fled to safe distance.'[6] Civil police personnel also deserted their posts, and days of lawlessness and looting followed in Imphal; the situation was finally restored and the police force reconstituted by the end of the month. By the end of July 1942, the situation was almost back to normal.

As the official Administration Report for that period noted, the Manipuris could hardly be blamed for reacting this way, to what was the first-ever bombing of their town:

> This debacle was due to a belief that the Japanese were coming; Imphal had no anti-aircraft defences and all that the civilian population had seen were Japanese planes, a retreating army and a rabble of refugees.[7]

From May 1942 to May 1944, there were 17 air raids on Imphal and the valley. A total of 170 civilians, excluding refugees, were killed, while

154 were wounded; some of the wounded later died.[8] The breakdown of incidents is as follows:

- 10 and 16 May 1942: 71 killed and around 80 wounded. At least 50 refugees were also killed, including in lorries on the road and in the European refugee camp.
- 20 and 21 April 1943: 90 killed and 49 wounded.
- 9 November 1943: 3 killed and 3 wounded.
- 16 and 17 March 1944: 1 killed and 16 wounded.
- 3, 10, 15, 17, 22 and 26 April 1944: 1 killed.
- 1, 6, 10 and 11 May 1944: 4 killed and 6 wounded.[9]

Besides the first Japanese air raids on Imphal in May 1942, the incident that lives on in popular memory of the Second World War in Manipur is the bombing of 20 April 1943. This was when a couple of hundred people who had gathered at a temple in Imphal for a religious feast were bombed from the air. Some 90 people were killed, the largest loss of civilian lives in a single incident in Manipur during the war.

There is today a local memorial at the same Khurai Chingangbam Mandap, where a ceremony is organised every year to remember the victims of the bombing of April 1943. There is also an oil painting that hangs at the same spot today; it is a reproduction by a Manipuri artist of an old photo showing British officials inspecting the site after the bombing.

Khuraijam Nimaicharan Singh was around nine years old at the time and his father had gone for that particular feast. He was to discover later that day that his father was badly wounded in that bombing; he died of his injuries in hospital later that night. Nimaicharan Singh has written a wonderfully personal book on his childhood memories of the Second World War in Manipur. The book, *The Second World War in Manipur and My Childhood*, is available in English and helps to at least partly fill a glaring absence of written works that deal with Manipur and its people's experience of the war years.

Imphal as a forward supply base

With the Japanese restricting themselves to east of the Chindwin River, the situation in Manipur became calmer as time went on. The main focus of the Allies was to develop Imphal as a forward supply base for the eventual push back into Burma. In February 1943, 4 Corps headquarters moved from Jorhat in Assam to Imphal. First thousands and then tens of thousands of Indian, Gurkha and British soldiers began pouring into Manipur. Their main task was to patrol the Chindwin River area (beyond the Tamu–Palel Road) and the Chin Hills (around Tiddim, at the end of the Tiddim Road).

As numbers of soldiers swelled in Manipur, accommodation had to be found for them. By late 1943, around 8,000 homesteads containing over 20,000 buildings had been requisitioned for the army in Imphal.[10] The Administration Report of the time notes blandly: 'The owners, including many state servants, had to "double up" with friends and relations in the surrounding countryside.'[11] The soldiers also had to be fed and a lot of food was procured locally as part of a 'Grow More Food' campaign. From October 1942 to September 1943, this included 78,014 maunds of vegetables, 317,744 maunds of firewood, 3,177,426 lbs of milk, 622,343 lbs of fish, 26,963 maunds of potatoes, 131,940 eggs, 10,991 maunds of fruit, 11,435 maunds of charcoal and 82,322 ducks and chickens.[12]

Construction and infrastructure activity in Manipur picked up dramatically in the latter half of 1942 and through 1943. The six airfields in the Imphal Valley that were to play a key part in the Battle of Imphal sprung up. Supply dumps and depots, hospitals and all the logistical infrastructure required to sustain a large military force in Manipur and prepare for its advance eastwards into Burma was created.

Roads were rehabilitated and constructed across the state. The tarmac road from Imphal–Kohima–Dimapur was upgraded from single track to double track; the road from Imphal to Palel was converted to tarmac, while the bridle path from Palel to Tamu and that towards Churachandpur were made into motorable, all-weather roads. Finally, other bridle paths such as that to Ukhrul, Tiddim and the Silchar–Bishenpur Track were made passable for jeeps.[13] Ironically, in 1944 these very same 'roads and jeep-tracks which had been laboriously prepared for a British advance south and east greatly facilitated the Japanese advance north and west'.[14]

All of these infrastructure works and economic activities created jobs and earning opportunities of all kinds for the people of Manipur. Local contractors, labourers, overseers and suppliers of local produce, among others, were all in much demand, and remunerated generously by the army. By mid-May 1942, most of the Marwari business families had left, only to return towards the end of the war.

Unprecedented amounts of money flowed into and circulated within Manipur. From about two lakh rupees a month, treasury transactions skyrocketed to between thirty and forty lakhs a month.[15] This had its downside, too, as inflation followed in the wake of so much money. The prices of food commodities rose, a situation further complicated by an acute shortage of local transport used to import goods into Manipur. The price of rice, the staple food of Manipur, was of particular concern. At the outset of the Second World War, it had been just over Rs 1 per maund; in

1940 it rose to Rs 2 per maund; in 1941 it was Rs 2.8 per maund; in early 1943 it was Rs 3 per maund; by the end of April 1942 it was up to Rs 7 per maund; and in August 1942 it rose to Rs 25 per maund.[16]

The heightened economic activities affected the Imphal Valley and the hill areas of Manipur. By late 1942, in the hill areas of Manipur alone, some 11,500 labourers were being employed daily for military projects.[17] The Administration Report of Manipur State for 1943–44 notes that although exact figures for that year for labour impressed in the hills were not available, they 'were far in excess of anything experienced in peace time'. It continued:

> Hill men worked not only as labourers on the Dimapur, Tamu and Tiddim roads and the Kharasom, Ukhrul, Sita, Mombi and Bishenpur-Jiribam Jeep-tracks but also as porters for parties of Assam Rifles, V Force and other military and air force formations operating in the Hills.[18]

Perhaps the best text to date on Manipur and the Second World War is a paper written by a historian from the state, Prof. N. Lokendra Singh, and brought out by the Manipur State Archives in 1993.[19] In it he delves into some detail on Manipur's experience of the war and the changes wrought by the latter. One of things he looks at is the work of the Manipur State War Fund Committee, which was set up in 1940 on the initiative of the then maharaja Churachand Singh in support of the Allied war effort. He notes that, in line with the Assam War Fund Committee, its main activities were to collect war funds, push for the sale of National Saving Certificates, propagate pro-Anglo-American propaganda among the civilian population and motivate locals for recruitment to the armed forces.[20]

As the war had yet to directly affect Manipur then, the committee was not active through 1940 and 1941. It was activated in mid-June 1942, this time on the initiative of the new maharaja Bodhachandra Singh, who had succeeded his father the previous year. Propaganda was again a key activity and, in line with the guidelines issued by the National War Front, its focus was 'on the defence of India and appealed to the people to face and defy every peril threatening India's honour and security'.[21]

As 1943 progressed, the propaganda work was stepped up, as was the sale of National Saving Certificates and the Grow More Food campaign. 'Tunisia Day' to mark the Allied victory in North Africa was celebrated in Manipur on 21 May 1943. Among other activities, meetings were held in which 'issues relating to the origin and the changing situation of the war were highlighted to impress upon the masses that the Anglo-American allies were on the verge of victory'.[22]

On 23 January 1944, on the initiative of E.F. Lydall, the president of the Manipur State Darbar, and under the chairmanship of the maharaja, a Manipur branch of the National War Front was inaugurated in Imphal. This continued and stepped up the work that had been initiated by the Manipur State War Fund Committee. As before, pro-Allied propaganda among the people of Manipur was a key area of activity.

Voices from Manipur on the Second World War

It would not be an exaggeration to say that everyone in Manipur has a Second World War story. Known in the local lingua franca as *Japan laan* or the Japanese war, the Second World War touched almost everyone, either directly or indirectly. This is understandable. Any place in the world would have been marked by the dramatic sequence of events from 1942 to 1945 – let alone a small one like Manipur, tucked away as it is on the India–Burma border, at a fair distance from any large population centre.

Fortunately, people who lived through the war years and can recall their experiences are still to be found in Manipur, although their numbers dwindle with each passing year. There are also some written testimonies by and about survivors of the 1942–45 period. Except for Nimaicharan Singh's book, these accounts are scattered and tucked away in different places and are not easy to find. What emerges from these oral and written accounts, however, is a fascinating picture of a society and people that suddenly found themselves at the front lines of the Second World War.

The following account gives a good feel of the situation in Manipur in the initial days of the war, and of the first bombing of Imphal on 10 May 1942. It is from an essay by the late M.K. Binodini Devi in Imphal on her own interview of the late Yengkhom Ongbi Hemabati. It was translated from Meiteilon (Manipuri) by Pradip Phanjoubam and is produced here with the permission of Imasi: The M.K. Binodini Devi Foundation, Imphal:

> We came to learn of the imminence of the war reaching Manipur months before it actually broke out. There were plenty of rumours, some plausible, others wild. One of them said if the Japanese took Singapore, they would arrive in Manipur before your day's laundries dried.
>
> Prophesies from the purans (Meitei ancient books of prophesies) began floating freely, with nobody actually knowing how they originated. The one that caught the people's paranoid imagination most was that the flight of 18 white egrets across the Manipur sky would signal the beginning of the war. When the phenomenon was sighted the advice was to flee and take

shelter at places with names beginning with the consonant 'K'. Everybody watched the skies day after day for the white birds with anxious expectation and apprehension. My son Jotin, the eldest of 11 siblings was 11 years old at the time.

The Allied troops began arriving into Manipur in endless convoys. Soldiers of different colours and built that we have never seen before, huge armoured military vehicles, tanks and antiaircraft battery began filling up our roads. It all made up for a very awesome and intimidating picture.

The war time administration then began bombarding the place with pamphlets, instructing the civil population of the dos and don'ts during the war. One of the many advices was to dig trenches to hide during bombing raids. Trainings were also imparted on these precautionary measures. Amidst the growing nervous tension, we continued to watch the skies for the 18 egrets in flight.

My husband was then posted at Thoubal. He left me and the children in the relative safety of Lilong but he became so busy those days that he was unable to visit us for extended periods. It was a time when refugees of Indian origin began pouring into Manipur from Burma. Many of them, especially women and children, were sick and on the verge of death from starvation and fatigue. He was busy attending them.

One day he showed up at our residence at Lilong briefly. He seemed depressed. He told us the story of a refugee then on his last leg, brought to him for treatment. The unfortunate man had been suffering from cholera for some time during the trek to India. My husband treated him but was too late to rescue the dying man. On his deathbed, the man presented my husband a tin box which he had lugged all the way from Burma and said it contained money, weeping that he was to die without seeing his family. My husband said he took the box and although the dead man had gifted it to him handed it over to the British wartime authorities, telling them to do what they thought was the needful.

My husband was honest to a fault and had no particular cravings for unearned money. His story however made us all grieve for the dead man.

(Did the white egrets appear? I interrupted impatiently at this point.)

Yes, yes! They did come flying. But they were not the birds that we were expecting. Instead, they were white airplanes. The first time they came they did not unleash their loads of fire and brimstone. As per instructions we ran and jumped into our trenches but the planes simply turned and flew away. The first day gave us a very wrong impression of the war. We could not figure out why the White men were so fussy about airplanes and the trench routine.

A few days later, on May 10, the airplanes returned and shocked us all out of our complacency, pouring on us bombs that exploded like unending thunder claps. Many said there were 18 of them. So perhaps the puran prophesy did come true.

It rained bombs continuously from then on for a long time. A lot of familiar landmarks were flattened. A refugee camp too took a load and many unfortunate souls were killed. The spectacle of terror was simply beyond words.[23]

As time went on, and before the Battle of Imphal in 1944, things stabilised somewhat in Manipur, and the men of 4 Corps settled in. Nimaicharan Singh notes that on the whole the interaction between the civilians and Allied soldiers was warm and cordial. He writes about the experience of life during the war years in his own village, Kanglasifai, which lay near the Kangla Airfield, off the Ukhrul Road:

> Despite occupation by Indian and Anglo-American armies in and around the places of the village, civilians and army men could lead a peaceful life without any such disturbances that might spoil in the social well-being. No doubt, certain small things happened between the army personnel and civilians at times, but they were all negligible types. Twice of thrice, there had been cases of theft and intrusion in civilian houses but those wrong doers were heard strictly punished under military law of those days.
>
> On the other hand, most villagers did not suffer for want of food materials like rice, dal, salt, sugar and oil etc. There was an abundant source of acquiring those things from the stocks of armymen without any such trouble on the part of most villagers. Facilities and advantages of this kind would have been prevailed everywhere in Manipur where there were army camps.[24]

Soibam Angangyaima Singh, from the Tulihal area off the Tiddim Road, is quoted in describing the many first experiences he had during the war, which also holds true for countless others across Manipur:

> Once when I was on my way to give hookah to my father who was ploughing our field at Sagollou, I saw something flying in

the sky. On that, my father said 'it is God, pray' and so I prayed. Later on, when I saw a plane landing for the first time at the area of the present day flying club [Tulihal Airport] I realized that it is not God but something operated by man. During the war I ate many tasty foods which I have never had in my life before, transported by aeroplane. The soldiers gave the food or we picked it up at the time of unloading from the plane. Some of the foods are – fish and meat packed in flat containers, bread, biscuit, butter, cream and coffee.[25]

Yendrenbam Bijoy had a similar experience:

I was the helper of an American pilot who was posted at the Phura Makhong hill top. I went in the morning and came back and went again in the evening. The pilot gave me new shirt, pants, boot, towel, blanket and soap. I ate whatever he ate. Some of the things which I saw for the first time were – big bread, biscuit, tin fish, butter and coffee. I felt healthy after eating those things. Being a dhoti and shawl wearing simple boy, I felt so happy in getting such new clothes and food.[26]

Kangjam Mera Singh is quoted as follows:

Before the War, people in the plains, carrying lengcoat basket (a big basket made of bamboo), used to go to Laimaton and Maram hill ranges to take cotton for making clothes. In return for the cotton they used to give back Meitei salt (locally-made salt) and a variety of pots. The tradition was to fill the baskets of both the parties. Making clothes out of the cotton brought in this way was a time-consuming process. After the proper construction of roads in the Japan Laan, imported yarn was abundantly available in Imphal. Later on, gradually people gave up the process of spinning and the use of cotton was reduced drastically. . . . Since the arrival of imported buttons after the war, making of buttons also stopped.[27]

To the extent possible, the normal rhythm of cultural life in the Imphal Valley continued during the war years. Nimaicharan Singh remembers that despite the hardships, 'the place or the form of cultural festivals and religious ceremonies relating to birth, death, new year and days of other religious importance were not totally lost from the Manipuri society (Hindus)'.[28] Elsewhere he writes, 'Festivals like *Yaoshang* (*Doljatra*), *Kaang*

(*Rathjatra*) and *Janmashthami* etc. had their normal observations carried out almost everywhere with religious norms and gaiety.[29]

Then came the Battle of Imphal. The Administration Report of Manipur State for 1943–44 has a revealing passage on how some Manipuris reacted to the rapid advance of the Japanese Army towards Imphal in 1944:

> The behaviour of the Manipuris in the face of these whirl-wind advances was in remarkable contrast to their behaviour in May 1942. Nobody ran away and except for the Ukhrul Sub-Division which had been overrun, all the departments of the State continued to function normally. During the second half of March the auction of State Fishery leases produced bids ten times those of peacetime, the bidders being quite undeterred by the presence of the Japanese some ten miles away.[30]

Others do not paint quite such a relaxed picture. The Battle of Imphal and the Second World War in general caused massive displacement of the people of Manipur. This included those whose houses had been requisitioned for Allied soldiers.

Nimaicharan Singh describes the situation:

> For every house, there were ditches dug out for their shelter to protect themselves from bombardment. When almost all the dwelling houses on the plains of Manipur were requisitioned for the British, Indian and American army men, and as were said earlier, majority of the people were then leaving their home-steads and took shelters in places where the war was not likely to reach. According to their conveniences, people from villages also come to somewhere in Imphal area and contrary to this, inhabitants of Imphal also went afar to distant villages as their shelter, vice versa. . . .
>
> . . . At certain places, many different families had to live together in a single homestead of their unknown brethren at distant villages. A number of wearied looking men, women and children following a bullock cart laden with their belongings and driven by an innocent looking elderly person were the common sights on the dusty roads of the plains of Manipur in those hectic days.[31]

According to Yengkhom Ongbi Hemabati, as told to M.K. Binodini Devi:

> What a tumultuous time it was! People having to vacate their homes and flee to rural areas, leaving behind much of their

belongings, letting loose their pets and cattle in the hope they would fend for themselves until the war got over and they could be reclaimed.[32]

In addition, villages in the main battle areas were evacuated, where possible, sometimes at very short notice. A case in point is the evacuation of all villages between Moirang and Bishenpur in mid-April 1944 when the main British-Indian defensive position on the Tiddim Road was shifted from the Torbung area to Bishenpur. Some 25,000 people were given just two days to move out.[33] Moreover, the British followed a policy of denial and all of the rice stocks left behind in those villages were burnt.

Ian Lyall Grant, a sapper who served with the 17th Indian Division at the time, describes this action:

> Most of the rice was stored in granaries raised several feet above the ground on timber piles. They were largely made of bamboo with thatched roofs and a match was all that was needed to destroy them and their contents. In addition many villagers had buried a store of rice in their gardens or more often under the mud floor of their houses. In these cases the rice had to be dug up and exposed, sprinkled with petrol and burnt. The timber-framed houses with mud-plastered bamboo walls and thatched roofs of course nearly always caught fire as well. Most of the villagers had departed but there were a few left and not surprisingly, though not obstructive, they couldn't be called enthusiastic helpers either.[34]

Pukhrambam Birachandra of Ningthoukhong recalls:

> It was on Cheiraoba day, the British came and announced that the war has reached Moirang. They ordered us to vacate our houses. 'Leave this place, your houses will be burnt down tomorrow' was what they said. We started digging pits to bury our things. Many people started moving towards Loktak and Thanga Chingjao but three families stayed back. On the next morning we moved out and fled. In the afternoon, the British arrived and burnt down the houses. One woman of one of the families which stayed back gave birth inside the trench. British big guns started firing. . . . They even used planes and drop bombs suspecting that the Japanese have arrived and are hiding inside the trenches. Then the families also fled. One child was left behind. He was nowhere to be found after the war.[35]

Of this action, N. Lokendra Singh informs that many of the affected villagers moved to the east of Loktak Lake, while some came to Imphal. He adds that since the area had been badly affected by fighting which lasted until July 1944, by the time the villagers returned it was too late to cultivate.[36] Agricultural activities were similarly disrupted on the Imphal–Kohima Road between Kangpokpi and Sekmai and in other areas where the fighting raged over long periods.

Pukhrambam Birachandra of Ningthoukhong continues:

> Four days after we fled, the Japanese arrived. They started digging trenches and positioned their weapons. The British secured their boundaries with barbed wire. At night time, there were many colourful bright lights fired up from both parties. Several tanks were destroyed in this area. We saw everything from Thanga Chingjao. One day when I was picking Heikak (water chestnut) at Loktak Lake, two big British planes came and three Japanese planes also suddenly came. The Japanese planes were actually six in numbers when they spread out and they started firing towards the British planes. The latter did not get time to turn back and they were encircled. One of the British planes caught fire and it went down in the lake. The Japanese plane again followed the other plane and fired on it. It also went down later. After some days of light fighting, the British fired their guns non-stop one day. Since the Japanese suffered badly in terms of diseases and casualties, they started retreating.
>
> We also faced problems of food. We didn't eat normal rice. It was half burnt rice with water chestnut. When we came back after the war, some men found two live bombs and they played with it. The bombs went off and two men died on the spot. Their bodies were torn into pieces.[37]

In some cases, such as in Shangshak off the Ukhrul Road, the sudden outbreak of fighting in 1944 made an orderly evacuation of civilians impossible. Shankazip Varu remembers the scenes at the time:

> There was chaos everywhere. The Indian soldiers, 'Maratha' as we called them, told us that they will be fighting here and asked us to leave. Our village playground was filled with vehicles. We could see from a distance that many soldiers had reached our village. Nothing was certain. Was the fighting going to take place today or tomorrow? What will we eat? Everybody was running on all sides, crying. The Indian soldiers also didn't tell us when the fighting will happen exactly. They just drove us out.

But when we reached the jungle at night we could see guns firing sending out bright lights from a distance. It was, in one way, great fun to watch the fireworks for young children like us. It was very colourful. But the elders were crying assuming their houses were burnt and their granaries and livestock gone. The Indian soldiers informed us that we won't be able to go back to our village for some time since they will be there and they are fighting with the Japanese Army. So, we took shelter in the ditches.[38]

N. Luikham recalls the arrival of the Japanese in Ukhrul:

I vividly remember that it was Sunday morning on the 20th March 1944, when we saw hundreds of vehicles of Allied forces in Ukhrul to transport the things left behind by the soldiers at the Ukhrul HQ. After a day or two, hordes of Japanese soldiers reached Ukhrul HQ without a fight, as Allied forces had left two days earlier. But before entering the Ukhrul HQ – one brave Japanese soldier came without a shirt holding a sword. But there was no enemy force to shoot him, except children and civilians looking at him with curiosity: 'only one soldier without gun'. He then sat down. Few minutes after, we saw many Japanese soldiers coming out from all sides. Occupation of Ukhrul was complete.

After occupation of Ukhrul HQ, the chief and his council members and all leaders met the Japanese commanders – who were very friendly and said that Japanese and Tangkhuls were brothers (of Mongoloid stock); not many days later the people were given many cows, free of cost for food by Japanese. . . . It was a great economic elation as people got to eat beef (by every house); we praised the Japanese as Allied forces never gave us things free of cost like that. We saw the generosity of the Japanese forces in the midst of the war devastation.[39]

As the Battle of Imphal wore on, however, the problem of supplies for the Japanese worsened. While at least some supplies could be brought up to the soldiers of the Japanese 33rd Division on the Tiddim Road, the Silchar–Bishenpur Track and Tamu–Palel Road, the Japanese 15th Division to the north and north-east of Imphal, who had travelled across the grain of the country over high hills, fared particularly badly. Unsurprisingly, the Japanese turned to the civilian population to meet their needs. According to one report, as the situation became more desperate in the hills the Japanese seized any available paddy and killed livestock; if they paid, it was said to be via Japanese Burma notes or forged Rs 10 British India notes.[40]

N. Lokendra Singh notes that the villages on the Japanese communication lines were the worst hit in this regard.[41] On coolies, he writes:

The treatment of the local coolies in the hills, although was fine in the beginning, became more torturous. Coolies were made to carry loads for long distances and occasionally they used to be tied up at night to prevent escaping.[42]

According to Prof. Lal Dena, as a result of dwindling supplies in the Churachandpur area:

The Japanese and INA personnel had to depend more and more on the ration and livestock of the local people. An eye-witness account maintains that all the male folk and young women in the occupied villages were engaged in pounding rice day and night to feed the soldiers. At other times, the male folk also served as coolies and porters carrying ration and ammunition to different camps. Zathuoi, who was a volunteer, also testified that he and his two friends one day carried a wounded Japanese soldier whose leg was completely torn asunder just below his knee, from the Saidan peak to the Saikawt camp. Deeply impressed by his forbearance, Zathuoi further stated that not even once did the soldier groan.[43]

And yet many others did not have an unpleasant experience dealing with the Japanese. Yengkhom Ongbi Hemabati recalls her time at Thanlon village, near Churachandpur:

Then one day news reached that the Japanese were in the vicinity and a fight was imminent. We were very scared, but my husband said he would go and see the Japanese who were camping a little distance away in the jungle. He said he had no enemies, the Japanese or the British.

We also saw the Japanese occasionally. They were very likeable. We made friends with the British but so what, we can equally be friends of the Japanese. It was not our war.

The Japanese soldiers went about in phanek (sarong) in the daytime and it was easy to mistake them for local tribal women. Once some of them in sign language indicated they were hungry. We boiled eggs and offered them on plantain leaves. They relished the meal.

The Japanese were not too many in number and it appeared that they were in hiding, looking for an escape route. Some would come and others would move away. It had seemed the war had intensified elsewhere in the state and the Japanese were not faring well. I felt sorry for them. My husband was right, neither the Japanese nor the British were our enemies. . . .

. . . The war concluded while we were in Thanlon. I was told the Japanese were thoroughly defeated and they had to flee Manipur. We were also told later that so many Japanese died everywhere in Manipur.[44]

A.S. Arthur gives an account of his village Shangshak:

The Japanese occupied the area for about four months. But they were kind people, they did not harm or torture anyone. During those days the Christians lived further down and there were only about six houses where the main village now is, where the haos (non-believers, non-Christians) lived. The Japanese occupied that entire area. Apart from those houses, the entire area was a jungle. In fact, the V Force informed the British soldiers about their location. That's when a fighter plane crashed in the area when they were trying to bomb the jungle. The pilot died, I don't know what happened of the other one. My father and some others buried the pilot in a trench because the Japanese would not bury him for several days.

There were two Japanese soldiers who were trying to flee. They came and took shelter in our hut. One had a knife with him. The other one was very sick and looked like he would die soon. We decided to hand them over to the British soldiers otherwise the sick soldier would have died. We knew the British, who had just recaptured Shangshak, would not kill them but treat them as prisoners of war. But that soldier, who could barely walk, left the hut and took shelter in the field. The other soldier was waiting in the hut for us to give him some rice. He asked for a matchbox and when he was trying to light it, my cousin reached for his knife, but the soldier jumped up, grabbed his knife and ran off.

We went to look for the other one, found him and first brought him back to the hut to feed him. My sister, who was feeding him, reached up to clean the rice from his chin, but it turned out to be maggots which had infested the lower portion of his face. We later took him to the British camp. We know they took care of him, but I don't know what became of him.

The only time the Japanese killed someone in the village was when a gentleman from Lungphu, his name was Yarteo, promised

to give them about forty coolies but did not keep his promise.
They shot him. Apart from that one incident, there was never
any trouble with the Japanese.[45]

L. Achung Kom from Upper Kom Keirap recalls his experience:

> I had studied up to Class VI at Chinga High School in Imphal.
> So I was able to speak a bit of English, Hindi and Bengali. One
> day, we got the news that the Japanese had arrived in our area
> and we were asked to leave our homes. That time I was very
> strong and brave. We sent off all the women, children and elders
> of the village to safer places while some of us stayed back. After
> sometime, we got the news that some Japanese soldiers have
> looted the things from a girl of our village. Since I was not
> afraid of anything in those days, I went to face the Japanese and
> help the girl. They could not understand what I said so I used
> signs to take back the things. One of them tried to hit me but
> I showed my anger and he backed off. That time, I didn't even
> believe that a small bullet of the gun can actually kill a strong
> man like me.
>
> Somehow, I succeeded in getting the things back and they
> went back. They reported the incident to their officer and he
> sent five soldiers the next day to pick me up. I went with them
> because I wanted to see what they do. I knew that they will not
> kill me. I thought they wanted to know something from me.
> They took me to their camp in the hills, deep in the jungle.
> There, I met a tall Japanese officer. He asked me (in Hindi),
> 'Master, do you speak Hindi?' and I said 'A little, Sir'. But there
> was always a problem in communication because neither of us
> was perfect in both Hindi and English. He asked me to stay with
> him.
>
> We stayed together, we moved around together. He appointed
> me as their cashier and handed me lots of Japanese currencies.
> I guided him to many places like Moirang, Khoirentak etc. I can
> still identify the place where we slept. He gave me a certificate
> for my services to be used after the war. But I lost it when my
> house caught fire. After the war, I got 5 Japanese rifles and 5 Brit-
> ish rifles and some pistols but the government collected from me
> later. After some months, the Japanese started retreating and I left
> the Japanese officers and soldiers and came back home.
>
> One day British soldiers arrested me along with four villag-
> ers for helping the Japanese. To them, I was the leader because

I was close to the Japanese and I knew Hindi and English. They tied our hands with telephone wire very tightly and kept us at Bishenpur. Luckily, one British officer passed by us and he started talking to me in Hindi and English. He asked me many things about the Japanese soldiers and their locations. I told him that there is a hospital and INA camp at Laimanai and army camp at Sadu. He gave us food and set us free.[46]

Ningthoukhongjam Moirangningthou, of Keibi village (next to Nungshigum) in the Iril River Valley, recalls:

In our area the Japanese came via Pukhao side and started climbing the hills. They occupied three strategic points on the hill. Once the British realized that the Japanese have arrived on the hill the big guns posted at Heingang hills started firing continuously for days. British soldiers tried hard to remove the Japanese from the hill top but the Japanese threw grenades upon them.... Then the big gun from Lamlai Umanglai started firing on the hill. Six planes from Kangla airfield came and dropped bombs on the Japanese positions. Three tanks – we called them 'Iron Elephants' – came and started climbing the hills and attacked the Japanese.

I saw all these scenes for some days sitting beside the main road with our elders. While the battle was going on here, one day, some policemen came and ordered us to vacate the village immediately. There was a *Shradha* ceremony going on but it was winded up in the middle. We climbed the hill just after the battle and saw, apart from the trenches, many body parts, weapons, canteens, stretchers, ammunition in big sacks and many other items. I got only a bottle of kerosene oil.

When we go to our fields after the battle in July we found many Japanese items and the small huts used by them. They have all fled by that time.... I didn't see any Japanese personally. I was close to meeting one who was hiding at my friend's place situated at another locality but my friend stopped me from meeting him as the soldier was already asleep after having dinner.[47]

M.K. Binodoni wrote about her own experience:

I too, even though I belong to the Manipur royalty, had harrowing experiences. We had to flee home along with my mother the queen and a good part of the war years were spent as refugees

29

in makeshift arrangements in somebody else's portico or some such places.

Apart from the booming guns and terrifying explosions, amidst the chaos and lawlessness, there were also numerous gangs roaming around looting people and homes. Insecurity was the name of the game for everybody those days, even at home. But Manipuris must distinguish themselves for the ability to make the best of the worst situation. Even amidst all the machine gun clatters and daily reports of deaths, fun and merrymaking did not stop. The lone cinema in Imphal still ran full house, *Ras Lilas* were performed on schedule, religious ceremonies never stopped.

One thing was conspicuous. Inflation was at a peak because of the soldiers who created an unprecedented market for commodities. Prices escalated and those pecuniary minded minted money.[48]

Asem Tomchou Singh of Maibam Chingmang (next to Red Hill) off the Tiddim Road gives his account:

In 1944, many people started telling each other that we are surrounded by Japanese on every side. Then, the war reached Moirang and Ningthoukhong. One day a plane dropped bombs at Oinam area. A man picked up a live bomb which fell down from the plane and hit it hard on the ground. The bomb went off and three people died on the spot.

No Japanese planes came this time. But their infantry reached areas like Keinou, Tingkai and Irengbam. One day during day time, some 5–6 Japanese came in disguise as local people with the traditional baskets filled with fruits and vegetables (Shams) and did a reconnaissance of the British area at Oinam bazar and they went back. At midnight, the Japanese came back and attacked the British position. Many British died. So the Japanese reached Maibam via Keinou and Oinam. The area was filled with Japanese after some time.

Once the British knew the Japanese have arrived, they started firing towards our village from different directions. We hid ourselves in the trenches. Some Japanese started dismantling the doors of the houses. We don't know the reason why. In the morning, we started preparing to flee from our village. When we start packing up our things, the Japanese stopped us and took the things and kept half for themselves of each of the items like rice, oil, molasses, etc.

Some British soldiers were there on top of Lotpaching [Red Hill/Point 2926] with the holes as their boundary. As soon as the Japanese reached the area they attacked them and killed some of them. They fixed up one big gun here just near my house. The British tank came and destroyed the gun. After the war, I collected some parts of that gun but now it is nowhere to be found. A British plane came and burn down some houses. The battle here was about one week.... Our village faced the wrath of the war, no tree and bamboo was left standing.[49]

Local support to the warring sides

Another oft-overlooked story is the response of the people of Manipur to the different sides. In the case of the Battle of Kohima, a fairly clear narrative has emerged of the locals throwing in their lot with the British. The answer to the question of who supported whom in Manipur is less black and white or straightforward. As in most aspects of life in Manipur, this question has seen some debate, and differences of opinion remain even today. What is clear, however, is that there were many in Manipur who played an active part in supporting one side or the other in 1944 in particular and the Second World War in general.

To start with, the maharajas of Manipur and their administration firmly supported the Allies through the war period. In September 1939, then maharaja, Churachand Singh, who remained on the throne until September 1941,

> ... placed the resources of his State at the King Emperor's disposal for the prosecution of the war, the Darbar, a year later, voting Rs. 85,000 from the State funds as a gift to His Majesty's Government towards the purchase of aircraft.[50]

His successor, Maharaja Bodhchandra Singh, continued to extend all possible assistance to the war effort, including – as noted earlier – through his leadership of first the Manipur State War Fund Committee and then the Manipur State National War Front.

In the book *The Merger of Manipur* by H. Bhuban Singh, there is an intriguing account about the interaction between Maharaja Bodhchandra Singh and the British during the Battle of Imphal. It is reproduced as follows:

> When Imphal was encircled, the military authorities suggested to Maharaja Bodhchandra Singh that the royal family be evacuated and take shelter at a safe place in India. They arranged an

aircraft for that purpose. But the Maharaja politely turned down the offer and preferred to stay with his people. The Maharaja said: 'I can't leave my people and the State at this hour of danger. I shall fight to the last.'[51]

It goes on to state that the maharaja had a secret verbal agreement with Lord Louis Mountbatten, the supreme commander of Allied Forces in South East Asia. The latter promised to do everything to defend Imphal during any Japanese offensive, while the former vowed not to abandon the city under any circumstances.[52] As events were later to show, both men upheld their respective ends of the bargain.

The then viceroy Lord Wavell thanked the maharaja for his support during the Battle of Imphal in a telegram in August 1944, part of which is quoted here:

> I send your Highness my cordial congratulations on expulsion of Japanese armies from Manipur soil. During the arduous campaign which has now ended so satisfactorily, my thoughts had been much with Your Highness and your subjects. I was particularly pleased that Your Highness refused to leave Imphal, even when the capital was under serious threat from enemy forces. As you are aware, the Central Government have arrangements to give your people ample assistance and I am sure that normal conditions would soon be restored in Manipur.[53]

The maharaja also received a message of thanks from the British King Emperor on 8 October 1945, after the surrender of Japan:

> In recognition of Your Highness's and your people's services towards Allied Victory, the tribute of Rs. 50,000/ (Fifty thousand) payable by Your Highness since 1891 is remitted in perpetuity forthwith – George R.I.[54]

The delighted Maharaja went on to declare October 8 as a State holiday and called it *Bodh Leisemba* (nation-building) Day.[55]

During the war, another form of local support for the British came in the form of V Force. This involved a few thousand men in the hills of Manipur – from among the Nagas and Kukis – gathering information about the Japanese and their movements in their respective areas. A local name associated with V Force that continues to be remembered in Manipur is that of Major Ralengnao (Bob) Khathing, who was a captain in the Indian Army at the time. After the Second World War, he became famous as the person who established Indian control over the area of Tawang in present-day Arunachal Pradesh on the Indo-China border in 1951.

A.S. Arthur comments:

> Major Bob Khathing had control over the entire hill area. He would send his soldiers beforehand to each village before he reached, instructing the villagers they had to meet him with information about Japanese movement. So that he would not be suspected of being a soldier, he used to travel with a basket on his back, and it had a spade in it. He'd pretend to be a villager.
>
> The sole responsibility of the V Force was to report on the movement of the Japanese soldiers. They stayed put in the villages and passed on every information they gathered about the Japanese.[56]

A look through the war diaries and intelligence summaries confirms the role played by then captain Khathing and his V Force in the north-east sector of Manipur during the Battle of Imphal. The following are some of the wartime documents of the 20th Indian Division, which was deployed in this section from mid-May to July 1944, which contain references to Captain Khathing:

• An intelligence summary of 17 May 1944 mentions a report received from him on Japanese movements in the Shangshak area.[57]
• A sitrep of 19 May 1944 mentions information from him about Japanese movements in the Leishan area.[58]
• A special sitrep of 22 May 1944 mentions a report from him about the widening of the track Humine–Kamjong–Gamnom and the daily movements of vehicles and elephants on it.[59]
• A sitrep of 24 May 1944 mentions information from him about Japanese staging camps in the Humine area.[60]
• A sitrep of 31 May 1944 mentions a confirmation from him about the Japanese concentrating in the Humine area.[61]

This account about the people of Manipur and 1944 would be incomplete without mentioning the men of the 1st Assam Regiment who fought against the Japanese 31st Division at Kharasom and Jessami. Although this is connected to the Battle of Kohima, the two villages are in Manipur, and some of the men of that battalion came from its hills. Their experience of being directly involved in fighting the Japanese at Kharasom, Jessami and Kohima constitutes an important part of Manipur's own experience of the Second World War.

All in all, the response of the main communities of Manipur – the Meiteis, Nagas and Kukis – to the Japanese-INA and British forces was varied. According to N. Lokendra Singh, there have been differences of opinion among scholars about the extent of support among the majority community, the Meiteis, for the Japanese-INA. While some have argued that a considerable number of Meiteis worked to help Bose's men, others dispute this and point to more limited support.[62] After reviewing the different arguments put forth and available literature, Singh concludes, without putting a number on it: 'The available sources show that quite a good number of people from among the different ethnic groups supported the INA-Japanese forces.'[63]

Much attention has been paid to the supplies and intelligence provided to the Japanese-INA by the Meiteis around Moirang and the Tiddim Road; the most famous being in the raising of the INA flag in Moirang on 14 April 1944. Among others, some of the names mentioned in this context are of M. Koireng Singh, I. Sanaba Singh, K. Kanglen Singh and M. Mani Singh.[64] The INA Museum at Moirang has an entire section on the local support extended to the Japanese and the INA during the Battle of Imphal.

Singh also mentions an account of over a dozen Meiteis of Mandalay, led by a L. Guna Singh, who entered Manipur with the Japanese off the Tamu–Palel Road and worked to gather supplies and intelligence for them in the Palel area. It is difficult to extrapolate from these instances of specific support and project them as reflective of the views of the entire Meitei community in Manipur, however.

In the case of the hills, some people among the Tangkhuls are said to have supported the Japanese around Ukhrul. In particular, there is mention of the formation of a co-operation committee, divided into three departments, to provide intelligence, supplies and labour to the Japanese in the area.[65] Singh notes, however, that for the most part the Tangkhul Nagas did not help the Japanese-INA.[66]

The Administration Report of 1943–44 seems to corroborate this view. In the section that deals with the eviction of the Japanese from Manipur at the end of the Battle of Imphal, it states:

> This ejection was first taken in hand in the Ukhrul area where the local hillmen had throughout been a thorn in the side of the Japanese of whom a preliminary count showed that they captured 79 and killed 95. Shortly before they left, the Japanese held meetings in the villages of Maipi and Khengoi at which a Japanese Officer told headmen: 'We came 5,000 strong but we have had 3,000 casualties. We are withdrawing to Mawlaik and

will return in December. When we came we trusted Kukis and Nagas but they deceived us. Next time we come we will have no mercy on the civilian population.'[67]

Notwithstanding the preceding quote, a substantial number of Kukis in the hills are believed to have worked in favour of the Japanese and the INA. A scholar, Jangkhomang Guite, writing in the *Indian Historical Review* in 2010, presented a detailed account of the role of the Kukis in the Japanese offensive and attributed their actions as 'mainly for their freedom from the [British] colonial rule'.[68] He describes their support for the Japanese and the INA as a 'political action' and talks of it as 'made with a conscious, pre-meditated and tactful resolution based on their own reasons and understanding of the situation'.[69]

Again, one has to be careful of attributing a larger, community-wide motive to the actions of select groups of people. But having said that, the actions of some Kukis in 1944 (and earlier) did cause enough concern among the British authorities in Manipur. Hundreds of Kukis are said to have deserted the V Force.[70] After the Battle of Imphal, some 70 Kukis were identified as having actively supported the Japanese and the INA; of these, sufficient evidence was found against only eight, who were then recommended for trial.[71]

The range of charges against them makes for a revealing read about the different ways in which local support was extended: Tongkhothang, chief of Chassad, and his Minister Otkhodam – the former, assisted by the latter, is believed to have crossed the Chindwin in 1943 and asked the Japanese for 400 rifles to fight the British, besides forming a V Force for the Japanese. Palet, assisted by Jamshei (both from Lamyang Tombi village), acted as a scout for the Japanese and planted landmines on the road to Sita village which destroyed some Allied jeeps. Kolvel of Saikot is believed to have supplied rations to the Japanese; Seilet Kuki is said to have been behind the establishment of the Tangkhul Cooperation Committee in Ukhrul; Pakang of Tonglhang is said to have deserted the V Force and joined the Japanese before the Battle of Imphal, passing on valuable information to them; while Lamkhothang of Vayang Lankhoyam is said to have deserted the Assam Rifles to join the Japanese.[72]

Prof. Lal Dena captures the essence of the dilemma between the Japanese and the locals:

The immediate problem for the Indo-Japanese leaders was how to get the support and confidence of the local people. For the people, supporting the Indo-Japanese soldiers meant being an enemy of the British and vice versa. To get local support, the Japanese commanders initially adopted two methods – intimidation and friendship.[73]

In this regard, there is a revealing passage in a Japanese operations instruction found by the 5th Indian Division on the sort of messages given to their soldiers at the outset of the offensive in 1944. Dated 19 March 1944, it was issued by Colonel Miyamoto of the 124th Regiment, Japanese 31st Division:

> Our enemies are the British and Americans. If you have to fight the Indians, persuade them as much as possible to surrender and when they do, treat them kindly. They should be evacuated to the nearest INA HQ.

It continues, with special reference to the native population on the other side of the India–Burma border: 'After crossing the Chindwin, treat all the natives kindly. Do not steal, and above all, don't get wrong ideas about the women.'[74]

Like the British through the war, the Japanese made use of propaganda where possible to try and win over the local people, especially in 1944. N. Lokendra Singh describes the range of methods used, which included everything from emphasising racial similarities to drawing on Manipuri prophesies to highlighting the alliance with the Bose and his INA:

> The Japanese claimed that they came to give 'Swaraj' (Independence) to India. They carried pictures of Subhash Bose addressing or inspecting the INA army; displayed Congress colours on arm bands; carried Congress flags and also uttered 'Jai Hind' as a sign of greeting. In order to get sympathy and support from the local people, the Japanese army used to respond to any of the genuine socio-economic problems of the people. For instance, they said that there would not be 'house tax' and 'forced labour' under them and such propaganda certainly attracted the Kukis.
>
> The Japanese force also tried to appeal to the emotion of the Kukis by claiming that they descended from 'chongji' brother of 'chongthu' from whom the Kukis claimed their descent. There was yet another form of propaganda. A widely known prophesy 'Nongpokthong hangani' (eastern gate will be opened) had been convincingly interpreted by the Japanese and claimed that they represented the eastern power.[75]

Some of these methods worked, at least initially, and the Japanese forces found some local support, especially among the Kukis.

Kukis' Japan gal la (songs of the Japanese War)

There are still songs preserved among the Kukis about the Japan Gal (or Japanese War), many of which are full of praise for the Japanese. The following are some such songs, collected by another scholar, Alfina Haokip, and presented and translated by Jangkhomang Guite:

> *Theilou koljang toni lep banna;*
> *Ging deng deng'e Japan lenna huilen kong;*
> *Peogo lhemlhei saigin bang;*
> *Mao deng deng'e vanthamjol Japan lenna;*
> *Amao deng deng'e Japan lenna;*
> *Mongmo vailou kon sonsot selung hemtante,*
> *Atwi theikhong taa bang ging deng deng;*
> *Ging deng deng'e Japan lenna huilen konggin.*

From the horizon of Burma plain;
The Japanese plane floats its sweet note;
Like the sweet note of the bamboo flute;
Japanese plane hums in the sky above;
When the Japanese plane floats its sweet note;
The depressed farmer forgets the sadness;
Like the sweet melody of the watermill;
The Japanese plane floats its sweet note.

And another:

> *Agam thimthu jing nan jong;*
> *Huilen kong chunga lunghem jangvan ahung lenge;*
> *Lunghem ja a nahung len leh;*
> *Tolkum tado lunglha gol tongkai sah na ding;*
> *Japan mangpa tolsonin tolsonin;*
> *Vankikhup noi namtin cha lonlhi longlou umponte.*

In the darkness of the land;
The Japanese plane comes like the charming bird;
If you come because of my sorrow;
To the ground, to console your disgraced friend;
Mighty Japan! To the ground! To the ground!
All nations will be overjoyed with tears.

Finally, he continues:

Noija hungkon Japante;
Nahun tolthing sem neme

Japanese who come from foreign land;
Your glory humbles the people.

Pummei chang dang ijat nin hatjong leh;
Japan Meipum chang sanga hatjo ding umlou;
Hungkon uvo Japante;
Thingmang damnoi sunsot hijang kangah uve.

Of all the cannons;
Japanese cannon is the strongest;
Japanese! March on;
We are waiting for you in the deep forest.

Hungkon uvo Sapkangte;
Nalailo ding Japan sepai kikhou somme.

March on Britishers;
Japanese soldiers are here to kill you.

Japan galhat meltheisa;
Tulai solkar mangkang in thonom;
Lungdei gol angkoi ponte.

I knew Japanese bravery;
British power wants to imitate them;
But it will be impossible.[76]

In a way then, one can argue that the answer to the question of who supported whom in Manipur in 1944 depended on several factors. First, maybe it was linked to how one was personally affected by the battle and the two sides. For example, someone near Ukhrul who was subject to looting by hungry Japanese soldiers could perhaps be less disposed to support them. Similarly, villagers living between Bishenpur and Moirang whose entire rice stocks were burnt by the hurriedly evacuating British-Indian forces might not subsequently be the most willing to help the latter.

Second, perhaps it depended on existing historical grievances against one side or the other. For instance, there was already much antagonism and bad blood among the Kukis against the British colonial authorities, including about the suppression of the Kuki Rebellion (or Kuki Uprising) of 1917–19 and the different taxes collected from them. Jangkhomang Guite saw this as key to understanding why some groups of Kukis sided with the Japanese and INA.

Ultimately, however, the point must be made that Imphal was such a brief, intense and diffuse battle that in many cases how people reacted may have owed most to where they found themselves during the fighting in Manipur and whom they had to deal with.

As in all such situations, at times the loyalties of some civilians may have been flexible. Tucked away in the war diaries of the 20th Indian Division from May 1944 is an abstract from the Pacific theatre of the Second World War. Mentioned in the subsection 'Enemy Methods', under the heading 'Japs Use of Locals for Spying', it is quite telling that this text was included in an intelligence summary about the Battle of Imphal. It reads as follows:

> These and many similar entries in captured documents indicate quite clearly that the Japanese obtain a good deal of intelligence about Allied Forces from natives who are not necessarily employed by them as spies. Indeed, the majority of them seem to be merely natives of no fixed loyalties who are willing to work for and give information to whichever side pays and feeds them, but who may at one time be assisting our force as carriers and on another occasion tell the Japanese all about them.
>
> That the Japanese themselves are aware of the possibilities that the natives with whom they come into contact may at some later stage tell our forces all about them is indicated by a captured order, dated 24 July 1943, marked 'Military, Very Secret', and issued at Buna which stated: 'For security reasons, no natives will be allowed to enter the base.'[77]

Post-Battle of Imphal

It was estimated that some 6,000 houses in 409 villages across Manipur were destroyed due to the fighting in 1944. Singh gives the breakdown as follows: Moirang (550 houses), Bishenpur (26 houses), East area (2,100 houses in 160 villages), valley area (1,463 houses in 59 villages), Sadar area (1,636 houses in 163 villages), Mao area (137 houses in 8 villages) and west area (209 houses in 19 villages).[78]

Entire areas in Manipur were affected. This is evident in a letter in February 1945 by Christopher Gimson, the British political agent in

Manipur, to an official in Assam in which he underlines the army (and government's) liability in all the areas affected by the fighting of 1944. His overall point was that government assistance should be aimed at all areas hit, instead of just the Bishenpur-Moirang axis on the Tiddim Road. The context was that in this particular area the villagers had been told to leave their homes at the last minute in April 1944 and their rice stocks burnt in a denial policy aimed at the Japanese. Gimson notes:

> If a legal liability exists at all, it applies just as much to that area, where acts of denial were practiced on a large scale, as it does anywhere else. In the areas noted below as well as in other places the villages were turned out by the Army for military reasons:
>
> (1) Saombung to Pukhao [Iril River Valley]
> (2) Saombung to Yaingangpokpi [Ukhrul Road]
> (3) Sengmai to Kangpokpi [Imphal–Kohima Road]
> (4) Buri Bazar to Bishenpur [Tiddim Road]
>
> In all these areas it will rarely by possible to decide how houses were destroyed, whether by our troops or by our bombing or by our artillery or by the Japanese. The villagers were evicted, and when they were allowed to return, they found their homes destroyed. Their houses were not requisitioned. Their fields were uncultivated, because they were not allowed by the Army to cultivate them. There is no essential difference between these areas and the Bishenpur-Moirang area.
>
> All these losses were the result of the Japanese incursion.[79]

N. Luikham gives a glimpse of what life was like around Ukhrul after the Battle of Imphal:

> After the war there was a dip in the social and economic life of the people. It had left a devastating effect in all areas of life. The environment was grim as the remains/bones and skulls of Japanese soldiers were scattered like toys everywhere by the road side, some in full uniform without guns. There were no Japanese soldiers left to bury their comrades. Allied soldiers perhaps had no time to attend to circumstance as they went pursuing the retreat of the enemy. The locals did not and could not attend to it after they had lost everything in the bombs and ravaging fire; granaries were burnt or ransacked. Barring just few families,

almost all others went hungry. Leaves and roots collected from the jungle could not fill their hunger.[80]

He goes on to note that cholera, dysentery and fever, among other sicknesses, were rife around Ukhrul:

In Ukhrul (Humpun) village alone within three months i.e. July to September, close to two hundred people died. Initially there were tearful partings, but as the death toll rose dying and parting did not seem to matter much anymore and was taken as part of everyday life. It was no longer tearful, heart-rending parting. But at least the dead were buried according to Tangkhul customary rites. Sorrow and pain was for the Japanese soldiers who fell for their nation but their bones lay scattered without burial, unsung, no loved ones to give them final farewell with honour.[81]

The government of India did put in place relief and rehabilitation measures for affected people across Manipur. By August 1944, relief depots had been opened in the hills and the Imphal Valley, with Imphal as the main base. N. Lokendra Singh informs that 24 depots were opened and rations supplied to 622 villages, with 103,573 people being fed.[82] The depots were closed only in 1945.

Other measures by the government of India included compensating villagers who had lost their belongings, distributing agricultural implements and seeds, supplying livestock, sanctioning materials for reconstructing houses and providing cash relief.[83] Again, local contractors and businessmen benefited from the procurement process of all these relief materials.

The end of the Battle of Imphal did not mark the conclusion of Manipur's experience of the Second World War, however. The opening lines of the Administration Report of Manipur State for 1944–45 succinctly capture just what its people were witness to for almost a year afterwards:

During the year 1944/45 the war continued to dominate the affairs of the Manipur State. The Japanese having been cleared from State territory, Imphal became an important base for the further advance of our armies into Burma. Hundreds of thousands of troops poured into the area and the resources of the State were strained to their uttermost in providing supplies to the Local Purchase organisations and labour for Military works. The circulation of money increased to an extent never dreamt of in Manipur and prices continued at an abnormally inflated level.

The army requirements of accommodation led to over 40,000 houses being requisitioned and the provision of accommodation for the families ejected produced a serious problem.[84]

References to hundreds of thousands of soldiers passing through Manipur in 1944–45 are staggering. These are in addition to the estimated 190,000 refugees who came through Imphal from Burma in 1942 and, of course, the Japanese Fifteenth Army that invaded in 1944. One can safely assume that a mass of people at least the size of the entire state's population at the time passed through Manipur during the Second World War.

Impact of the Second World War

The Second World War was thus a momentous period in Manipur's history. In his book *Wounded Land* John Parratt puts it well: 'By the time the war ended, Manipur had been forcibly dragged into the modern era.'[85] In a few short years its infrastructure was dramatically improved and its economy transformed by a massive infusion of money. Natives got a massive leg up in business during the war years; many of the main local business families in Manipur today made their beginnings in trade during the Second World War.[86]

The year 1944 saw its people being plunged into the maelstrom of the Battle of Imphal. Several found themselves drawn into either directly or indirectly supporting the different battling sides. Many had to evacuate their homes and seek shelter elsewhere; villages were bombed; and houses were destroyed during some the bitterest fighting the world had ever seen.

There was a psychological impact too. The people of Manipur were suddenly exposed to the presence and thinking of hundreds of thousands of people from different parts of India and the world for the first time – and all within a very compressed time period. For it was the war from 1942 to 1945 that brought, for the first and the last time, people from around India and the world to Manipur in such large numbers. There were the Indians who made up the Indian Army, as well as those who fought on behalf of the INA. The British and the Americans were there, as were the Japanese and even soldiers from East Africa, who passed through to fight in the Kabaw Valley in Burma and beyond.

The people of Manipur were further subjected to intense propaganda in favour of both the Allied war effort and, to a more limited extent, the Japanese and the INA. Besides opening their eyes to the wider world, this politicised the people like never before.

Manipur was also left awash with weapons after the Second World War. In April 1951, a good seven years after the end of the Battle of Imphal, a Mr Sidhva raised some questions in the Indian Parliament about the status of weapons left over in Manipur from the war. The official response he received underlines the extent of the problem at the time. The following is an excerpt:

> After the last war the Japanese and the Allied Armies left large quantities of arms and ammunition of all types (including modern rifles, automatic weapons and Hand Grenades) in the Hill areas of Manipur. It is difficult to estimate the exact quantity and categories of arms and ammunition thus left over; but the number of these arms is estimated to be not less than 10000. The villagers residing in these areas collected such of these arms as they discovered and kept them with themselves for private use. Most of these are understood to be in the possession of tribal people and communists. A vigorous drive has been made for the recovery of these arms and ammunition and so far 3000 arms of various types and 100,000 rounds of ammunition have been recovered. The Police forces of the State are being assisted in this drive by the Assam Rifles.[87]

It is unclear how many of the remaining arms were finally recovered. It is also unclear whether 'Hill Areas of Manipur' here actually refers just to the hills of the state or is shorthand for all of Manipur. One suspects it is the latter.

The people of Manipur themselves have a range of views about the Second World War and its impact. M.K. Binodoni sums up her point of view:

> It was a meaningless war for most of the people of Manipur. A lot of those who suffered the worst fate possible, displaced from homes, maimed, or had relatives killed, etc., still vividly remember what suffering they went through, but not many comprehend why the war was fought on their home ground at all. . . .
> . . . It was a war like no other war the place has ever seen till then. The scale and magnitude of destructive violence was incomprehensible. . . . It was even more incomprehensible because it was a war in which the native population shared no issue.[88]

Dr Y. Shyam Singh notes that significant changes were brought about in the dressing style and eating habits of the people of Manipur due to their interaction with people from different parts of the world. More significantly, people's mindset changed, especially towards English-language

43

education. He concludes: 'People realized that the narrow minded living of the days before the war was foolish and soon began to shift their focus on modern education and scientific way of living.'[89]

A.S. Arthur says:

> The War brought development to Manipur; without the War the state would not have advanced as much. The War opened our eyes; we would be living in darkness otherwise. That's how they learnt how other people lived and about other cultures. We had no contact with the outside world before that. Then the foreigners came and taught us about the ways of the world. Roads were built. Before that, we just had foot tracks, bridle paths. It was only after that that vehicles could ply in the area [around Ukhrul].[90]

Dr N. Lokendra Singh offers a broad conclusion about the impact of the Second World War on Manipur:

> The war period was a time of intense socio-economic and political cross-currents. The changes during the war time provided material as well as ideological basis for a strong political movement during 1946–49 period. It was during such a time of tremendous socio-economic change that the economic base of the nascent Manipuri middle class was strengthened through massive investments in transportation, supply and construction works. Ideologically, the Manipuri middle class was exposed to the national and international political trends and was, therefore, on the lookout for opportunities to fight for broad socio-economic and political changes in the state.[91]

This conclusion is significant. Whether in the Imphal Valley or the hills, no one had been left untouched by the Second World War. The transformation in the period from 1942 to 1945 had been at all levels: economic, social, political and psychological. Whichever way one looks at it, it was clear that the war had changed Manipur and its people forever. Other parts of what we today call North East India, including the Naga Hills of then Assam and the Lushai Hills (Mizoram today), had also been affected, although not as much as Manipur.

Had these changes occurred at any point in the state and the region's history, they would have been considered noteworthy. But all of this happened at a particularly crucial time for Manipur, the North East region and India as a whole. By the time the war ended in 1945, India was a mere two years away from independence. A churning would start to get under way about the North East's place in India, starting with the Nagas, later followed by the Mizos. Manipur would also question the terms and conditions in which it became a part of India. Over time this churning would engulf the entire North East. The origins of this process of churning owed at least partly to the politicisation and militarisation experienced by the people of the region during the Second World War, including in the Battle of Imphal of 1944.

Notes

1 E.F. Lydall, *Administration Report for the Manipur State for the Year 1943–44*, Imphal: State Printing Press, 1945, Manipur State Archives, Imphal, p. 2.
2 Geoffrey Evans and Antony Brett-James, *Imphal: A Flower on Lofty Heights*, London: Macmillan, 1962, p. 24.
3 Ibid., p. 25.
4 Lydall, *Administration Report for the Manipur State for the Year 1943–44*, p. 2.
5 Ibid.
6 Ibid.
7 Ibid.
8 Ibid., p. 15.
9 Ibid.
10 Ibid., p. 4.
11 Ibid.
12 Ibid., p. 3.
13 Ibid., p. 30.
14 Ibid., p. 4.
15 Ibid., p. 3.
16 Ibid., p. 16.
17 Ibid., p. 3.
18 Ibid., p. 17.
19 N. Lokendra Singh, *Manipur during World War II (1941–45): Socio-economic Change and Local Responses*, Imphal: Manipur State Archives, 1993, pp. 1–31.
20 Ibid., p. 2.
21 Ibid., p. 4.
22 Ibid., p. 6.
23 M.K. Binodini Devi, 'The Late Yengkhom Ongbi Hemabati', Imasi: The M.K. Binodini Devi Foundation, Imphal (original interview in Meiteilon transliterated by Pradip Phanjoubam).
24 Khuraijam Nimaicharan Singh, *The 2nd World War in Manipur and My Childhood*, Imphal: Kh. Ratankumar Singh, 2012, p. 95.
25 'Japan Laan and the People of Tulihal', *Poknapham*, Imphal, 15 October 2014, Y. Shyam Singh (translated from original Meiteilon edition by Yaiphaba Kangjam).
26 Ibid.
27 Ibid.
28 Singh, *The 2nd World War in Manipur and My Childhood*, p. 83.
29 Ibid., p. 93.
30 Lydall, *Administration Report for the Manipur State for the Year 1943–44*, pp. 4–5.
31 Singh, *The Second World War in Manipur and My Childhood*, p. 137.

---

32 M.K. Binodini Devi, 'The Late Yengkhom Ongbi Hemabati'.
33 Lydall, *Administration Report for the Manipur State for the Year 1943–44*, p. 5.
34 Ian Lyall Grant, *Burma: The Turning Point*, Chichester: Zampi Press, 1992, p. 122.
35 Interview with Pukhrambam Birachandra by Yaiphaba Kangjam, January 2015.
36 Singh, *Manipur during World War II (1941–45): Socio-economic Change and Local Responses*, p. 11.
37 Interview with Pukhrambam Birachandra by Yaiphaba Kangjam, January 2015.
38 Interview with Shankazip Varu, January 2014.
39 N. Luikham, *Transformed Headhunters: The Pioneers of Tangkhul Education*, Ukhrul: El Shaddai Resource Centre, 2011, p. 75.
40 Lydall, *Administration Report for the Manipur State for the Year 1943–44*, p. 6.
41 Singh, *Manipur during World War II (1941–45): Socio-economic Change and Local Responses*, p. 22.
42 Ibid., p. 23.
43 'Indo-Japanese Soldiers in the Khuga Valley of Churachandpur', *Hueiyen Lanpao*, Imphal, 28 March 2014, Dr Lal Dena.
44 M.K. Binodini Devi, 'The Late Yengkhom Ongbi Hemabati'.
45 Interview with A.S. Arthur, November 2014.
46 Interview with L. Achung Kom by Yaiphaba Kangjam, January 2015.
47 Interview with Ningthoukhongjam Moirangningthou, February 2015.
48 M.K. Binodini Devi, 'The Late Yengkhom Ongbi Hemabati'.
49 Interview with Asem Tomchou Singh by Yaiphaba Kangjam, January 2015.
50 Lydall, *Administration Report for the Manipur State for the Year 1943–44*, p. 7.
51 H. Bhuban Singh, *The Merger of Manipur*, Imphal: Pritam Haobam, 1988, pp. 53–54.
52 Ibid., p. 54.
53 Ibid., pp. 54–55.
54 Ibid.
55 Ibid.
56 Interview with A.S. Arthur 1 November 2014.
57 Intelligence Summary I.6554, War Diary of 'G' Branch, H.Q. 20 Indian Division, File No. 601/250/WD/Part II-A, History Division, Ministry of Defence, New Delhi.
58 Sitrep I.7119, War Diary of 'G' Branch, H.Q. 20 Indian Division, File No. 601/250/WD/Part II-A, History Division, Ministry of Defence, New Delhi.
59 Special Sitrep, I.8672, War Diary of 'G' Branch, H.Q. 20 Indian Division, File No. 601/250/WD/Part II-A, History Division, Ministry of Defence, New Delhi.
60 Sitrep I.7864, War Diary of 'G' Branch, H.Q. 20 Indian Division, File No. 601/250/WD/Part II-A, History Division, Ministry of Defence, New Delhi.
61 Sitrep I.6803, War Diary of 'G' Branch, H.Q. 20 Indian Division, File No. 601/250/WD/Part II-A, History Division, Ministry of Defence, New Delhi.
62 Singh, *Manipur during World War II (1941–45): Socio-economic Change and Local Responses*, p. 12.
63 Ibid., p. 13.
64 Ibid., p. 15.
65 Ibid., pp. 20–21.
66 Ibid., p. 21.
67 Lydall, *Administration Report for the Manipur State for the Year 1943–44*, p. 6.
68 Jangkhomang Guite, 'Representing Local Participation in INA-Japanese Imphal Campaign: The Case of the Kukis in Manipur, 1943–45', *Indian Historical Review*, 2010, 37(2): 308.

69 Ibid.
70 Singh, *Manipur during World War II (1941–45): Socio-economic Change and Local Responses*, p. 19.
71 Guite, 'Representing Local Participation in INA-Japanese Imphal Campaign: The Case of the Kukis in Manipur, 1943–45', pp. 296–97.
72 Ibid., pp. 296–98.
73 'Indo-Japanese soldiers in the Khuga Valley of Churachandpur', *Hueiyen Lanpao*.
74 Intelligence Summary No. 140, April 1944, War Diary of 'G' Branch, H.Q. 5 Indian Division, File No. 601/221/WD/Part IX-B, History Division, Ministry of Defence, New Delhi.
75 Singh, *Manipur during World War II (1941–45): Socio-economic Change and Local Responses*, pp. 18–19.
76 Guite, 'Representing Local Participation in INA-Japanese Imphal Campaign: The Case of the Kukis in Manipur, 1943–45,' pp. 300–301.
77 Intelligence Summary No. 6, May 1944, H.Q. 20 Indian Division, File No. 601/250/WD/Part II-A, Historical Division, Ministry of Defence, New Delhi.
78 Singh, *Manipur during World War II (1941–45): Socio-economic Change and Local Responses*, p. 25.
79 Letter to Dr N.L. Bor from C. Gimson, 23 February 1945, in Rehabilitation of the dispossessed population of Manipur State and Naga Hills, Assam, File No. Progs., Nos. 5(50)-P.A., 1951, National Archives of India, New Delhi.
80 Luikham, *Transformed Headhunters: The Pioneers of Tangkhul Education*, p. 76.
81 Ibid., pp. 76–77.
82 Singh, *Manipur during World War II (1941–45): Socio-economic Change and Local Responses*, p. 23.
83 Ibid., pp. 23–25.
84 F.F. Pearson, *Administration Report for the Manipur State for the Year 1944–45*, Imphal: State Printing Press, 1946, Manipur State Archives, Imphal, p. 1.
85 John Parratt, *Wounded Land*, New Delhi: Mittal Publications, 2005, p. 93.
86 Singh, *Manipur during World War II (1941–45): Socio-economic Change and Local Responses*, p. 26.
87 Question in Parliament by Shri Sidhva Regarding Arms and Ammunition Left Over by the Allied Armies in Manipur Hills after the Termination of World War II and the Steps Taken to Recover Unlicenced Arms and Ammunition in the State, File No. Progs., Nos. 5(50)-P.A., 1951, National Archives of India.
88 M.K. Binodini Devi, 'The Late Yengkhom Ongbi Hemabati'.
89 'Japan Laan and the People of Tulihal', *Poknapham*.
90 Interview with A.S. Arthur, November 2014.
91 Singh, *Manipur during World War II (1941–45): Socio-economic Change and Local Responses*, p. 28.

3

IMPHAL 1944

The Fourteenth and Fifteenth Armies clash

The Japanese Fifteenth Army

On the Japanese side in the Battle of Imphal was its Fifteenth Army, commanded by General Mutaguchi Renya. This consisted of two infantry divisions: the 15th Division, commanded by Lieutenant General Yamauchi, and the 33rd Division, commanded by Lieutenant General Yanagida; the latter was replaced by Lieutenant General Tanaka in May 1944. This force consisted of some 70,000 men. A third division, the 31st, commanded by Lieutenant General Sato, passed through Manipur en route to Kohima in the Naga Hills of then Assam. This included some 15,000 soldiers.

A Japanese infantry division, commanded by a lieutenant general, had under its command three regiments, which were the British equivalent of brigades. A regiment was commanded by a colonel. A division also had an Infantry Group Commander, a major general, who could command independent operations. At Imphal, the Japanese 33rd Division's Infantry Group Commander was Major General Yamamoto, who commanded Yamamoto Force. Like the British, each infantry regiment in turn had under its command three battalions.

The Japanese weaponry used at Imphal consisted mainly of mountain and field guns. This included the 75 mm Mountain Gun, the 105 mm Field Gun and the 150 mm Medium Howitzer. On occasion, the Japanese were also found in possession of anti-tank guns, including the 37 mm gun and the 47 mm gun. In terms of armour, the 14 Tank Regiment was active at Imphal. This consisted of three Medium tank (Type 2597) companies and one Light tank (Type 2595) company.[1] In the air, Fifteenth Army was supported by 5th Air Division of the Japanese Army Air Force, commanded by General Tazoe.

By the time the Fifteenth Army's divisions launched their offensive towards Imphal in 1944, the Japanese had built up a fearsome reputation as jungle fighters. Far from looking at the jungle as an obstacle or hindrance, the Japanese were able to use it to their advantage and had mastered the art of jungle warfare. They were able to move swiftly through the jungle, often undetected. Their ease of movement was helped by the fact that they travelled light, carrying with them only the bare minimum of arms and supplies required. They also used the sights and sounds of the jungle, initially unfamiliar to the British-Indian forces at the start of the Burma Campaign in 1942, to instil fear in them.

When on the offense, a favourite Japanese tactic was to strike deep behind their opponents' bases/positions and cut their lines of supply and communication. The forces thus cut off would be rendered acutely vulnerable and that feeling of vulnerability, more often than not, induced panic. The besieged forces would conduct a disorganised and disoriented retreat, only to be attacked and cut off again by the Japanese farther behind. This pattern had repeated itself on several occasions in 1942 when the Japanese chased and inflicted a humiliating defeat on the retreating Allied forces through Burma.

As defenders, especially in mountainous and jungle terrain, the Japanese Army was arguably the best in the world during the Second World War, barring none. Once in place and given sufficient time, the Japanese would dig in deep, creating a vast network of tunnels, bunkers and trenches. Defensive positions were often interlocking, making them well-nigh impregnable. Dislodging Japanese defenders required the combined effort of the infantry, artillery and armour, almost always supported by air strikes. Even after a defensive position was captured, a watchful eye had to be kept for barely alive Japanese soldiers who would emerge hours or even days later from the rubble to try and attack their opponents.

What made the Japanese Army truly formidable at Imphal was the unfailing – indeed fanatic – determination and dedication to the cause of the individual soldier. A Japanese soldier sought to abide by bushido, the code of the ancient samurai. For him, giving himself up or surrendering was not an option; fighting to his death was the only honourable and acceptable way out. He believed that he was fighting to defend the honour of his emperor; his war cry *banzai* referred to his wish that the Japanese emperor live 'a thousand years'. And so whether he was defending his own position or launching himself in a wave of attacks – attacking in waves being another preferred tactic – the Japanese soldier fought to the end.

The Japanese Army had used its prowess in the jungle and its tactics to devastating effect against Allied forces in Burma in 1942. As a result, there was a certain arrogance or at least overconfidence about its own fighting abilities in 1944, and a related disdain for its previously vanquished foes. This was reflected in the time frame the army set for itself to capture Imphal and in its disregard for a more secure and reliable supply line for its offensive. Initially, General Mutaguchi sought to have the job over and done within just over three weeks; a subsequent deadline became the emperor's birthday on April 29. In any event, Fifteenth Army were to have been in Imphal before the rains began.

The tight deadlines meant that speed was of the essence to the Japanese units advancing towards Manipur's capital in 1944. It also meant adopting a risky strategy when it came to supplies. Keeping tens of thousands of soldiers supplied over the hills of the India–Burma border and across the Chindwin River was always going to be a challenge. Instead of ensuring that this was adequately addressed at the outset, the emphasis on speed required the men to carry the bare minimum of supplies, backed up by an unreliable and untested supply line. The assumption was that they would be able to help themselves to the bounty of the Fourteenth Army's supply depots and bases that were expected to fall into their hands in little to no time.

If Imphal would have been taken by the Japanese Fifteenth Army according to its original timeline, the problem of supplies would have automatically been solved. Unfortunately for the Japanese, Imphal did not fall in a matter of weeks. In fact, Imphal did not fall at all. And the fundamental reason for this was that the British-Indian forces they faced in 1944 were quite unlike those they had so roundly defeated only two years prior.

The British Fourteenth Army

On the British side was the Fourteenth Army, commanded by General Slim. At Imphal, this consisted of its 4 Corps, commanded by Lieutenant General Geoffrey Scoones. The corps was initially made up of three infantry divisions – the 17th Indian Division, commanded by Major General D.T. 'Punch' Cowan; the 20th Indian Division, commanded by Major General Douglas Gracey; and the 23rd Indian Division, commanded by Major General Ouvry Roberts. Also in Manipur was the 50th Indian Parachute Brigade. As the battle progressed, two brigades of the 5th Indian Division, commanded by Major General Harold Briggs, and one of the 7th Indian Division were flown into Manipur's airfields from the Arakan in Burma. This was a total of over 120,000 men.

Unlike the ethnically homogenous Japanese forces, 4 Corps was made up of British, Indian and Gurkha soldiers. Added to the mix was the intelligence-gathering V Force of Manipur's natives in the hills east and north-east and west and south-west of Imphal. Mention must also be made here of the Chindits. Although they did not play a major role in the Battle of Imphal, one unit – the 23rd Long Range Penetration Brigade – became involved in the Ukhrul sector (north-east Manipur) in late June/early July 1944. It was tasked with disrupting Japanese supply lines between Ukhrul and Burma and cutting off the retreat of thousands of Fifteenth Army soldiers as they made their way back from the battlefields of Imphal and Kohima.

An infantry division of the Fourteenth Army was commanded by a major general. He had under him three brigades, led by brigadiers, and each of these had under his command three battalions. Several of the brigades at Imphal had a mix of battalions: usually one British battalion, like the 2nd West Yorkshires, 2nd Suffolks and 1st Northamptons, together with two Indian or Gurkha battalions. The majority of the fighting forces at Imphal were Indian and Gurkha units.

The Fourteenth Army infantry at Imphal had the support of the guns of several Field and Mountain Regiment units. The weapons at their disposal included 6-pounders, 25-pounders and 3.7-inch Howitzers; also in action were anti-aircraft and anti-tank gun units. Armoured support came from the 254th Indian Tank Brigade, which included the Lee-Grants (Medium tanks) of the 3rd Carabiniers, Prince of Wales's Dragoon Guards and the Stuarts (Light tanks) of the 7th Light Cavalry.

In terms of men and firepower, the Fourteenth Army at Imphal in 1944 was a far cry from the Allied forces who had retreated from Burma in 1942 or those who were ground down in the first Arakan offensive of 1943. And yet some of the units were the same, such as the 17th Indian Division. This was not happenstance. The Fourteenth Army, which had been created from the erstwhile Eastern Army in August 1943, had put in some hard work since its formation. Or to be more precise, since General Slim assumed its command a couple of months later. For here was a man who had first-hand experience of fighting the Japanese in Burma. Of greater import, he had learnt from his forces' defeat, and he sought to draw on it in subsequent months as he prepared the Fourteenth Army for the next major encounter with the Japanese.

Slim worked on the morale and material needs of his men. He laid emphasis on training, especially in jungle warfare. He was convinced that with rigorous and sustained training the Fourteenth Army's soldier would be more than a match for the Japanese. Once he became similarly accustomed to surviving and combat in the jungle, he was less likely to perceive the Japanese as some sort of extraordinary jungle fighter. Slim also saw to it that the soldier on the ground had better access to medical care and that a strict programme on malaria prevention was put in place.

Furthermore, Slim paid attention to logistics and supplies. He knew that matters of supply were critical in the mountainous, jungle terrain of the India–Burma border, and beyond. He worked to ensure that his fighting units were backed up by secure lines of supply and communication.

He also sought to devise ways to counteract the preferred Japanese tactic of cutting off these lines behind units. Key to this was supply from the air. No longer would Fourteenth Army units be found wanting in food, ammunition and other supplies, even if they had been isolated or surrounded by Japanese forces. Better coordination between his land and air forces was therefore an important part of his army's training. It would pay off handsomely at Imphal.

The Royal Air Force's 221 Group, under the command of Air Vice-Marshal S.F.Vincent, together with the squadrons of the Troop Carrier Command, supported the Fourteenth Army in this 'Air Battle of Imphal'. The pilots and crews came from the Royal Air Force, the United States Army Air Force, the Indian Air Force, the Royal Canadian Air Force, the Royal Australian Air Force and the Royal New Zealand Air Force. It was a well and truly Allied force.

And so the army the Japanese Fifteenth Army faced off with in the Battle of Imphal was shades different from its earlier avatar. Moreover, Fourteenth Army followed the doctrine of using overwhelming firepower as and when it could afford to – against its opponents, who were well known for their offensive and defensive capabilities. This involved using infantry, artillery, armour and the air force in tackling Japanese positions, a feat demonstrated repeatedly in the many minor and major battles that unfolded around Manipur in 1944.

The Indian National Army

There was a third fighting force at Imphal, albeit a miniscule one compared to the Fourteenth and Fifteenth Armies. This was the Indian National Army (INA). The INA was involved in the Battle of Imphal on the side of the Japanese in two ways. The first was through the deployment of the 1st INA Division, consisting of some 6,000 men. This included the Gandhi and Azad Brigades, and part of the Subhash Brigade. Manipur is the only place in India where the INA's 1st Division was deployed and fought during the Second World War. The second way was through INA Special Groups of several hundred men who were attached to each of the Japanese divisions.

It is hard to overstate the importance of the Battle of Imphal for the INA. Imphal in 1944 was the moment the INA had been created and been waiting for: to try and liberate India militarily from British rule. This was from where its planned march on to Delhi was to begin and where territory in India would be captured and start to be administered.

The first detachments of the 1st INA Division had been rushed up to Manipur to ensure that they were at the vanguard of the Japanese offensive in 1944. Many of them were ill-equipped and under-trained for the task and terrain at hand, however. They were also largely dependent on the Japanese for logistical support who, in turn, struggled to keep their own fighting troops as the battle wore on. This would exact a heavy price on the INA men who fought at Imphal.

Imphal 1944

These then were the forces that clashed in the hills and valley of Manipur from March to July 1944 in what has since become known as the Battle of Imphal. The battle involved the Japanese Fifteenth Army, together with INA units, attacking towards Imphal from three broad directions in mid-March 1944: the 15th Division from the north and north-east; Yamamoto Force, made up primarily of the 33rd Division, from the south-east; and the bulk of the 33rd Division from the south and south-west. The date set for the capture of Imphal was mid-April 1944.

The 31st Division crossed Manipur through and around the area of Ukhrul and headed towards Kohima in the then Naga Hills of Assam. Its aim was to take Kohima and cut the Imphal–Kohima–Dimapur Road which kept the British-Indian forces in Imphal supplied.

The overall – and authorised – objective of the Japanese U Go operation in North East India in 1944 was to capture Imphal. As a result, some military historians consider the battle at Kohima as being part of the overall Battle of Imphal.[2] However, this book, as well as many other historians and authors, treats the two as separate, simultaneous battles, albeit part of the same Japanese offensive into India. The focus here is on the Battle of Imphal, in particular on the fighting that took place in the then princely state of Manipur from March to July 1944.

Before Imphal, the Japanese first attacked the Arakan in Burma in early February 1944. Mutaguchi aimed to divert British attention from the much larger planned offensive towards Manipur. It was also hoped that the Arakan operation would draw in British reinforcements, making it easier for the Japanese Fifteenth Army to take a less well-defended Imphal. Much to their surprise, the British-Indian forces held off and repulsed their attack, with besieged units cut off on land relying on Allied air supply for their success. The template for the eventual British-Indian victory at Imphal had been set. Undeterred by the reverse in the Arakan, epitomised by what has since become known as the Battle of the Admin Box, Mutaguchi continued to plan for Imphal.

In the weeks leading up to March, Fourteenth Army and its 4 Corps had received intelligence about the impending Japanese offensive. At the time, one division – the 23rd – was in reserve at Imphal, while two divisions had been deployed forward along the India–Burma border – the 20th Indian Division at Tamu and the Kabaw Valley and the 17th Indian Division at Tiddim. Since 1942, six airfields had come up in the Imphal Valley. The two all-weather airfields were Imphal Main (or Koirengei Airfield) and Palel, while Kangla, Wangjing and Sapam were fair-weather airfields; Tulihal, the current Imphal airport, was somewhere in between.[3]

General Slim's strategy was to withdraw his forward divisions to the edges of the Imphal Valley at the first sign of a Japanese attack. He wanted to fight the Japanese on ground of his choosing and in conditions favourable to the Fourteenth Army. He felt they could be beaten if he concentrated his army around the Imphal Valley, thereby forcing the Japanese to fight at the end of a long and precarious supply line extending all the way back over the hills to the Chindwin River in Burma. The British-Indian forces, in contrast, would be well supported by shorter and more secure supply lines, besides being able to rely on the airfields and supply depots scattered around the Imphal Valley.

Despite some scares for Fourteenth Army in the opening stages of the Battle of Imphal, this is ultimately what happened. Although the Japanese had cut all land routes to the Imphal Valley by mid-April 1944, this did not affect the British-Indian forces much. Until the Siege of Imphal was lifted on 22 June, 4 Corps relied on supplies from the air. Much-needed reinforcements, in the form of the two brigades of the 5th Indian Division and one of the 7th Indian Division, were flown in to the Imphal Valley from the Arakan. They relied on American aircraft hurriedly diverted from the Hump operation in eastern Assam.

All British and other military accounts acknowledge that without support from the air, the Battle of Imphal would have been very hard for the British-Indian forces to win. Thus, it was as much an air battle as one fought on land. Allied planes maintained complete superiority in the skies of Manipur in 1944 over the Japanese Army Air Force. The six airfields served as a lifeline to 4 Corps in and around the Imphal Valley during the Siege of Imphal. They allowed for rations, supplies, ammunition and reinforcements to be flown in and for the seriously injured to be evacuated. Allied planes flying from these airfields provided close air support, bombing Japanese supply lines and supporting infantry operations. All of this was done in some of the most difficult weather conditions imaginable.

On the ground, Fourteenth Army units, fresh from their jungle training, no longer viewed the Japanese as invincible. They did not panic or scatter, but stood their ground and repulsed attacks, eventually turning to the offensive as the days and weeks wore on. The supplies expected to easily fall into Japanese hands and sustain them never materialised in any large quantities.

Another problem that came to the fore as the fighting dragged on was the deep-seated mistrust between Mutaguchi and his division commanders, both at Imphal and in Kohima. Quarrels between them and, at times, between commanders such as Major General Yamamoto and his own subordinates only became worse as the Fourteenth Army proved more than a match for the Japanese Fifteenth Army. In the case of the Japanese 33rd Division, things got so bad that Mutaguchi replaced its commander half-way through the Battle of Imphal. These differences between the various levels of command only worked against Japanese objectives at Imphal and hampered their operations on the ground.

Confronted with mounting logistical difficulties, the onset of the monsoon and a better trained and supported – medically and from the air – opponent than expected, the Japanese offensive failed. Fourteenth Army delivered a resounding victory and the Fifteenth Army, together with INA units, was forced to return to Burma in mid-July 1944 in a disastrous retreat. The Japanese in Burma were never able to or given the chance to recover from this defeat in North East India in 1944. It paved the way for a string of successes for the Allied forces; in less than a year after this battle, Fourteenth Army was in Rangoon (Yangon).

The combined battle of Imphal–Kohima is considered the largest defeat on land for the Japanese Army. It is also considered the turning point of the Burma Campaign. Robert Lyman, who successfully argued for its naming as 'Britain's Greatest Battle' by United Kingdom's National Army Museum, writes: 'It is clear that Kohima/Imphal was one of the four great turning-point battles in the Second World War, when the tide of war changed irreversibly and dramatically against those who initially held the upper hand.'[4] He considers the battles at Stalingrad, El Alamein and in the Pacific as the other three.

The Japanese suffered some 53,000 casualties at Imphal–Kohima.[5] Of these, some 30,000 are thought to have died and 23,000 injured. This includes men killed due to fighting and disease and, importantly, those who died in the disastrous retreat back to the Chindwin River after the battle. Of the total, some 7,000 is estimated to be the number of casualties for Kohima. Given the vastly greater number of Japanese forces at Imphal, one can assume that the bulk of the remainder in the tens of thousands were sustained at that battle, and in the retreat back to Burma.

For the Fourteenth Army, there is, by and large, some agreement on the total number of casualties for the combined battle of Imphal–Kohima. These are usually estimated to be around 16,000, including dead and injured. Of these, 4,000 is the approximate figure for Kohima, while the vast majority of casualties, some 12,000 men, are believed to have been sustained at the Battle of Imphal.

Notes

1 Ian Lyall Grant, *Burma: The Turning Point*, Chichester: Zampi Press, 1992, p. 236.
2 Louis Allen, *Burma: The Longest War, 1941–45*, London: Phoenix Giant, 1984, p. 191.
3 Norman Franks, *The Air Battle of Imphal*, London: William Kimber, 1985, p. 20.
4 Robert Lyman, *Japan's Last Bid for Victory*, Barnsley: Praetorian Press, 2011, p. 262.
5 Ibid., p. 254.

4

THE BATTLEFIELDS

Hub and spokes

It is not simple to chart the course of the Battle of Imphal, however. The fighting took place in many parts of Manipur and was simultaneous. The situation is particularly confusing when one tries to plot the battlefields of 1944 on a present-day map of Manipur. One is confronted with a wide range of locations spread across the state in different directions, many clusters of battlefields seemingly disconnected and isolated from each other. How does one explain how Potsangbam, Nungshigum, Shenam and Kanglatongbi fit into the overall picture of the Battle of Imphal?

There is a way to put the battlefields of 1944 in perspective, however. It has been provided by the person perhaps best placed to do so: Field Marshal Viscount Slim, who as a then general commanded the Fourteenth Army to victory at Imphal. One can call it Slim's 'hub and spoke' analogy. He likened Imphal to the hub of a wheel, with the main roads leading to the town as its spokes.[1] According to him, these were the routes used by the Japanese to approach Imphal in 1944 and so it was on or along them that most of the fighting occurred, simultaneously.

Slim's hub and spoke analogy is useful to have at the back of one's mind as one heads out of Imphal to explore the battlefields of 1944. This part of the book has been structured on the basis of these different spokes: it therefore starts with looking at the battlefields on the Tiddim Road, which heads south out of Imphal, and then considers the other routes, ending with the Imphal–Kohima Road heading north.

Ironically, the city of Imphal saw little fighting during the 1944 battle to which it lends its name. Clashes raged all around Manipur's capital and even occurred as close as Nungshigum, some 5 miles (8 km) to the north, and Red Hill or Maibam Lotpaching, some 10 miles (16 km) to the south. However, barring some aerial attacks targeting the Imphal airfields by the Japanese Army Air Force, the city emerged relatively unscathed from the over four-month-long battle. Perhaps what affected Imphal most was that it was under siege – for over two months it was cut off from the rest of the world by land and kept supplied by air.

Militarily, of course, Imphal remained the nerve centre from where 4 Corps headquarters directly ran and coordinated the Battle of Imphal, under the overall command of the Fourteenth Army and General Slim in Comilla (in present-day Bangladesh). 4 Corps headquarters area, known as the 'Keep', was just to the north of Imphal and included Imphal Main (or Koirengei Airfield). Slim gives a sense of what it was like for Lieutenant General Scoones, the 4 Corps Commander, at the time:

> … it should be remembered that encounters on all of the spokes [leading to Imphal] were going on simultaneously. At no time and in no place was the situation, either to commanders or troops, as clear even as I can make it now. Into Scoones' headquarters, from every point of the compass, day and night, streamed signals, messages, and reports, announcing successes, setbacks, appealing for reinforcements, demanding more ammunition, asking urgently for wounded to be evacuated, begging for air support.[2]

Slim's own Fourteenth Army headquarters moved from Comilla to Imphal for a few months towards the end of 1944 to coordinate the unfolding operations in Burma. The cottage in which Slim stayed can still be seen in the Kangla Fort in Imphal today (Figure 4.1).

The city is also home to two Second World War cemeteries maintained by the UK-based Commonwealth War Graves Commission (Figures 4.2-4.3). The first is the Imphal War Cemetery in the Dewlahland neighbourhood. This is home to some 1,600 graves of Commonwealth soldiers, including Britons, Australians, Canadians, New Zealanders, Indians and East and West Africans. The second cemetery is the Imphal Indian Army War Cemetery in the Hatta neighbourhood. This contains 828 graves, most of which are of Muslim soldiers of the Indian Army. It is also home to the Imphal Cremation Memorial, which commemorates 868 Sikh and Hindu soldiers of the Indian Army who were cremated.

Two caveats are in order here. One, this book limits itself to the Battle of Imphal and the related battlefields around Manipur. It does not look at the simultaneous – albeit shorter – Battle of Kohima which took place in the then Naga Hills of Assam next door. It recognises, however, that the two are closely linked and were part of one overall clash between the Fourteenth and Fifteenth Armies on the India–Burma border in 1944.

Two, this is not intended to be an exhaustive listing of all of the battlefields around Manipur. Only some of the main ones have been presented here and, as and when possible, their photos included.

Figure 4.1 Slim Cottage, Imphal
Source: Photo by Ranjit Moirangthem

Figure 4.2 Imphal Indian Army War Cemetery
Source: Photo by Ranjit Moirangthem

Figure 4.3 Imphal War Cemetery
Source: Photo by Ranjit Moirangthem

The spokes

The routes leading to the hub at Imphal from different directions constituted the spokes of Slim's analogy for the battle. The alignment of these routes are, of course, a result of Manipur's particular geography. The tiny oval-shaped Imphal Valley, which makes up some ten percent of the state's total area, is the main stretch of flat land in a territory overwhelmingly dominated by hills. Imphal sits at the northern end of this valley. As such, for most of their length in Manipur the roads and paths into and out of Imphal are twisting mountain trails. They all flatten out; only once they hit the Imphal Valley.

It is these routes that have always connected the other parts of Manipur and the rest of the world to Imphal, the largest population centre in the state. As the primary seat of power for the former princely state, it has also been – and remains – its centre of political and economic gravity. Naturally then, these routes have played a significant role in Manipur's history. Their link to the Anglo-Manipuri or Khongjom War of 1891 has already been described. In present times, it is on the back of these very roads that the potential for greater connectivity between India and South East Asia is sought to being realised.

It was during the Second World War, however, that these routes were witness to the most dramatic series of events (Figure 4.4). Indeed, the outcome of the entire Japanese offensive of 1944 into India depended on what transpired on or near these very roads leading into and out of Imphal. They

Figure 4.4 Khurai Chingangbam Mandap in Imphal, the site of an aerial bombing on 20 April 1943

Source: Photo by Hemant Singh Katoch

and their environs were the scenes of some of the bitterest fighting of the Second World War as the Japanese advanced towards the town.

The Tiddim Road: White Tigers, Black Cats and a springing tiger

Historical Overview

The old Tiddim Road used to connect Imphal to the town of Tiddim in Burma's Chin Hills, some 164 miles (264 km) to the south, of which some 72 miles (116 km) lie in Manipur on the Indian side of the border. The fighting on the Tiddim Road in 1944 pitted the Japanese 33rd Division against the 17th Indian Division which, in early March, was based around Tiddim. The latter was commanded by Major General D.T. 'Punch' Cowan, while the Japanese were commanded by Lieutenant General Yanagida until May 1944, after which he was replaced by Lieutenant General Tanaka Nobuo.

Imphal was not the first time that the Japanese 33rd Division and the 17th Indian Division faced off with each other. They had also clashed in

Burma in 1942 when the Japanese had roundly defeated the British. It was on and near the Tiddim Road in 1944 that the two battle-hardened divisions were to meet again. Adding to the sense of drama of this clash were the names the two were sometimes referred to as: 33rd Division was also known as the 'White Tigers' due to an old Japanese legend about a group of heroic martyrs called the Byakka Tai (or White Tigers) in an area where one of its regiments came from; the 17th Indian Division was called the 'Black Cat Division' because of a black cat on its formation sign.

The 33rd Division was the first off the mark in the Japanese U Go offensive in 1944, launching its attack towards Tiddim on 7/8 March. This was a full week before the other divisions – the 15th and 31st – began crossing the Chindwin River. The aim was to cut off and destroy the 17th Indian Division and, by attacking early, draw in reinforcements from Imphal, leaving it more vulnerable to attacks by the other Japanese columns. The main infantry units of the 33rd Division involved in the fighting on and along the Tiddim Road in Manipur were 214th Regiment, commanded by Colonel Sakuma Takanobu, and 215th Regiment, commanded by Colonel Sasahara. There was also 2nd Battalion, 213th Regiment (less two companies). As the Battle of Imphal progressed through May and June 1944, these forces were joined by other reinforcements as well, including 1st Battalion, 67th Regiment; 2nd Battalion, 154th Regiment; and 151st Regiment.

The 17th Indian Division was supposed to withdraw to the Imphal Valley as the Japanese attack developed, but instructions from 4 Corps Headquarters in Imphal to do so came too late. By the time the division started withdrawing from Tiddim, the Japanese had already got behind them and cut the road back to Imphal. From then until early April, the 17th Indian Division made a fighting withdrawal to the Imphal Valley. It was helped in the process by two brigades of the 23rd Indian Division that had been sent down the Tiddim Road from Imphal. Most of the key battles during this period – Tonzang, Singgel, Sakawng – took place in the hills on the Burmese part of the Tiddim Road and are not covered here. In early April, the 17th Indian Division arrived safely in the Imphal Valley after severely weakening the Japanese 33rd Division.

This book covers the subsequent fighting on the Tiddim Road from early April to mid-July 1944. This is the only route in the Imphal Valley itself that witnessed heavy fighting during the Battle of Imphal. This involved the Japanese 33rd Division's attempts to capture Imphal and the 17th Indian Division's – together with 32nd Brigade of the 20th Indian Division – thwarting of and pushing back against these efforts. It is understood to have taken place in three broad phases: the first, from early April to early May 1944, was when the Japanese 33rd Division advanced up

Figure 4.5 The Tiddim Road near Bishenpur

Source: Photo by Ranjit Moirangthem

the Tiddim Road to the main British-Indian defensive positions before Imphal at Bishenpur (Figure 4.5).

The second, from early May to early June 1944, was the most crucial phase and involved the clash of the British and Japanese strategies in this sector. The British attempted a hammer and anvil approach to crush the Japanese by pushing them southwards from Potsangbam (the hammer) towards a roadblock at Torbung (the anvil). The Japanese simultaneously attempted to capture Bishenpur from the north, south and west.[3]

The third and last phase, from early June to mid-July 1944, involved an exhausted 33rd Division, together with reinforcements, continuing to launch attacks on British-Indian positions along the Tiddim Road, notably on the villages of Potsangbam and Ningthoukhong. The fighting on the Tiddim Road at this time has to be seen in conjunction with that in the hills along the Silchar–Bishenpur Track, which is where the 33rd Division had concentrated the bulk of its forces.

Commenting on the Japanese attacks around Bishenpur, Slim wrote:

> There can have been few examples in history of a force as reduced, battered, and exhausted as the 33rd Japanese Division delivering such furious assaults, not with the object of extricating itself, but to achieve its original offensive intention.[4]

He went on, after reviewing the order signed by the 33rd Division Commander on which these attacks were based:

> Whatever one may think of the military wisdom of thus pursuing a hopeless object, there can be no question of the supreme courage and hardihood of the Japanese soldiers who made the attempts. I know of no army that could have equalled them.[5]

The battlefields today

To get a good feel of the different types of terrain in which the Battle of Imphal was fought, there is perhaps no better route to explore in Manipur than the Tiddim Road. This book covers some 35 miles (56 km) of the road between Imphal and Torbung, the main arc of fighting on the Imphal Valley in 1944. This stretch, together with the town of Moirang just off the road, also contains a good mix of sights to see: battlefields, memorials and a museum, as well as Manipur's premier tourist attraction, Loktak Lake.

The Tiddim Road up to Torbung today is a tarmac road that is in fairly good condition. It is a major artery for Manipur as it connects Imphal with the state's second-largest city, Churachandpur, which lies just beyond Torbung. The road here is flat and for the most part cuts straight across the Imphal Valley until its southern edges at Torbung, where the hills begin. The villages and towns along the route are separated from each other by expanses of paddy fields; one veteran described them as 'looking much like a kebab with the road as the skewer'.[6]

To the west of the road runs a parallel range of hills that skirt the western edges of the Imphal Valley; parts of this are locally called the Thangjing Range. At a slight distance to the east of the road, beyond the town of Bishenpur and up to Moirang Lamkhai (or the Moirang Fork), lies the Loktak Lake. A casual comparison of the present-day Tiddim Road on this stretch with maps of 1944 shows that its alignment broadly remains the same some 70 years on.

The following is a brief sequence of events in this sector in 1944, involving the main battlefields covered in this book:

7 March	Japanese 33rd Division attacks Tiddim and the road to Imphal
5 April	17th Indian Division arrives safely in the Imphal Valley
14 April	INA flag hoisted at Moirang
29 April	Japanese move into Potsangbam on the Tiddim Road
1–10 May	Four Japanese air raids on Bishenpur

10–15 May	Fighting for the bridge at Potsangbam on the Tiddim Road
17–24 May	Battle of Torbung Roadblock
20–29 May	Battle of Red Hill/Point 2926 (Maibam-Lotpaching)
20–26 May	Japanese attack junction of the Silchar Track and Tiddim Road at Bishenpur
6–7 June	Japanese attacks on Potsangbam and Ningthoukhong Action at Ningthoukhong for which Hanson Victor Turner is awarded a Victoria Cross
12 June	Japanese attack on Ningthoukhong Action at Ningthoukhong for which Ganju Lama is awarded a Victoria Cross
16/17 July	Ningthoukhong Kha Khunou on the Tiddim Road cleared of Japanese forces

TULIHAL AIRFIELD

Heading out of Imphal on the Tiddim Road, one crosses on the city's outskirts its current airport – Tulihal. Tulihal's origins date back to the Second World War, when it came up together with five other airfields in the Imphal Valley. The fact that it eventually became the main airport for Imphal instead of the all-weather Imphal Main (or Koirengei Airfield) might have had something to do with its original length of about 4,000 yards.

The story goes that its length owes to a miscommunication between the British and the Americans at the time of Tulihal's construction. The Americans had wanted it to be 'four thousand long', but they had meant that to be in feet. The British engineer in charge mistakenly assumed the unit of measurement to be yards. And so came up a much longer air strip.[7] This came in handy in March 1944 in particular when Tulihal was also among those used for flying out men of the second Chindit expedition, Operation Thursday.

Tulihal continues to serve Imphal and Manipur well. It is today among the busiest airports in North East India, and the government of India has recently designated it an international airport. It received its first charter flight from Mandalay in Burma in 2013, and efforts are under way to make this a regular service.

RED HILL OR POINT 2926 (MAIBAM LOTPACHING)

The first battlefield one encounters on the Tiddim Road is what was known as Red Hill or Point 2926 during the Battle of Imphal. It is locally known as Maibam Lotpaching and lies to the immediate east of the Tiddim

Figure 4.6 Red Hill (Point 2926) or Maibam Lotpaching
Source: Photo by Ranjit Moirangthem

Road after the town of Nambol (earlier called Buri Bazar). The side of the hill facing the road is covered by trees, while the other slopes are bare. Red Hill rises up abruptly in the surrounding countryside, and it can be distinguished from miles around by the four mobile phone towers that dot its heights today. The village of Maibam lies to its south, with its first few houses separated from the base of Red Hill by a country road (Figure 4.6).

At the base of Red Hill lies India Peace Memorial, the only official Japanese memorial to the Second World War in India (Figure 4.8). It was constructed by the government of Japan in 1994 to mark the 50th Anniversary of the Battle of Imphal. Located just off the Tiddim Road in an enclosed park, the memorial, with its concrete walls and red sandstone flooring is minimalist and stark in design. At its northern end are three uncut blocks of red sandstone. One explanation goes that these signify the drops of blood of Japanese, Indian and British soldiers, respectively, who were lost in the Battle of Imphal.

Adjacent to India Peace Memorial and often overlooked by visitors due to a poorly situated shed that obscures it from view is another, much older and more atmospheric Japanese war memorial. Its design and construction in 1977 is said to have been funded by the survivors of the Japanese 33rd Division that had fought on and near the Tiddim Road. With its more

Figure 4.7 Japanese War Memorial, Maibam Lotpaching
Source: Photo by Ranjit Moirangthem

traditional design and moving Japanese inscriptions honouring the memory of those who lost their lives in the Battle of Imphal, this older memorial makes for a more poignant place of reflection (Figure 4.7). It is also, thankfully, located a little further away from the Tiddim Road and is therefore quieter.

The choice of location of these Japanese memorials is deliberate. For Red Hill and the village of Maibam, like many of the Second World War battlefields along the Tiddim Road, may convey a sense of tranquillity and rural idyll today. It was anything but in May 1944 when a fierce battle raged on Red Hill and its surroundings. Indeed, this was the closest the Japanese came to Imphal from the south during the Battle of Imphal.

Red Hill was attacked on the night of 20/21 May by over 500 Japanese soldiers of the 33rd Division. Belonging mainly to 2nd Battalion, 214th Regiment, they descended down towards the Tiddim Road from the Thangjing Range and approached the hill and the village of Maibam from the south. The Japanese stormed the hill and made repeated attempts on the first night to capture Point 2926, the highest point of the feature, which was being held by a platoon of the 7/10th Baluch. The platoon successfully defended the position through the night, and the platoon commander, Subedar Ghulam Yasin, was later awarded the Military Cross for his action. The Japanese had by now occupied most of the southern

Figure 4.8 India Peace Memorial
Source: Photo by Yaiphaba Kangjam

part of Red Hill, including the two positions of First and Second Pimple, and the adjacent part of Maibam village.

This attack, together with a simultaneous move on the northern end of Bishenpur, was part of the Japanese plan to capture Bishenpur by strikes from the north, west and south. In the end only the northern prongs of the Japanese attack went ahead, while the southern and western actions were put on hold as the British simultaneously launched their own offensive on Japanese positions in the area. Red Hill was part of the northern strike, and it was aimed at cutting the Tiddim Road to prevent reinforcements from Imphal from reaching Bishenpur.

Unbeknownst to the Japanese, however, the hill had gained considerable importance since early May 1944 when the 17th Indian Division's headquarters had moved to Chingphu, a hamlet to its immediate north. The sudden arrival of the Japanese in such numbers and so close to a strategic target was discomforting for the British-Indian forces, to say the least. It became imperative for Major General Cowan to evict the Japanese from Red Hill at the earliest. Intense fighting followed over the next nine days.

The British-Indian forces made several attempts to evict the Japanese. Initially, a scratch force from 17th Division headquarters was used but it was unsuccessful. The second attack was in battalion strength on 22–23 May and involved the 9/12th Frontier Force Regiment (less two companies) from 20th Indian Division, supplemented by two companies from 6/5th Mahratta Light Infantry. Attacking down the Tiddim Road and south-east into Maibam, they were supported by two troops of light tanks from 7th Cavalry and a battery of 25-pounders. The British-Indian units suffered many casualties, and although the attack made some progress, it was called off.

A third attempt was made on 25 May and involved an attack from the north on the southern parts of the hill by two companies of the 7/10th Baluch. Another company, together with four tanks from the 3rd Carabiniers attacked Maibam from the west.[8] Both attacks captured some ground, but the one on the hill was held up by Japanese bunkers on the reverse slope of First Pimple. The Japanese recovered some of the ground lost in the village in a strong counter-attack.

By now it had become clear that a much stronger force was required to clear the Japanese from Red Hill. This came in the shape of headquarters of 50 Indian Parachute Brigade that was commanded by Brigadier E.G. Woods (popularly known as 'Lakri' Woods). They took over on 26 May and were supported by 3/1st Gurkha Rifles of 20th Indian Division, 1/4th Gurkhas from 32nd Brigade and two troops of tanks from 3rd Carabiniers. The composite body of infantry, armour, sappers and artillery he commanded was named after him and was known as 'Woodforce'.[9]

Attacks by Woodforce went in on 27–28 May and after fierce fighting at close range, Red Hill and Maibam village were finally recaptured by 29 May. For getting his tank up on to Red Hill on 27 May and directly supporting the infantry, Lieutenant A. Weir of the 3rd Carabiniers was awarded the Military Cross.

Hundreds of – mostly Japanese – soldiers died in the fighting on Red Hill. Of the 500-strong Japanese force that attacked Red Hill, it is estimated that only about 40 men made it back.[10] The Japanese also suffered casualties in the nearby village of Irengbam, a little further south down the Tiddim Road and to its west. A small memorial there marks the loss of Japanese lives in the fighting of end of May 1944.

BISHENPUR

As one continues on the Tiddim Road, the countryside turns more scenic, with the Thangjing Range, running parallel and to the west, looming ever closer. It is the right setting for the next busy little town: Bishenpur. It was in this then village that the British had set up their main defensive position on the Tiddim Road during the Battle of Imphal. The decision was dictated by terrain: Bishenpur is bounded by hills to its immediate west and by the upper reaches of the Loktak Lake to its east. As Evans and Brett-James noted: 'This was the sole place capable of prolonged defence on the southern approach to Imphal'.[11]

The Japanese needed to capture this then village and the part of the Tiddim Road running through it in order to launch an assault on Imphal with all their heavy guns and armour. It was all the more strategic because in 1944 Bishenpur was the starting point for a jeep track – a battlefield in its own right – that headed westwards and wriggled through the hills all the way to Silchar in Assam (also known as the Silchar–Bishenpur Track in war accounts or Tongjei Maril or Old Cachar Road locally). Bishenpur became the base of 32nd Brigade (20th Indian Division) that had been attached to 17th Indian Division to deal with the Japanese threats on the Tiddim Road and in the western hills. This was where the brigade artillery was located, in a position known as 'Gun Box', around where the present-day Indian Army's Loktak Brigade is located near the junction between the Tiddim Road and the Silchar–Bishenpur Track. It included an impressive array of guns, including eight 25-pounders, four 3.7 Howitzers, six 6-pounders and three A/A guns. From Bishenpur, they 'poured fire into the Japanese positions in the hills'.[12]

Bishenpur was therefore vital to the British-Indian defences in the Tiddim Road sector. It was naturally an attractive target for the Japanese, too, and they attached much importance to its capture. Indeed, one British military historian characterises the fighting on and near the Tiddim Road during this period as the Battle(s) of Bishenpur.[13] Like Imphal that similarly lent its name to the overall battle in Manipur in 1944, however, Bishenpur itself was not much affected directly by the fighting raging all around it.

The exception was the month of May 1944. In the first half of that month the Japanese Army Air Force attacked Bishenpur. Their main target was Gun Box. In the first ten days of May, four air raids were made with between 12 and 25 planes in each attack.[14] Bishenpur was also directly attacked from the north on 20/21 May by 214th Regiment of the 33rd Division. As noted before, this attack was launched simultaneously with that on Red Hill. The area targeted was at the northern edge of the village where the Silchar Track branches off. The British furiously counter-attacked the Japanese positions over the next few days, including with tanks. An entire Japanese company was wiped out. Another 70 men sent in on 26 May met with the same fate. It is estimated that 1st Battalion of 214th Regiment which carried out the attack ended up losing some 360 of their 380 men.[15]

A 20th Indian Division intelligence summary describes the whole area as a 'carpet of dead' by the end of the operation made up of the decomposing remains of dead soldiers and mules.[16]

POTSANGBAM

Just down the road from Bishenpur is Potsangbam, the northernmost village on the Tiddim Road occupied by the Japanese during the Battle of Imphal. The Japanese had entered the village at the end of April and dug themselves in well. Christened 'Pots and Pans' by British troops, Potsangbam witnessed fierce fighting through that month as the British sought to recapture it.

An excellent description of the village at the time comes from the British veteran and military historian Ian Lyall Grant. He writes:

> Like all Manipuri villages Potsangbam was a chequer-board of ditches and banks studded with many clumps of giant bamboo. Mango and banana trees proliferated and were interspersed with other fruit and spice trees. The thatched mud houses were usually on raised mud platforms and many had a square pond outside for water supply. There was plenty of cover to be exploited and the Japanese were adept at using it.[17]

This description continues to apply to parts of modern-day Potsangbam (and Ningthoukhong), although there are many more houses today and they are mostly concrete structures.

Initial attempts by 32nd Brigade to recapture Potsangbam were unsuccessful. The village was subjected to heavy artillery bombardments at this time. Together with Ningthoukhong, it was also bombed from the air. For example, three squadrons of Vengeance dive bombers bombed Potsangbam on 7 May, while Strategic Airforce Liberators pattern-bombed both Potsangbam and Ningthoukhong with 1,000-lb bombs.[18] A combined force of infantry (9/14th Punjab) and Medium tanks attacked the village from the north-west. It captured some ground but was held up by Japanese anti-tank guns and machine guns. A constant concern for the British in their efforts to recapture Potsangbam and Ningthoukhong was shelling from Japanese positions in the hills to the west, especially Kokadan.

A key feature of relevance to the Battle of Imphal in Potsangbam is the *turel* or stream over which the Tiddim Road passes. The stream runs west to east through the village and divides it into northern and southern halves. The bridge over the stream on the Tiddim Road and the area on both sides of the stream east of the road was where much of the fighting took place in May 1944. Today one can still walk along the Potsangbam turel, east of the bridge on the Tiddim Road, to get a feel of the scene of much fighting in May 1944. This part of the turel is not yet built up, and bamboo clumps and lush vegetation still line its banks.

There was a British-Indian operation from 10 to 15 May aimed at securing the bridge over the Potsangbam turel and the areas surrounding it. The operation was led by 63rd Brigade of the 17th Indian Division, commanded by Brigadier Guy Burton. It involved two battalions, the 1/3rd Gurkhas and 1/10th Gurkhas, each supported by artillery and a troop of Medium tanks from the 3rd Carabiniers. After the initial attack by the 1/3rd Gurkhas on the main village east of the road, the Japanese had withdrawn across the stream into southern Potsangbam. This area on both sides of the stream then became the focus of the fighting.

After full frontal attacks failed to make much progress against the strongly held Japanese positions, the 63rd Brigade commander decided to change tack. He devised a plan whereby an artillery bombardment from the Gurkhas' front in north Potsangbam across the turel made it appear that the direction and tactics of their previous attacks were being repeated. Instead, the 1/10th Gurkhas passed secretly behind the main front held by the 1/3rd Gurkhas and attacked the bridge over the Potsangbam turel and the area immediately surrounding it east of the Tiddim Road.[19] The plan worked and, despite the expected counter-attacks by the Japanese, the bridge and the surrounding parts of the village were in British-Indian hands by 15 May. The Tiddim Road through Potsangbam was open, although some Japanese continued to hang on in the south-eastern corner of the village for another couple of weeks.

The Japanese defence of Potsangbam in May 1944 is significant because it frustrated the British strategy for the Tiddim Road at this time: to push back the Japanese from Potsangbam onwards (the hammer) against the roadblock at Torbung (the anvil). Faced with the delay at Potsangbam, Major General Cowan decided to abandon the push southwards down the road and instead ordered 63rd Brigade to attack the Japanese positions in the hills. To deal with this British incursion in the hills, the Japanese finally withdrew from Potsangbam, and Ningthoukhong became the main Japanese defensive position on the Tiddim Road. The last major Japanese attack on Potsangbam took place on the night of 6/7 June and involved an approach from the south-west across the paddy fields. It proved unsuccessful in the face of well-defended British-Indian positions.

Beyond the village one finds countryside that is fairly typical of the Imphal Valley: beautiful paddy fields flank both sides of the road, interrupted by villages often situated in tall bamboo clumps, with bluish-green hills never too far away from view. It is no wonder that Evans and Brett-James characterised the fighting in the area as 'village and paddy field fighting'.[20] For battlefield tourists and historians, the scenery is a clear bonus – exploring the battlefields not only allows one to get a better sense of the fascinating Second World War history of Manipur but also lets one enjoy the beauty of this little-known North East Indian state.

A stop on the Tiddim Road just beyond the turn off heading eastwards for Potsangbam is a case in point. It involves walking about a hundred yards or so into the paddy fields to the west of the road. From this vantage point, one is confronted with a breathtaking panorama of villages set amid bamboo, gleaming paddy fields and the western hills up ahead, the peaks – such as Point 5846 – often shrouded in mist. It is from here that one is able to grasp not just how the fighting in this sector unfolded in 1944 but also the reasons for the Japanese defeat. One sees how the Japanese generals had taken a huge risk by assuming a timeline of under a month for the capture of Imphal, with their supply and communication lines strung out over very difficult terrain. It was a timeline that was to go awry, thanks to a better trained and logistically supported enemy than the Japanese had imagined, with devastating consequences for the thousands of soldiers fighting in these very hills and fields.

NINGTHOUKHONG

Continuing on the Tiddim Road, one arrives in Ningthoukhong. At first glance, it is hard to imagine that this bustling town has anything to do with the Second World War. In fact, quite the opposite is true. The then village of Ningthoukhong saw the most intense fighting between the British-Indian forces and the Japanese in the Imphal Valley during the Battle of Imphal – and for the longest period of time. Evans and Brett-James, setting their comment in April 1944, write: 'During the next three months Ningthoukhong was the scene of many a battle, and along with Shenam, it probably received more shelling than any other area in Burma or Assam.'[21]

The terrain in Ningthoukhong is much like Potsangbam, and it was similarly well suited for defence rather than offensive actions in 1944. The Japanese used this to their advantage, and parts of the village were under their continuous control from mid-April to mid-July 1944. In another parallel with Potsangbam, the banks of the turel here, which also runs west to east and bisects the village into northern and southern halves, were again the scene of much action (Figure 4.9). If anything, the Ningthoukhong turel saw a lot more fighting and of a greater intensity and duration. Also, unlike at Kohima and some of the other sectors of fighting around Manipur, it was in the fighting on the Tiddim Road around Bishenpur that tanks were used by both the British and the Japanese. The Japanese were able to bring them up the Tiddim Road, something that was not feasible around Kohima.

Figure 4.9 The Ningthoukhong turel
Source: Photo by Bishwajeet Hemam

The key month in Ningthoukhong was June 1944. Initial attempts by the British-Indian units to recapture the village after the arrival of the Japanese in mid-April had been largely unsuccessful. They had consisted of infantry and tank actions, supported by artillery and preceded by air strikes, aimed at the northern part of Ningthoukhong.[22] The well-hidden Japanese were able to repulse these actions.[23] By June, however, the turel divided the two sides east of the Tiddim Road: in North Ningthoukhong were the British-Indian forces, while the Japanese were ensconced in South Ningthoukhong. Despite their mounting losses and reverses around Manipur, the commander of the Japanese 33rd Division ordered all-out attacks around the Silchar Track and on the Tiddim Road in early June. The stage was set for especially heavy fighting along the Ningthoukhong turel in the first half of June in which two men would later be awarded the Victoria Cross.

The first major Japanese attack on the British-Indian positions came on the night of 6/7 June. At the time the 1st West Yorkshires were in North Ningthoukhong, together with two companies of the 2/5th Gurkhas. The Japanese used a company of newly arrived reinforcements in the shape of 1st Battalion, 67th Regiment. The plan was for the company to head out west, cross the turel and then move east along the turel to attack North Ningthoukhong across the Tiddim Road. They were to be supported by light tanks that would cross the turel along the road.

The Japanese attack could not make much progress, thanks in no small part to Sergeant Hanson Victor Turner of the 1st West Yorkshires. He was one of the section commanders of the platoon that was defending the targeted position. He went back and forth on five occasions to gather grenades with which he attacked the Japanese, thereby single-handedly repulsing them. On the sixth occasion, he was killed while throwing a grenade. For his actions on that day, he was posthumously awarded the Victoria Cross. He is buried at the Imphal War Cemetery.

A second major Japanese attack went in on 12 June, this time frontally across the turel from South to North Ningthoukhong. The war diary of 2/5th Gurkha Rifles gives a good feel of the village and paddy field fighting of that day:

> **12 June**: T.a from the 2 pdrs. Enemy attacked 0520, about two coys supported by six tanks. Tanks moved along perimeter blasting our forward bunkers with 47 m.m.H.E. at point blank range. Then turned in with infantry and over ran our forward positions causing our men to fall back on the S.W. corner for a depth of 200 yards. The 2 pdr shot the barrel off the leading tank, which turned aside to allow another tank to advance. This was completely knocked out by the 2 pdr. Two others of the enemy tanks trying to evade this grave yard bogged themselves. A fifth tank advancing up to the right of our perimeter over ran our other 2 pdr before it was ready in action, and bogged itself just by the gun. This latter tank was piated by Lieut Little of D Coy. The enemy tanks all having been brought up to a standstill, our troops were able to hold the enemy infantry attack. By 0930 hrs this position was stabilised with the enemy holding an area 200x X 300x of our S.W. corner. During the whole action, the enemy fired his mortars to good effect on our rear areas killing Lt. P.C. Lewin, our Q.M., S.M. Dile amongst others.
>
> At 1430 hrs counter attack was started under heavy arty barrage of 8 minutes and supported by our six tanks firing from the road. The counter was put in by 2 Coys of 1/7 G.R. At first advance was slow due to enemy shelling giving our troops the impression that they were right up under our barrage, but after about ½ an hour the 1/7 went in at the run and had great fun piating the bogged tanks and setting them on fire and shooting running Japs. By 1600 hrs the whole of the position was again in our hands with considerable enemy equipment, including 4 medium tanks and 1 light tank and 70 counted dead.[24]

For single-handedly knocking out two of the Japanese tanks and killing or injuring their crews, despite being injured himself, Rifleman Ganju Lama of the 1/7th Gurkha Rifles was later awarded the Victoria Cross. These attacks in June were the last attempts by the Japanese to advance up the Tiddim Road. Although they did not succeed, the Japanese continued to hang on to their positions in Ningthoukhong until mid-July.

Ningthoukhong has grown into a small town today. To get a sense of the fighting in the village in 1944, one needs to turn off the Tiddim Road and head east along the turel for a few hundred yards. This was where some of the most intense fighting described earlier took place. Although there are many more houses here now and during the dry season the turel becomes little more than a trickle, there are areas near the small bridges over the turel where the bamboo clumps and trees close in at least on one side. It is here where one gets a feel of the conditions in which the fighting unfolded, especially in June 1944. The closely packed bamboo and the houses hidden by trees in South Ningthoukhong in particular reinforce the point that these parts were ideally suited for defence rather than offence. It is no wonder then that the tenacious Japanese were able to stubbornly maintain their positions here for several months against all odds – and much greater firepower on the side of the British-Indian units.

A perfect case in point is the adjoining village of Ningthoukhong Kha Khunou. Driving down the Tiddim Road after Ningthoukhong, one barely notices when this village passes by. Yet, it was here that the Japanese held out the longest in mid-July 1944 to cover the retreat of their forces from the hills around the Silchar Track and along the Tiddim Road. In 1944, Ningthoukhong Kha Khunou was small, some 200–300 yards wide and 500 yards in length.[25] It was this tiny space that on 16 July was subjected to what has been described as 'one of the heaviest artillery concentrations yet fired in Burma'; some 9,000 shells were fired into it in less than an hour by seven batteries from different British artillery regiments.[26] At the end of it, Grant writes, 'The village itself was an amazing sight. It was a sea of huge water-logged bomb craters, shell-holes and sticky mud, with not a house and scarcely a tree or bank standing.'[27]

Hardly easy at the best of times, conditions for soldiers of both sides in the villages along the Tiddim Road became increasingly difficult in the monsoon rains. One notices references to this in the war diary of the 2/5th Gurkha Rifles for June 1944:

14 June [Potsangbam]: Heavy rain last night. The river rose and flooded its banks. There was not a single bunker or slit trench that could be used. The mess was full of water and considerable damage done. All mortar amn spoilt, much equipment washed away including A Coy's rum issue. During the day things began to dry out again, but more rain about mid-day, caused the river to over flow its banks again in the afternoon.

On 16 June, it notes, 'More rain. Conditions appalling.' For 19 June, it says, 'Trench feet, fever and dysentery on up grade. 23 men evacuated.'[28]

With even less logistical and medical support and fewer supplies, the soldiers of the Japanese 33rd Division on an off the Tiddim Road fared far worse in 1944.

TORBUNG

Moving on south from Ningthoukhong, one traverses more villages – Thinungei, Phubala, Naranseina – all of which saw fighting of varying intensity during the Battle of Imphal. At the end of July 1944, the detritus of war lay scattered everywhere in these parts. For example, 14 abandoned Japanese tanks were found in the two villages of Ningthoukhong Kha Khunou and Thinungei.[29] Around 15 minutes after driving past Moirang Lamkhai (the Moirang Fork) in the direction of Churachandpur, just beyond the village of Torbung comes the area where the 'anvil' of the British strategy was put into effect: the site of the Torbung Roadblock of May 1944.

Torbung was the original choice for the main British-Indian defensive position on the Tiddim Road. It is at one end of the Imphal Valley if one is travelling south from Imphal – or at its entrance if one is heading northwards from Tiddim. Depending on the direction one is coming from, this is where the hills begin and the valley ends or the other way round. The defensive position was changed to Bishenpur in mid-April when on a recce Brigadier D.A.L. Mackenzie, the commander of 32nd Brigade, observed that the Japanese were outflanking the Torbung area by approaching Imphal via the western hills above it.

In the second half of May 1944, it was decided that 48th Brigade, commanded by Brigadier Ronnie Cameron, would site a roadblock behind Japanese lines on the Tiddim Road at Torbung. This would be the anvil against which the Japanese 33rd Division would be pushed from Potsangbam. Or so the plan went. As it turned out, the push southwards by 63rd Brigade of the 17th Indian Division (the hammer) was frustrated by the Japanese defence of that village in the first half of May. It was ultimately called off. But the Torbung Roadblock was set up as scheduled by 48th Brigade, which arrived in the area in mid-May. It had reached the Tiddim Road by a circuitous route: from east of the Loktak Lake it had moved

Figure 4.10 Site of the Torbung Roadblock, with Point 3404 in the background

Source: Photo by Hemant Singh Katoch

southwards, secretly crossed the Manipur River and then made for the road. It had two infantry battalions, the 1/7th and 2/5th Gurkha Rifles, as well as 21 Mountain Artillery Regiment and two mule companies.

The original aim was to have two roadblocks, some 1½ miles (2½ km) apart. Ultimately, only the southern roadblock was set up around some nullahs at the then Milestone 33.2, as the northern site was found to be occupied by the Japanese. The brigade headquarters was set up at Point 3404, a hill overlooking the area of the roadblock and an adjacent, lower hill. The roadblock was established by men of the 1/7th Gurkha Rifles on 17 May, and it was held for an entire week, until 24 May (Figure 4.10).

The nullahs between which the roadblock was set up near Torbung can still be seen today. The easiest to spot is the bridge over the nullah at the then Milestone 33. This was to be the northern perimeter of the roadblock, but another nullah to the south, which was to be the southern perimeter, was chosen instead. This was because the Gurkhas found four tanks heading their way down the Tiddim Road before they had had a chance to dig in. A lesser nullah became the new southern perimeter. All three can be still be identified, although many houses have now sprung up on the road between them.

The Torbung Roadblock and its surrounding areas were the scene of fierce fighting from 17 to 24 May 1944. Because it prevented the movement of vital Japanese supplies and reinforcements up and down the Tiddim Road and had been established behind their lines, the Japanese reacted furiously to its discovery. Infantry attacks were launched against the roadblock and artillery fire was directed towards it and Point 3404. The British responded with counter-battery fire against the Japanese gun and mortar positions in the surrounding hills. The Gurkhas destroyed eight lorries and two Japanese tanks at the roadblock; one tank was destroyed by Rifleman Ganju Lama of the 1/7th Gurkha Rifles, for which he was awarded the Military Medal. He went on to win a Victoria Cross less than a month later at Ningthoukhong.

The war diary of 1/7th Gurkha Rifles of May 1944 sheds some light on the fighting at the Torbung Roadblock and the waves of Japanese attacks launched at it after its discovery:

17 May: 2000 hrs. 4 Japanese light tanks approached from north. Engaged with P.I.A.T.s, Molotov cocktails and L.M.G.s. 2 tanks knocked out and one damaged.

2200 hrs. 8 lorries approached from south and allowed to enter perimeter when engaged with L.M.G.s, grenades, Molotov cocktails. 52 Japs in lorries were killed and much equipment, arms, ammunitions and food captured. All lorries destroyed.

18 May: 2200 hrs. One platoon enemy attacked from west. Attack driven off with heavy casualties. 'Jitter' patrols by Japanese throughout night.

19 May: 15 Japs counted dead as result of last night's attack.

1100 hrs. Hurricanes strafed us with cannon as result of which we suffered following casualties – Killed: 5 Gurkha Other Ranks (G.O.R.s), 15 mules.

2000 hrs. Heavy attacks from south and west put in by Japs and persisted throughout the night but all attacks repelled. C.O. (Lt. Col. A.R. Robertson) wounded by grenade discharger shell.

20 May: 105 Jap bodies counted near perimeter as result of last night's action and there are many more which we cannot reach in the jungle. Our casualties: CO wounded and evacuated. Killed: 7 G.O.R.s. Wounded 16 G.O.R.s.

2000 hrs. Further attacks by Japs from west all repulsed and 15 dead Japs counted in morning. Our casualties: Killed 3 G.O.R.s. Wounded 10 G.O.R.s.

21 May: 1800 hrs. Japs attacked heavily from south west and penetrated perimeter at our sector. 'B' Coy put in immediate

counter-attack led by Major Wyatt and restored situation. At least 35 Japs killed. Our casualties: Killed 6 G.O.R.s. Wounded 13 G.O.R.s.
22 May: Fairly heavy shelling and mortar fire. No attacks by Japs except patrols, are driven off.
23 May: Intermittent shelling during day.
1900 hrs. Heavy shelling and mortar fire. Own casualties up to midnight: Killed 3 G.O.R.s Wounded 12 G.O.R.s.[30]

An entry in the war diary of 48th Brigade on 22 May 1944 gives an idea of the casualties sustained by the Japanese in the attacks on the Torbung Roadblock and Point 3404:

> **22 May**: 1630 hrs. Enemy casualties since start of scheme 'Ayo' counted killed at road block 238 and Pt. 3404 killed 58. These figures do not include killed and wounded in nalas and jungle. Estimated figures at least 500 killed.[31]

The roadblock had worked in that it had disrupted the movement of Japanese supplies on the Tiddim Road and inflicted heavy casualties. However, since it was supposed to have been the anvil to 63rd Brigade's hammer and the latter did not materialise, it was decided to abandon this position. 48th Brigade then embarked on a fighting march along the Tiddim Road all the way back to Bishenpur, engaging with the Japanese all along the way.

THE INA MEMORIAL COMPLEX

One has to take a U-turn after Torbung, head back towards the Moirang Lamkhai and this time take the road leading to Moirang. Moirang, a town on the southern edge of Loktak Lake, is home to the only such INA Memorial Complex in the world (Figure 4.11). It includes the INA War Museum, an auditorium, a library, a statue of Netaji Subhash Chandra Bose and a replica of the original INA Memorial whose foundation stone was laid by Netaji in Singapore in 1945. Inscribed on the top of the memorial are the three watchwords of the INA: Ittefaq (Unity), Itmad (Faith) and Qurbani (Sacrifice).

The complex is a reminder of the importance of the Battle of Imphal to the INA story. The INA was involved at Imphal through the deployment of its 1st Division on the flanks of the Tamu–Palel Road and through its Special Groups. Also known as Bahadur ('courageous') Groups, they were units of between 200 and 250 men attached to each of the Japanese divisions making their way towards Imphal and Kohima. Acting as spies, guides and propagandists, their main job was to 'penetrate British lines, make contact with sepoys, and persuade them, whole bodies of them if possible, to

Figure 4.11 Indian National Army (INA) Memorial Complex, Moirang

Source: Photo by Ranjit Moirangthem

come over'.[32] It was the men of these units who were active in Moirang and its vicinity; they had come along with the Japanese 33rd Division.

The INA Memorial Complex is located here because this was where – the spot is still preserved – INA men of the Bahadur Group, under the command of Colonel S.A. Malik, hoisted their army's flag for the first time on the Indian mainland on 14 April 1944. Its flag is said to have featured the figure of a springing tiger, one of the symbols of the INA. Moirang is also where the Advance INA headquarters for their operations in Manipur and the then Naga Hills was set up.[33] The house in which these headquarters were based still survives on the town's outskirts.

For decades, the INA War Museum was the only museum dedicated to the Second World War in Manipur. Besides containing photographs of the INA and Netaji Subhash Chandra Bose, it also displays relics of war that were discovered around Manipur by locals and donated to the museum. There is a separate section at the museum that touches on the support given by some people in Manipur to the INA.

SENDRA AND KEIBUL LAMJAO NATIONAL PARK

The last stop for most visitors after the INA Memorial Complex is the nearby Sendra Resort that offers magnificent views of Loktak Lake, the largest freshwater lake in North East India. Top of the to-do list of every visitor to Manipur, Sendra has become an even more attractive destination, thanks to its takeover by a private hospitality company that has cleaned the area up. Although of no direct relevance to the Second World War, from the viewpoints at Sendra one can pinpoint and retrace in the distance the route just taken along the Tiddim Road all the way back to Red Hill.

Finally, for those who have the time and the inclination, one can continue on to Keibul Lamjao National Park. It is said to be the only floating national park in the world, thanks to the floating mass of soil and vegetation – locally called phumdi – that makes up a large part of its area. It is also the sole home of the endangered brow-antlered deer called the Sangai. The Sangai is a shy animal, however, and is often difficult to spot during the day from the park's watchtowers. The park is still worth a visit for the stunning views of the surrounding areas it affords.

CASUALTIES ON THE TIDDIM ROAD

The Tiddim Road is the only sector of fighting in the Battle of Imphal where there is some clarity on casualty figures for both sides. This is due to the work of the British veteran and military historian Ian Lyall Grant. He estimates that the number of Japanese killed and injured in the Tiddim Road sector is as follows: 7,900 killed; 2,100 dead from wounds; 4,300 dead from sickness; and some 12,000 wounded. This comes to a total of some 26,300 casualties (14,300 killed, 12,000 wounded) or around half the overall number estimated for Imphal–Kohima.[34]

It should be noted, however, that Grant takes into account all of the fighting on/around the Tiddim Road, including the Burma portion of it and pre- and post-Battle of Imphal. For the Allies, he estimates 6,740 casualties, including dead and injured.

For the other sectors of fighting, figures can be obtained for some individual battles, such as at Shangshak and Nungshigum. But it remains difficult to get more precise overall numbers by sector.

The Silchar–Bishenpur Track: picquets and Point 5846

Historical overview

This was the dirt track that branched off west from the Tiddim Road at Bishenpur, climbed over the hills on the western rim of the Imphal Valley and – in 1944 – wriggled over more hill ranges and valleys to reach

Silchar in eastern Assam, some 110 miles (177 km) away. British military memoirs refer to this route as the Silchar–Bishenpur Track or the Silchar Track. The people of Manipur know it as the Old Cachar Road or, in Manipuri, Tongjei Maril. This book will use the simple nomenclature 'Silchar Track' for the most part.

Like the Imphal–Kohima Road, the Silchar Track was another route connecting Imphal to Assam and the rest of India during the Second World War. The volume of traffic on this track was, however, miniscule compared to that which came to Manipur via Kohima and the main railhead at Dimapur. It was nevertheless a target for the Japanese as they sought to encircle Imphal in 1944 and cut off all land routes to 4 Corps in the Imphal Valley. A raiding party from the Japanese 33rd Division, together with some INA men, blew up the 300-foot suspension bridge spanning the Leimatak River on the night of 14/15 April. This was where the track descended from the western hills into the Leimatak River valley. The Silchar Track was so cut and the Japanese siege of Imphal truly begun.

As on the Tiddim Road, it was 214th Regiment, commanded by Colonel Sakuma, and 215th Regiment, commanded by Colonel Sasahara, of the Japanese 33rd Division that were active in this sector. In May and June 1944, these units were joined by reinforcements in this sector, including 2nd Battalion, 213th Regiment (less two companies); 1st Battalion, 67th Regiment; 2nd Battalion, 154th Regiment; and 151st Regiment.

The men of these units faced off with the 17th Indian Division, in particular 32nd Brigade – originally from the 20th Indian Division – that had been attached to it. 32nd Brigade was commanded by Brigadier D.A.L. Mackenzie. Owing to their geographic proximity, the fighting on the Silchar Track was closely connected and interlinked with that on the Tiddim Road. It was also equally fierce. As Slim commented in the context of the Battle of Imphal: 'It was along the Tiddim Road and the Silchar–Bishenpur track, the southern and western spokes of the wheel, that some of the heaviest fighting of this Battle of Attrition took place.'[35]

The importance of the Silchar Track, particularly the stretch from its starting point on the Tiddim Road up to the top of the western hill range (at Point 5846), a distance of some 7 miles (11 km), was also closely linked to Bishenpur. As noted earlier, Bishenpur was the main British defensive position on the Tiddim Road and its capture would have allowed the Japanese to move practically unopposed to Imphal. This stretch of the Silchar Track overlooked Bishenpur, and had it fallen into Japanese hands, the defensive positions around the then village would have become very difficult to hold.

The fighting on and around the Silchar Track in 1944 involved determined Japanese attempts to approach Imphal from the west and to block their opponents' use of the track – and similarly dogged British-Indian efforts to thwart these twin objectives. For the Japanese, the shortest way over the western hills towards Imphal was to cut across the Silchar Track. As the British-Indian units largely prevented this from happening, they had to use a more circuitous route around from the west. The overall flow of fighting in this sector mirrored that of the Tiddim Road. April 1944 saw the initial Japanese thrust towards Imphal being halted. The difference here was that in the second half of the month the two sides literally raced each other to occupy the main vantage points over the Silchar Track. The month of May saw the clash of the Japanese and British strategies over Bishenpur, which also affected the Silchar Track. And finally in June 1944, against all odds the much weakened Japanese 33rd Division launched its last major attacks in this sector. Throughout, the two sides patrolled aggressively, ambushed each other and, perhaps most important, sought to gain and maintain possession of favourable positions astride the Silchar Track. Given the terrain and conditions, it was campaigning at its hardest.

The battlefields today

Of all of the spokes that were the scenes of fighting during the Battle of Imphal, the Silchar Track is probably the most difficult one to travel on today. This is mainly to do with the bad condition of the track. The tarmac at Bishenpur quickly gives way to what is still more or less a dirt track. How a veteran then described it still holds true: "'Jeepable in Dry Season" the map said, and was just about right!'[36] One reason is that the route is no longer used to connect Imphal to Silchar via Bishenpur; a new road today heads west to Silchar directly from Imphal. The old track therefore goes only up to a few dozen kilometres today, connecting remote villages along the way.

The stretch of the track of particular interest is from Bishenpur up to the vicinity of the hill called Point 5846 (or Laimaton in Manipuri). Unfortunately, even this initial bit is in bad shape today. It is recommended to be tackled in a four-wheel-drive vehicle. Once the track starts climbing the hills above Bishenpur, it also becomes increasingly isolated and is best done with someone local who is knowledgeable or is, ideally, from the area. For foreign nationals, as a measure of precaution, it is also advisable to notify in advance the Bishenpur Police Station of any intended travel up the track.

Another point to bear in mind if doing the Silchar Track by car is that after the old location of the village of Ngariyan, the present-day track diverges from the old, war-era alignment. The old track, which is still there, albeit in even worse condition, rises steeply until it reaches a flat, grassy patch, with Point 5846 to its north on one side and the features of Wooded Ridge – what the Japanese called Mori – and Wireless Hill – or Japanese Antenna – to its south. It is not possible to proceed beyond this point on the old track as it has been taken over by the jungle. The new alignment takes a longer route, with a much gentler incline, that curls south of Wooded Ridge.

On the flip side, those who brave the Silchar Track by car are likely to encounter parts that are incredibly atmospheric and seem to have changed little since 1944. On stretches of the track the jungle presses in on both sides, making it difficult to discern what lies beyond. These are just the sort of conditions the British-Indian units and the Japanese encountered when they faced off here some 70 years ago.

Based on the condition of the Silchar Track at the time of writing, it is recommended that it is ideally approached on foot. Health and fitness permitting, the best way to explore the area is under the aegis of the Manipur Mountaineering and Trekking Association (MMTA), which organises treks that take one right up to the top of Point 5846. MMTA has a facility in the hills at Lamdan, which is easily and safely accessed on a tarmac road that branches off the Tiddim Road short of Ningthoukhong. They do all of the required notifications to the authorities in the area prior to the trek and use guides who are from the area and know it intimately. This is how the author has tackled the Silchar Track on several occasions, and the information on the battlefields given here is presented accordingly – as seen on a trek.

The following is a brief sequence of events in this sector in 1944, involving the main battlefields covered in this book:

13–26 April	Fight for Point 5846, Wooded Hill/Mori and Wireless Hill/Antenna on the Silchar Track
14/15 April	Japanese blow up bridge on the Silchar Track
20–26 May	Japanese attack junction of the Silchar Track and Tiddim Road at Bishenpur
10 June	32nd Brigade's first attack on Dome south of the Silchar Track
13/14 June	32nd Brigade's second attack on Dome south of the Silchar Track
21–26 June	Fighting rages for the picquets along the Silchar Track
26 June	Action at Mortar Bluff for which Netrabahadur Thapa is awarded a Victoria Cross
	Action at Mortar Bluff and Water Picquet for which Agan Singh Rai is awarded a Victoria Cross

Setting out from Lamdan, one follows a path northwards along the top of the ridge. In 1944 this was the route taken by thousands of Japanese soldiers of the 33rd Division who were approaching Imphal from the west. They had left the Tiddim Road and climbed these hills that make up the western rim of the Imphal Valley. This path on the ridgeline was also the main supply line for the men in the hills.

The men who had walked these parts some 70 years ago belonged to the 33rd Division's 214th and 215th Regiments, as well as other units that were brought in as reinforcements. They made up the bulk of the 33rd Division that was active here and on the Tiddim Road. The task of 214th Regiment was to get across the Silchar Track to the hills to its north, from where they were to be ready to strike at Bishenpur or Imphal.[37] These were the men who carried out the attacks on Bishenpur and Red Hill in May 1944. The objective of 215th Regiment was to secure a corridor from the villages of Kokadan to Khoirok – the shortest route to the hills to the north – which crossed the track around the old location of Ngariyan.

In some sections the path skirts along edges of the ridge with steep drops of several hundred feet. For the most part, however, the path today is well trod and allows for fairly easy passage, until the area of Wireless Hill/Antenna further north. Along the way, the first battlefield one crosses is what the British had then called Dome.

Dome is a hill approximately a mile south of Wireless Hill along the top of the ridge. Today, as in 1944, the approaches to this bare hill – especially from the north – are devoid of any cover. The Japanese had dug in positions on Dome, and the hill and its adjacent features were the object of a major attack by men of 32nd Brigade in the second week of June 1944. The attack was part of a broader push southwards by 17th Indian Division both in the Silchar Track area and on the Tiddim Road. In this case the two battalions involved in the attack, the 3/8th Gurkhas and the 1st Northamptons, were attemptir.g to push southwards along the ridge from their strongholds at Wireless Hill and Point 5846.[38]

The first attack went in on 10 June, followed by a second on the night of 13/14 June. In the first attempt, both Dome and a nearby feature were targeted. An air strike preceded the attack, but the units on the ground had difficulty with the approaches to their targets and it was called off.[39] Only Dome was the object of the second operation, which was carried out in pouring rain at night. Although some progress was made, the attack faltered the next morning in bright sunshine and was cancelled.

The lack of cover around Dome allowed the Japanese machine-gunners on the hill to successfully ward off the attackers. The Allies suffered 104 casualties, including 11 killed in the 3/8th Gurkhas and 19 in the 1st Northamptons.[40]

Walking the ground today, it is amazing to consider that battalion-strength attacks were carried out in this area in pouring rain and pitch darkness in 1944. Never mind the ever-present threat of Japanese snipers and machine-gunners, the terrain around Dome – especially to its west – is such that one wrong step would have sent men hurtling down the ridge to a near certain death.

Continuing on from Dome, the ground becomes surprisingly Alpine in feel, with open stretches of grass, gentle slopes and stunning views on both sides of the ridge. To the east one can catch glimpses of the Imphal Valley, with Loktak Lake gleaming in the distance on clear days (Figure 4.12). To the west, an endless series of mountain ranges stretch as far as the eyes can see. The prettiness of the terrain today sits in surreal contrast with knowledge of the kind of death and destruction that these parts witnessed some 70 years ago. Before long, one crosses the new alignment of the Silchar Track. Up a steep incline north from this road are the key features of what the British called Wireless Hill and the Japanese Antenna, and Wooded Ridge or Mori.

Figure 4.12 Looking on to Loktak Lake from the Silchar Track

Source: Photo by Ranjit Moirangthem

Figure 4.13 Point 5846 or Laimaton

Source: Photo by Hemant Singh Katoch

WOODED RIDGE/MORI AND WIRELESS HILL/ANTENNA

Wooded Ridge, so called because it was then forested, lay on the south-ern side of a saddle over which the old Silchar Track passed.[41] Point 5846 lay to the north of this saddle (Figure 4.13). It is because of their location, on either side of where the old Silchar Track passed over the hills that made up the western rim of the Imphal Valley, that both the British-Indian and Japanese forces attached such importance to these two positions in 1944. It also made them and their surroundings the scene of much fighting at the time.

Around mid-April 1944, as part of the Japanese push towards Imphal in this sector, the two sides scrambled to capture these two positions. Men of 32nd Brigade on the British-Indian side and of 214th Regi-ment on the side of the Japanese fought for possession of these two hills, and of Wireless Hill/Antenna. The latter, so called because it then had a wireless mast on it, lay some 200 yards to the east of Wooded Ridge/Mori (Figure 4.14). As Ian Lyall Grant puts it, 'It was a race to seize these key points, a race which the British were to win by a narrow margin.'[42]

Figure 4.14 Looking south from Point 5846 towards Wooded Ridge/Mori (right), Wireless Hill/Antenna (left), Dome (farther left) and the western hills

Source: Photo by Hemant Singh Katoch

The fighting here was often dramatic. The war diary of the 32nd Brigade describes a Japanese attack on Wireless Hill:

18 April: 1930 hrs. A strong attack was put in by the Jap on 3/8 GR and Northamptons coy posn. The enemy got into our posns, hand to hand fighting taking place. The enemy was driven out by a counter attack by 3/8 GR with help from the tks which switched on their headlights and used their MGs.
20.30 hrs. A further attack was put in on our posns by the Jap but although he again got into our posns, he was driven off with casualties.
19 April: 0600 hrs. 3/8 GR and Coy 1 Northamptons counted 23 dead Japs round in their posns after the night's activities.[43]

Standing near Wooded Ridge/Mori today, what one finds particularly striking about this excerpt is the use of tanks in such terrain. It was no mean feat, considering one is at an altitude of some 5,000 feet above sea level, among a tangled mass of jungle and hills. The British surprised the Japanese repeatedly with their bold use of armour during the Battle of Imphal – the battle at Nungshigum in the Iril River Valley sector is another case in point. One is also struck by the accurate use of artillery from distant locations to support the infantry in these environs. The British had guns sited at some distance away (at Bishenpur), as did the Japanese on many occasions. Yet both sides were able to repeatedly call in supporting fire from these guns to aid infantry attacks. It is remarkable that the overwhelming majority of this nature of artillery support was successfully provided.

Descending from the area of Wooded Ridge/Mori today, one has to cross a stream in a forested patch before climbing up a short distance again to reach the old Silchar Track. It is in this dimly lit area, where visibility is reduced and one keeps a wary eye for leeches crawling up the body, that one realises how intimidating these parts must have been for many a Japanese, Indian, British or Gurkha soldier some 70 years ago. It is through these thickets and in other forested patches still surrounding the present-day Silchar Track where men from both sides patrolled, ambushed and fought each other throughout the Battle of Imphal.

A short climb up from the thicket is the old Silchar Track. The spot, a large grassy clearing, has much historic significance. To the north looms Point 5846. To the south is Wooded Ridge. Looking west, the track disappears into the undergrowth after a short distance. Eastwards it soon starts its descent towards Bishenpur. Besides the fighting of 1944, one is reminded here that the war-era track was also an escape route for thousands of refugees in 1942. While the majority of refugees who had arrived in Imphal from Burma then took the Imphal–Kohima–Dimapur Road to proceed further into India, some 35,000 had used this track to move out of Manipur.

Coming back to 1944, it was close to this spot that the British-Indian units established a position they called Roadhead, where the supplies up from Bishenpur were brought (Figure 4.15). It was also – literally – the roadhead for jeeps and ambulances from Bishenpur at the time, and where the British Advanced Dressing Station was sited. Looming over this entire area, of course, is Point 5846.

POINT 5846

The best description of this hill is from a veteran of the 48th, the 1st Battalion, the Northamptonshire Regiment, who was there in 1944:

> 5846, which was to figure so conspicuously in the 48th's actions during the following weeks, can best be described as a crag.

Figure 4.15 The Silchar Track near the old British position of Roadhead

Source: Photo by Hemant Singh Katoch

> Certainly the top was a mere 200 yds by 100 yds wide covered with a few stunted trees merging into a dense bamboo thicket, perhaps no more than 10 ft high, but almost impenetrable except along animal tracks. Visibility was only a matter of yards. The bamboo thicket appeared to extend to the north and east without end. The western edge of the crag descended cliff-like for 1000 feet or so. Only on the south side was the hill open, grass covered and easily accessible, and it was up this slope that a path led for the final 1000 feet or so from the Silchar Track.[44]

Looking at Point 5846 today, it seems like those words were written just yesterday; so much of that description of this hill still rings true. Point 5846's importance at least partly lay in the fact that it overlooked the Silchar Track from the north as it crossed the western hills. The hill was, however, even more vital in 1944 as it looms over Bishenpur and the Tiddim Road and can be seen for miles around the Imphal Valley. A veteran of the Northamptons is quoted as saying: 'Whoever held this peak controlled one of the main approaches into Imphal.'[45]

The British established positions on Point 5846 around mid–April 1944; they were held despite coming under Japanese attack in the days that followed. These positions were later consolidated and control over them retained through the Battle of Imphal. The men on Point 5846 carried out extensive and active patrolling of the area to keep the Silchar Track open and to target the Japanese positions threatening it.

As one struggles up the final 1,000 feet to the summit today, it is sobering to realise that in 1944 soldiers climbed up and down Point 5846 laden with their packs and weapons. More often than not, they had to contend with incessant rains, as well as be subjected to constant Japanese harassment and sniping.

For the men stationed there during the Battle of Imphal for weeks and months at end, it was far from easy. Life on Point 5846 and its vicinity was challenging because of its topography and location. Water was a major concern, and the closest water source was a stream below the hill and further down the Silchar Track. Getting to it meant exposing one to Japanese sniping and so it was not always easy to come by. Point 5846 was also a constrained space, which meant that sanitation was a real concern. Unsurprisingly, diseases were rampant.

The Japanese would sometimes cut the Silchar Track, making it difficult for supplies to be sent up from Bishenpur. Air drops were arranged, but even this was not always possible because the peak would often be shrouded in thick mist and clouds during the rains. There was also much jungle near the hill, with all its attendant problems, including leeches.

Northamptons' veterans all recall the difficult conditions on Point 5846. One veteran, Michael Nott, has been quoted as saying: 'Apart from wounds there was the constant drain of men becoming sick, mostly from malaria and dysentery. Food was always short and we felt hungry all the time.'[46] Others remembered the shortage of water and the lack of any sanitation.

Leeches were particularly troublesome, something a visitor to the area even today will encounter. Another veteran, Ken Darlaston, recalled:

> There were leeches who would creep into any minute gap on gaiters and boots, burying their heads into the flesh. When filled with blood they would drop off, otherwise it was impossible to dislodge them, except by salt or best of all by touching them with a lighted cigarette. To pull them off would leave their head buried in the flesh. . . .
>
> … A further discomfort was the sharp bamboo shoots and thorns of the dense foliage which cut into the skin and festered, as did the leech bites. We all became covered with sores and boils and ugly scars.[47]

A specific focus of fighting in this sector in 1944 was the picquets established by the British on pimples or hills overlooking the Silchar Track to the north-east of Point 5846. These were often large enough to allow only a company or a platoon to be stationed on them. The two most important ones were Water Picquet, which covered a water source near the track, and Mortar Bluff. They were on a ridge that ran up to Point 5846 itself. They had already been attacked by the Japanese in early May and were frequently subject to artillery fire from the direction of Kokadan, south of the Silchar Track.

It was in the second half of June 1944, however, and the period 21–26 June in particular that these picquets came under fierce attack as the Japanese tried again to block the Silchar Track. Like the frontal attacks on British-Indian positions in Ningthoukhong on the Tiddim Road, these were part of the final offensive by the Japanese 33rd Division in this sector. The Japanese came around from the west of Point 5846 and closed in on Water Picquet from the north. The position fell on 21 June, while one called BP Picquet fell on 25 June; all of the other picquets in the area were also subjected to intense assaults.

A veteran of the Northamptons describes the situation at the time:

> The enemy were putting all they had into this final onslaught. In the next few days every hillock was occupied by either friend or foe, some changed hands daily. Round and round we went – it was a macabre dance, positions were so close, sniping became a daily route on both sides. Shelling also caused many casualties.[48]

To deal with the deteriorating situation, reinforcements from Bishenpur were called up. This included men of the 2/5th Royal Gurkha Rifles. Their war diary describes the events of 25/26 June:

> **25 June**: Orders received for Bn. to march from Bishenpur at 1000 hrs for Evans Knob (Hills overlooking Silchar Track). Arrived there 1600 hrs and occupied 1 Northants old positions. D Coy, less 1 Pl. and 2×3″ mortars moved forward to B.P. Picquet. 1 Pl. D Coy (Sub. Netrabahadur Thapa) plus two secs of C Coy moved forward to Mortar Bluff Picket. Enemy started attacking M.B. at 2000 hrs, practically all ammunition and grenades expended. The enemy, estimated one Coy, were attacking from all directions and many enemy had succeeded in getting inside the wire. 2 secs of B Coy were sent up with ammunition at 2230 hrs, all communication broken. Heavy rain all night.

26 June: At 0415 hrs information received that Mortar Bluff had been overrun and occupied by the enemy. A, C and Bn. HQ plus 2×3 mortars moved out at 0530 hrs and arrived at B.P. Picket at 0740 hrs, and were shelled there by 75 mm. Major McGill severely wounded in head and later died. 3 Havs also killed, 2 wounded and 1 Sub wounded all by one shell. Several men and mules also killed and wounded.

Bn. moved to the east of the Mortar Bluff. C Coy there formed up for the attack. Casualties were suffered by shots from own artillery. At 0950 hrs went in under concentration of mortars from B.P. Artillery concentration had to be abandoned owing to casualties caused to own men. C Coy went in excellently blitzing over difficult going made by tall grass and had taken their objective by 1020 hrs i.e. Mortar Bluff, capturing 1 MMG, 1×37 mm A/T Gun and 1 LMG. It was estimated that this was held by 1 Pl., most of whom ran when they saw C Coy climbing over the wire. C Coy then pushed on and took Water Picket by 1100 hrs and captured there 1×75 mm Regtl Gun 1 MMG and much equipment, grenades, ammunition, etc.[49]

These diary entries have been reproduced in detail because it was in this fighting for and the eventual recapture of Water Picquet and Mortar Bluff on 25–26 June that two men of this battalion were later conferred the Victoria Cross. Subedar Netrabahadur Thapa was posthumously awarded for defending Mortar Bluff for nearly eight hours against all odds until his death. His comrade, Naik Agan Singh Rai, was awarded for fearlessly leading his men in recapturing Mortar Bluff and Water Picquet. Interestingly, close-quarter combat in terrain made up of small, concentrated spaces – parts of the Ningthoukhong turel and the picquets off the Silchar Track – was common to four out of the five Victoria Crosses that were won in Manipur in 1944.

A location close to the main picquets and which also witnessed considerable fighting through the Battle of Imphal was what the British called Halfway House. In military memoirs it is described as the old location of the village of Ngariyan on the Silchar Track; today the village of Ngariyan is further down the track and is closer to Bishenpur. It was across the track here that the shortest route to the hills to the north ran from Kokadan village to Khoirok, where the Japanese 214th Regiment was present. The Japanese attacked this location and its vicinity on several occasions to secure this corridor, but these ultimately proved unsuccessful.

Intriguingly, there is a rock below Point 5846 and just off the old Silchar Track that has an engraved outline of a sword on it. The locals say this dates back to the Second World War, but its precise origins are less clear; some claim that it is a samurai sword, while a more recent theory gives it an Allied provenance. Other than that, remains of bunkers along the old alignment of the Track below Point 5846 can still be seen.

The Tamu–Palel Road and the Shenam Saddle: on the road to Burma

Historical overview

The Tamu–Palel Road of Second World War memoirs, or what is today referred to as the Moreh Road, is the shortest motorable route between Imphal and the border with Burma. This was the case in 1944, and it remains so 70 years later. The fighting on this road was concentrated on what the British then called the Shenam Saddle (or Shenam Pass), a collection of hills at the highest point on the road as it crosses the 5,000 feet-high range along the border between India and Burma. Palel is the last village in the Imphal Valley before the road climbs up to the Shenam Saddle. This book refers to the entire stretch from Imphal to Tamu as the Tamu–Palel Road.

On the British side, the 20th Indian Division (minus 32nd Brigade sent first as reserve to Imphal and later deployed on the Tiddim Road) was active in this sector from mid-March to mid-May 1944. It was commanded by Major General Douglas Gracey. It was subsequently replaced by the 23rd Indian Division commanded by Major General Ouvry Roberts. They faced Yamamoto Force, so named after Major General Yamamoto, the commander of the Japanese 33rd Division's infantry group. He also had under him most of the division's medium artillery, tanks and mechanised transport, and two battalions of the Japanese 15th Division.

The fighting in this sector involved repeated attempts from early April 1944 onwards by Yamamoto Force to get past the British-Indian defensive positions around the Shenam Saddle en route to Imphal. Positions exchanged hands in months of fighting in conditions likened to the Somme in the First World War. But the defences held. The Japanese tried to bypass the Shenam Saddle from the north, but this advance was also checked.

Yamamoto Force was evicted from its captured positions on the Shenam Saddle only in the last week of July 1944 after the British mounted a three-pronged offensive in this sector, led by the 23rd Indian Division. This entailed brigade-strength attacks in the centre on the Tamu–Palel Road – supported by all available artillery and tanks – as well as through the hills on the left flank and on the right that met up behind the main Japanese positions.

For those interested in the INA and its history, it is the Tamu–Palel Road sector that should be of most interest. While the first INA flag may have been planted at Moirang off the Tiddim Road in April 1944, it is in this sector where the INA's 1st Division was deployed during the Battle of Imphal. Its Gandhi and Azad Brigades were active on the left and right flanks, respectively, of Yamamoto Force on the Tamu–Palel Road. This was the only place on Indian soil where the 1st Division actually fought during the Second World War, pitting its soldiers against fellow Indians under the Indian Army.

It was from here that their 'March to Delhi' was to begin. Indeed, one author mentions a Japanese officer having witnessed the scene of INA men on the march up from Moreh on this very road. He recalls that they were 'wild with enthusiasm as they walked on Indian soil, holding their rifles aloft and yelling "Jai Hind! Chalo Delhi!" (India for ever! On to Delhi!)'.[50]

The battlefields today

This book covers an approximately 45-mile (72-km) stretch of what is today called the Moreh Road or, more ambitiously, Asian Highway 1, from Imphal up to the Shenam Saddle around the village of Tengnoupal. This is the main road that currently connects India to Burma (Myanmar) and the rest of South East Asia beyond. It is also the route of the proposed Trans Asian Highway and Trans Asian Railway that aim to seamlessly connect Asia in future.[51] It is quite literally where South Asia meets South East Asia.

The terrain up to Palel, the last village on the road in the Imphal Valley, is similar to the Tiddim Road: paddy fields on both sides of the road, interspersed by towns and villages, especially after one crosses the town of Thoubal. From Palel onwards, the road starts climbing steeply, goes past the village of Sinam (or 'Shenam') which lent its name to the main British-Indian defensive position, to reach the collection of hills near Tengnoupal which were called the Shenam Saddle or Shenam Pass. At around 5,000 feet above sea level, this is the highest point on the road over the hills on the India–Burma border. After this, the road descends steeply towards the last Indian town of Moreh in the plains on the other side. Tamu is the first town across the border from Moreh in Burma.

The following is a brief sequence of events in this sector in 1944, involving the main battlefields covered in this book:

1–16 April	Fight for Nippon Hill/Maejima on the Shenam Saddle
16 April–9 May	Yamamoto Force captures positions on the Shenam Saddle, including Crete East/Ikkenya Hill and Crete West/Kawamichi Hill
2/3 May	INA attack on Palel Airfield
10–11 May	Japanese attack and occupy part of Scraggy/Ito Hill
Mid-May	23rd Indian Division takes over from 20th Indian Division
23–24 May	Battle for Gibraltar/Hill 5185 on the Shenam Saddle
9–10 June	Japanese take crest of Scraggy/Ito Hill on the Shenam Saddle
3/4 July	Japanese destroy eight aircraft on Palel Airfield
24 July	Assault begins to clear Japanese positions on the Shenam Saddle

WANGJING AND SAPAM

As one heads south-east out of Imphal towards Palel, one difference with the Tiddim Road starts to become apparent: the distance between the road and the hills that form the rim of the Imphal Valley, in this case the eastern rim. Although there are parts where the road curves around hillocks before Palel, for the most part the hills to the east are at a fair distance away from the road – unlike the hills near the Tiddim Road. Even on the other side, there is a significant gap between the road and Loktak Lake to the west, again unlike the Tiddim Road. It is perhaps due to these large open spaces of paddy fields that of the six airfields in the Imphal Valley during the Second World War, three – Wangjing, Sapam and Palel – were along this road.

Warrant Officer H.W.R. Hepplewhite of 136 Squadron, Royal Air Force, is quoted as recalling what it was like at the time. He describes the system of 'boxes' that was adopted for the defence of these airfields.

Wangjing was a dirt strip in a paddy field and from here the squadron flew defensive patrols and escorted Dakotas, supply dropping to Wingate's Chindits who were operating behind Jap lines. Towards the end of March there was an enemy breakthrough into a section of the Imphal Valley and all 136 Squadron personnel vacated their domestic living area about one mile from the airstrip and which consisted of primitive bashas and moved onto the airstrip perimeter. Here dug-outs and foxholes were rapidly prepared and tarpaulins slung over the tops and these became our sleeping quarters. The squadron was 'now in the box'.[52]

Flying Officer R. King of 136 Squadron is recorded telling a similar tale about Wangjing Airfield:

My first impression was a sight more in keeping with the First World War. The pilots as well as guard crew had to dig their own sleeping quarters, covered with corrugated iron and sandbags. These quarters were interconnected by a series of trenches to form the basis of the defence of the airstrip and guard duties were carried out by pilots and ground crews alike.[53]

It would be a little deceptive to use the term 'airfield' to describe Wangjing and Sapam as one passes their approximate locations along the road today. For these were fair-weather airfields during the Battle of Imphal, which meant that they were essentially paddy fields that had been flattened and rehabilitated to make functional airstrips. After the war, the surrounding villages reclaimed this land, and they returned to being paddy fields. Therefore, as one looks east of the road at the fields just before the town of Wangjing and to the west after the town, one is gazing at the old locations of the fair-weather airfields of Wangjing and Sapam, respectively.

PALEL (KAKCHING) AIRFIELD

One has to rely less on one's imagination with what the British called the Palel Airfield or what is today known locally as Kakching Airfield or, more precisely, Kakching Garrison. Like Imphal Main (Koirengei Airfield), the old Palel Airfield is today also under the control of the Indian security forces, although in this case it is the Assam Rifles. Unlike Imphal Main, nearly three-fourths of the old runway has been built over and consists of apartment blocks and offices of the Assam Rifles. Only a small stretch of the old runway still survives, but the entire area is fenced off and guarded and, for security reasons, is not easy to access.

One of the best views of the old airfield can be had from Kakching Garden, a popular tourist spot on a hillock to the west of the airfield and on the outskirts of the town of Kakching (Figure 4.16). To get there one has to turn off the Tamu-Palel Road at the Kakching Lamkhai (or turnoff) short of the village of Palel and follow the signs for Kakching Garden. En route, one passes the entrance to the present-day Kakching

Figure 4.16 Distant view of the old Palel Airfield from Kakching Garden
Source: Photo by Hemant Singh Katoch

Garrison – the northern end of the old airfield. The vantage points of Kakching Garden afford the clearest views of the old airfield, large parts of the Imphal Valley and the imposing hills to the east atop which is the Shenam Saddle. One can easily make out the length of the old runway (around 2,000 yards); the buildings on it are aligned in a straight line, with the last stretch left as is.

Besides Imphal Main, Palel was the only other all-weather airfield in the Imphal Valley during the Second World War. It played an equally vital role in keeping 4 Corps supplied during the Siege of Imphal, and there were several supply dumps and depots in its vicinity in 1944. Naturally then, Palel was a key target for the Japanese in this sector, and its capture would have provided them an important source of supplies, besides giving them control of an airfield crucial to Allied air defences in Manipur.

The Japanese were unable to reach the airfield via the Tamu–Palel Road due to the defence of the Shenam Saddle; they responded by approaching it from farther north of the Saddle and east of the airfield. The most notable – and successful – Japanese attack on Palel from this direction happened on the night of 3/4 July 1944, when they blew up eight planes on the ground using Bangalore torpedoes and magnetic mines.[54]

Palel was also the object of an INA attack on 2/3 May. It was originally planned as a joint operation with the Japanese, but ultimately only the 300-odd INA men tasked were present on the appointed date and closed in for the attack. They belonged to the Gandhi Brigade of the INA's 1st Division. They approached the airfield from the south. There are two versions of what happened next.

In the first version quoted by the historian Louis Allen and sourced from the INA commander Shah Nawaz Khan's memoirs, the INA men managed to reach one of the picquets on the heights surrounding the airfield.[55] According to this – slightly more dramatic – account, the men at the picquet were Indians who, after the INA tried to kill their two British officers, counter-attacked. Another INA party is even said to have destroyed aircraft at the airfield, although Allen disputes this.[56]

A second version by Hugh Toye has the INA men reaching 5 miles (8 km) short of the airfield, where they encountered a Gurkha platoon.[57] The Gurkhas are said to have first attacked the approaching INA men, after which a parley followed where the INA tried to convince the platoon not to fire. This failing, the INA is said to have attacked the Gurkha platoon seven times, before finally withdrawing. Another INA group further to the rear, which included the Gandhi Brigade Commander, Lieutenant Colonel Inayat Jan Kiani, was attacked by the Frontier Force Rifles and subjected to an air strike. Toye estimates that two INA officers and several soldiers were killed in the attack by the Gurkha platoon, while some three dozen more surrendered or were captured; an additional 50 were killed in the air strike.[58]

Whichever version is true, what is undisputed is that the INA men were counter-attacked by the Indians and Gurkhas of the Indian Army as they approached Palel Airfield in early May 1944. Toye attaches great importance to this event:

> The failure at Palel and the subsequent casualties to Kiani's force were perhaps the most significant events in I.N.A. history since the arrival of S.C. Bose in the Far East. Bose had hoped, and his hope had become an axiom of I.N.A. propaganda, that when a formed body of the I.N.A. confronted British-Indian troops in the field, propaganda and not fire-power would decide the day. . . .
> . . . Now this cherished illusion was shattered; that they were regarded by their former comrades of the Indian Army as traitors was suddenly plain to all.[59]

Toye therefore believes that this failed attack on Palel Airfield affected INA morale considerably.

Getting back on the road, one crosses Palel, from where the climb up towards the Shenam Saddle begins. Groups of security personnel manning checkpoints are usually encountered on this stretch. They wear uniforms of varying hues that indicate whether they have been deployed by Imphal or New Delhi. It is a reminder that one is on the last stretch of the road before the India–Burma border at Moreh and that this is a high-security zone.

As one winds and curves up the hills towards the top, the scenery becomes ever more spectacular and the air cooler. It is the perfect time to reflect on the multiple layers of history associated with this stretch between Palel and Tamu. This was the route taken by close to 190,000 desperate refugees who fled Burma in the face of the Japanese advance in 1942 for the safety of India.[60] As the Japanese headed northwards in Burma, cutting off the sea route of escape, many refugees made for Imphal. Then, as today, the best route available to them to cross the mountainous frontier between Burma and India was via the Tamu–Palel route into Manipur. This is where many died along the way; already diseased, tired and hungry, they were unable to make it over the hostile hills to the Imphal Valley.

This is also the road where the longest retreat in British military history ended. Like the refugees, the Burma Army withdrew across the length of Burma in the first half of 1942, with the Japanese in close pursuit. It was a historic retreat of some 900 miles (nearly 1,500 km) in four months. General Slim gives a moving description of the moment the retreat ended:

> On the last day of that nine-hundred-mile retreat I stood on a bank beside the road and watched the rearguard march into India. All of them, British, Indian, and Gurkha, were gaunt and ragged as scarecrows. Yet, as they trudged behind their surviving officers in groups pitifully small, they still carried their arms and kept their ranks, they were still recognizable as fighting units. They might look like scarecrows, but they looked like soldiers too.[61]

Given that it was little more than a dirt track at the time, getting the stretch of the road between Palel and Tamu ready in time for the arrival of the retreating army from Burma in 1942 presented a major dilemma. It was largely thanks to the thousands of labourers of the Indian Tea Association in Assam, then the only large, organised source of labour in the region, that the task was completed in the nick of time. They worked furiously from early March onwards and got the road ready on 5 May 1942.

The association had also proved helpful in making arrangements to look after the newly arrived civilian refugees from Burma.

Halfway up the road to the top is the nondescript village of Sinam (or Shenam) which lends its name to the main pass through the hills further ahead. Continuing on, around a bend in the road just about a kilometre short of the village of Saivom, is the first view of the collection of hills that make up what the British called the Shenam Saddle. The ones that are immediately visible are Recce Hill, Gibraltar and Scraggy, with Nippon Hill in the distance. Malta, Crete West and East, Lynch and Cyprus are hidden from view. The names the British gave many of these hills are inspired from the Mediterranean, while the Japanese named them mainly after officers who captured them. Gibraltar was referred to by its height as Hill 5185 (or by its local name Laimatol); Scraggy was Ito Hill; Malta was Yajima Hill; Crete West was Kawamichi Hill; Crete East was Ikkenya Hill and Nippon Hill was Maejima Hill.

It is hard not to be moved by the sight of these hills (Figure 4.17). For these are arguably among the most spectacular Second World War

Figure 4.17 The Shenam Saddle and the Tamu–Palel Road. View from Recce Hill of Gibraltar/Hill 5185 (straight ahead) and Malta/Yajima Hill (left)

Source: Photo by Hemant Singh Katoch

battlefields in the world. Situated at a height of around 5,000 feet above sea level on the mountainous frontier between India and Burma, where South Asia meets South East Asia, these hills are on what one tourist called the Khyber Pass of the East. That many of them, with perhaps the exception of Nippon Hill/Maejima Hill and parts of Crete, remain nearly unchanged from 1944 only adds to their allure. However, what makes them even more remarkable is the fact that it was essentially within this very confined space of a few hills that fighting raged between the Japanese, British, Indians and Gurkhas from early April to the end of July 1944. As one veteran, John Hudson, puts it: 'How strange that such a vast area of mountains and jungle along the frontier between India and Burma lay undisturbed, whilst we beat the shit out of each other on this one small patch.'[62]

One way to get a good sense of the fighting here as it unfolded during the Battle of Imphal is to drive right up to the base of Scraggy/Ito Hill – and to later retrace one's steps. To get to this spot one drives across the Saddle, first past Recce Hill, which towers over Saivom village and around which the road makes a large loop (the hill is to the right), and then continuing past Gibraltar/Hill 5185, Malta/Yajima Hill and a part of Scraggy/Ito Hill on the left. The view from the vantage point just below Scraggy/Ito Hill, which is short of the Assam Rifles checkpoint and base at Tengnoupal village, is magnificent. On one side of the road lies Scraggy/Ito Hill, while Nippon Hill/Maejima Hill and Crete West/Kawamichi Hill are clearly visible up ahead. On the other side the ground falls steeply to an endless vista of green, forested valleys and hills as far as the eye can see. Behind these hills lie Burma and the Kabaw Valley. Walking back down the road throws up views of Malta/Yajima Hill and Gibraltar/Hill 5185 in the distance.

Apart from the noise of an occasional vehicle hurtling past in the direction of Moreh–Tamu or Palel–Imphal or the sound of an odd bird, nothing breaks the silence here. It was not so during the Battle of Imphal in 1944. As Hudson wrote:

> It was never quiet at Shenam. Bursts of mortar and shellfire racketed about our heads all the time. The heart-chilling tacker-tacker-tacker of automatic weapons and the sporadic crackle of rifle fire punctuated by grenade bursts echoed day and night from the valley walls.[63]

To understand the flow of the battle, it is perhaps best to start with the first hill on the Shenam Saddle that fell to the Japanese, Nippon Hill or Maejima Hill.

What the British called Nippon Hill and the Japanese Maejima Hill is the first major hill on the Shenam Saddle as one climbs up the road from the direction of Moreh and Tamu. It is today under the control of the Assam Rifles based at Tengnoupal. It saw nearly continuous fighting in the first three weeks of April 1944. During this time it exchanged hands several times between the British-Indian forces and the Japanese, before finally falling to the latter in the third week of April. The Japanese stayed in control of this hill until the fighting on the Shenam Saddle ceased at the end of July 1944.

Nippon Hill/Maejima Hill came under 80th Brigade of the 20th Indian Division as it withdrew from its base at Moreh at the end of March 1944. 100th Brigade moved to Palel, while 32nd Brigade moved to Imphal and then to the Tiddim Road under the 17th Indian Division. Yamamoto Force occupied the hill by 1 April, taking it from the 2nd Borders. Several attempts to retake the hill followed. The first was made the very next day by a company of the 4/10 Gurkha Rifles, without air cover, but it failed, as did other such efforts.

The decisive push to retake Nippon Hill/Maejima Hill came on 11 April. The task was entrusted to the 1st Battalion, the Devonshire Regiment. This time the operation was supported by all available guns and by Royal Air Force Hurribombers, both of whom bombed the Japanese positions on the hill before the infantry went in. Three companies of the Devons were involved in the attack. Their task had been made much harder than before because the Japanese had had enough time to dig in deep underground a 'rabbit warren of holes' out of which they kept up their fire.[64] After fierce fighting in which two officers and 17 men had been killed and all three company commanders wounded, the Devons finally secured Nippon Hill.[65] That night the Japanese put in three more attacks, but all of these were thwarted.

Nippon Hill/Maejima Hill is one such battlefield where, days after its recapture by British-Indian forces, the odd Japanese soldier would emerge from the rubble to try and launch a solitary attack.[66] This was after being buried underneath, with no food or water, and possibly with injuries. Such was the hardiness and determination of the Japanese soldier at Imphal. Moreover, this behaviour was not an exception but was fairly typical of how many soldiers of the Japanese Fifteenth Army conducted themselves.

The Japanese did not give up on capturing Nippon Hill/Maejima Hill. After another week of attacks by Yamamoto Force, some of which were aided by tanks, the hill fell again to them. This time no effort was made to try to recapture it, and the Japanese remained there until the end of

July 1944. Given its clear views of the other hills, the Japanese were able to constantly shell and harass the British-Indian forces on the Shenam Saddle from Nippon Hill/Maejima Hill for the rest of the Battle of Imphal. A week later and following fierce hand-to-hand fighting, the next positions to fall to the Japanese in April were Cyprus and Crete East/Ikkenya Hill; by 9 May, Crete West/Kawamichi Hill and Lynch Pimple had also been taken by Yamamoto Force. The front line had now moved to the hill the British knew as Scraggy and the Japanese as Ito Hill.

SCRAGGY/ITO HILL

Scraggy or Ito Hill today is quite possibly the most unremarkable looking of the hills of the Shenam Saddle (Figure 4.18). It does not have the height and sprawl of Recce Hill or the steep face of Gibraltar or even the clear shape of Malta. Instead, it is more a small, lumpy hillock, with the Tamu–Palel Road curving around it. It is covered in vegetation and there is dense undergrowth in parts, which makes passage difficult even for a single person. And yet this very same hill is perhaps the most iconic battlefield not just of the Shenam Saddle, but of the entire Battle of Imphal.

Figure 4.18 Scraggy/Ito Hill straight ahead and Nippon Hill/Maejima Hill on the right

Source: Photo by Hemant Singh Katoch

It is the fighting on this hill that has inspired the comparisons with the First World War battlefields of the Somme or Kohima. Those comparisons are entirely justified. For Scraggy/Ito Hill was witness to continuous, close-quarter fighting between the British-Indian and Japanese forces from early May right until the end of July 1944. Moreover, both sides maintained positions on this small hill for that entire period.

Yamamoto Force launched its first major attack on Scraggy/Ito Hill on the night of 10 May. The 3/1st Gurkhas were in position on the hill at the time. After some shelling, wave after wave of Japanese surged on to Scraggy/Ito Hill, overwhelming the first Gurkha defences. The Gurkhas fought back; yet the attacks continued through the night until the Gurkhas' commander called for artillery fire on his own positions to stem the Japanese advance. The tactic worked, but the Japanese had still managed to capture a part of Scraggy/Ito Hill. Hundreds of Japanese soldiers are said to have died in the attack on that night alone.[67]

From then on, the Japanese stayed on a part of Scraggy/Ito Hill for the remainder of the Battle of Imphal, facing off the entire time with the British, Indians and Gurkhas who were on the same hill, sometimes mere yards apart. Around the middle of May 1944, men of the 23rd Indian Division took over the positions on the Shenam Saddle from the 20th Indian Division. This changeover had little impact on the situation on the Shenam Saddle, and the fighting continued on and around Scraggy/Ito Hill.

The commander of the 3/3rd Gurkhas of 37th Brigade, 23rd Indian Division, noted that of the strongpoints that ran some 30 feet below the summit of Scraggy/Ito Hill, half of them were occupied by the Japanese and the other half by themselves, with no-man's-land being some 6 to 10 yards apart.[68] He remarked: 'Our position came under heavy artillery fire from Nippon Ridge in addition to grenade, rifle and mortars from Scraggy itself. Each side raided the other's trenches night after night.'[69]

The Japanese launched a second major attack on Scraggy/Ito Hill on the night of 20 May, but this was beaten back. An entry in the war diary of 3/10th Gurkha Rifles describes the attack:

> Night 20/21. Persistent attacks by enemy on all posns throughout night. Own DF extremely prompt and accurate. Attacks particularly heavy on Scraggy where own tps fired weapons practically all night against repeated attempts by enemy to rush posns.
> 0530 hrs. Climax of night's fighting occurred when enemy rushed Scraggy over crest in three waves throwing large numbers grenades and gelignite bombs but not carrying rifles. First time

this type 'trench raid' encountered. Own fwd pl (D Coy) beat off attacks by leaving trenches and meeting enemy half-way. Enemy cas heavy – 93 killed. Own cas 12 killed, 49 wounded.[70]

Another, full-scale attack was carried out on 9 June, and this time men of Yamamoto Force overran and captured Scraggy's peak and some forward British positions. There was a fierce counter-attack by the British forces, involving the infantry, tanks, artillery and even strafing by the Royal Air Force.[71] The 3/3rd and 3/5th Gurkhas fought on, and for their role in this fighting the former's lieutenant J.M. Carew and Subedar Dalparsad Gurung won the Military Cross.[72] One gets a sense of the intense fighting of 9–10 June from some of the entries of the 3/3rd Gurkhas war diary:

9 June

1755 hrs: Shelling of fwd slopes Malta-Pimple Scraggy by 1 × 105 M.M., 1 × 75 M.M.

1850 hrs: B Coy report casualties from shelling K.2 W.1 G.O., 21 G.O.R. Also 3 L.M.Gs. knocked out. Enemy came over top of Scraggy and entered posn occupying fwd posn.

1900 hrs: Bn Comd asked for one Coy reinforcement from Mob Reserve for counter attack.

1940 hrs: Local pl. counter attack put in.

1950 hrs: Counter attacks repulsed by enemy with high fire and showers of grenades. K.3 W.1 B.O., 23 G.O.R.s.

2155 hrs: Situation Pimple on Scraggy in enemy hands. Own tps have fallen back 40×.

10 June

1300 hrs: Supporting arty – L.M.G. + M.M.G. commenced firing. Fwd tps commenced withdrawal to line decided upon.

1430 hrs: Arty finished ranging Skyline Scraggy. M.M.G.L. M.G.s. Continued to fire as suitable targets present themselves.

1440 hrs. Tps in position to advance. Arty fire concs on Scraggy.

1451 hrs: Arty – L.M.G. – M.M.G. – Concs.

1453 hrs: Guns stop.

1500 hrs: Air strike on back of Scraggy-Lynch features. All bombs fell in T.A. Fwd elements advanced to attack. Enemy shelling mortaring grenading as we move up. It is not possible to deploy Coys as ground & front do not permit. Men must move from trench to bunker cleaning up as they go. During battle

comm to rear became dis. Also Signal Officer killed by shell. Coy taking part in attack were A + C Coy. Battle very fierce. Own tps moving ahead slowly under hail of enemy fire. Mortars – guns – M.M.G. – grenades.
1630 hrs: Battle died down own tps having regained greater position of lost ground. Estimated casualties inflicted on enemy 40. Own tps: 1 B.O. killed. 2 B.O. wounded. 1 G.O. killed. 2 G.O. wounded. 11 G.O.R.s killed. 53 G.O.R.s wounded.[73]

The Japanese nevertheless hung on to Scraggy peak. The British eventually decided to let them stay there as it was felt that the new Gurkha positions were even stronger than the earlier ones.[74] The Japanese remained in place until the end of July 1944.

All of the British military accounts and memoirs mention the difficult conditions on the Shenam Saddle. They talk of the surprisingly cold weather, the incessant rain once the monsoons began, the determination of their adversary, the wave upon wave of attacks they launched on certain positions and the constant threat of being fired upon from nearby locations. While this was true of the entire Saddle, the situation was undoubtedly the worst on Scraggy/Ito Hill. The additional factors here were that often the two sides were just yards apart from each other and bodies and body parts in varying stages of decomposition lay scattered all around. An entry about Scraggy from the war diary of the 3/10th Gurkha Rifles of 16 May 1944, adds: 'Occasional grenade battles. No movement except at night and absolute silence. Stench of bodies in "no man's land" most oppressive.'[75]

MALTA/YAJIMA HILL AND GIBRALTAR/HILL 5185

As one retraces one's steps back from Scraggy/Ito Hill, the next hill on the Saddle is what the British called Malta and the Japanese Yajima Hill. Malta/Yajima Hill seems to have been spared the kind of full-scale attacks hurled by Yamamoto Force at Scraggy/Ito Hill, largely because the latter bore the brunt of them. Life for the Allied soldiers on the hill during the Battle of Imphal was still difficult, though certainly more bearable than on Scraggy/Ito Hill.

Malta/Yajima Hill and Gibraltar/Hill 5185 were regularly shelled by the Japanese who had set up mountain guns on the nearby hills, especially to the east, beyond Nippon Hill. One memoir recounts a day when Malta received 250 shells and on another 100 shells within an hour crashed on Gibraltar/Hill 5185.[76] Hudson recalls the ever-present risk of fire from snipers, mortars and machine guns on these hills. According to him, the stretch of the Tamu–Palel Road across the saddle between Gibraltar and Malta was the most dangerous as it was exposed to Japanese fire; he remembers it being named 'Hellfire Straight'.[77]

Continuing on from Malta/Yajima Hill is the last major battlefield of the Shenam Saddle and the steepest of that collection of hills, Gibraltar/ Hill 5185. Looking somewhat like its namesake in the Mediterranean, Gibraltar towers above the Tamu–Palel Road and Malta/Yajima Hill. Hudson has a terrific description of the three hills together: 'They were our battle fleet, steaming in line ahead. The big dreadnought Gibraltar looked down on the cruiser Malta under her bows and Scraggy, the little destroyer, was in the van.'[78]

Gibraltar/Hill 5185 was the scene of a short but fierce battle in May 1944 on which, when it was happening, the fate of the entire British-Indian defensive position on the Shenam Saddle hung in the balance. The Japanese had first attacked Gibraltar/Hill 5185 on 20 May, but they were repulsed. Yamamoto Force achieved much greater success when it put in its second major attack on Gibraltar – bypassing Malta – just three days later on the night of 23/24 May. This time it was able to overcome the 5/6th Rajputana Rifles who held the hill. A 20th Division intelligence summary of May 1944 notes: 'In the early hours of 24 May, the Japs put in a powerful attack on Gibraltar with the whole of 1 Bn 60 Regt, and the enemy succeeded in planting their flag on the east peak.'[79]

This was a dangerous situation for the British because if the Japanese took Gibraltar/Hill 5185, it would have made the positions on isolated Malta/ Yajima Hill and Scraggy/Ito Hill untenable. The Japanese on Gibraltar were first subjected to artillery shelling that morning before C Company of the Rajputana Rifles attacked up the hill. The war diary of the 3/10th Gurkha Rifles mentions a Rajputana Rifles report on the fighting:

> **24 May**: 1015 hrs: Raj Rif report: Counter-attacks have reached the top of GIB and all but the top most posns have been re-taken. Hard hand-to-hand fighting in progress.[80]

As the day progressed, A Company of the 3/10th Gurkha Rifles were called upon to charge up the hill. Their war diary notes:

> **24 May**: 1250 hrs: Tanks and mtn arty put up five minute cover-ing barrage on N slopes GIB.
> 1300 hrs: A Coy report attack proceeding well. First wave pl on to Knife Edge posn on GIB reached. Summit but held up by enemy shelling and grenades. Some cas sustained. No. 3 pl under

Jem Bakhta Bdr Rai followed through, hand to hand fighting ensued and about fifty enemy broke and fled. These again shot up by 3/5 RGR from Malta and by Mtn Arty from Patiala. 1400 hrs: Now reported all posns on GIB retaken. Enemy cas very heavy. Enemy dead in all bunkers, transverse trenches and on wire. First count of enemy dead and booty as follows: three MMGs, 7 LMGs, five grenade dischargers, two Jap type TSMGs, RAP equipt, large number swords and uncountable rifles. Dead bodies – 119 ORs, 5 Offrs.[81]

Jemadar Bhaktbahadur Rai, who led the leading platoon in this action, won the Military Cross. Final casualties for the fighting on Gibraltar/Hill 5185 were estimated at 145 killed on the Japanese side, while 11 killed and 107 wounded for the Allies.[82] This was the last Japanese attack in force on Gibraltar/Hill 5185.

THE INA OFF THE TAMU–PALEL ROAD

As noted earlier, some 6,000 men from the INA's 1st Division participated in the Battle of Imphal. The commander of this division was Colonel Mohammad Zaman Kiani and its headquarters was set up in the village of Chamol, south of the Tamu–Palel Road past Tengnoupal (when coming from Imphal). Its Gandhi Brigade was deployed on the left flank of Yamamoto Force on the Tamu–Palel Road and set up its headquarters in the village of Khanjol in the hills at the end of April 1944. It was a group of some 300 soldiers of this brigade which set off via the village of Purum Chumpang for the attack on Palel Airfield on 2/3 May, an event whose significance for the INA has already been described.

Through May 1944, despite attacks by British-Indian forces, the Gandhi Brigade stayed in and around Khanjol and Mittong Khunou in the hills south of the Tamu–Palel Road. The INA's Azad Brigade, commanded by Lieutenant Colonel Gulzara Singh, was deployed in June on Yamamoto Force's right flank and set up its headquarters in the village of Narum.

Standing on the Shenam Saddle today and looking at the hills in the far distance on either side of the Tamu–Palel Road gives one at least a sense – however removed – of the terrain in which thousands of INA men lived and fought in 1944. It also allows one to ponder how difficult it must have been for those Indians, from the motherland and from the Diaspora in South East Asia, many of whom were civilian recruits, to remain in these hills for months – ill-equipped, under-trained, dependent on the Japanese for logistical support that they themselves were severely lacking in and, by a quirk of history, fighting fellow Indians on the British-Indian side.

Another point that comes to mind is how forgotten the INA is today. Netaji Subhash Chandra Bose might be remembered by many and his exploits feted in India, but the army he led remains a largely forgotten and unknown entity. Indeed, its foot soldiers are no less ignored today than those of the Indian Army who fought in the Second World War.

The INA is said to have begun its withdrawal from Manipur in mid-July 1944. Toye draws on official figures from General Headquarters in New Delhi in 1945–46 to get the following casualty figures for the INA: Of the around 6,000 men of the INA's 1st Division who had set out for Imphal, 2,600 returned, of which 2,000 had to be immediately sent to hospital. During the campaign 715 men deserted, some 400 were killed in battle, about 800 surrendered and some 1,500 died of disease and starvation.[83]

There is a poignant account by the INA's Abid Hasan of the moment he met Netaji Subhash Chandra Bose in Burma after his unit's retreat from Manipur:

> When my turn came Netaji said to me, 'nobody tells me what all you had to undergo. I want to know. You have long been close to me. I expect you to speak.' I had to gulp down a lump down my throat, but managed to recover. 'I am reminded, Sir', I told him, 'of the reply our Divisional Headquarters received when just prior to our retreat our staff officer went to the Japanese Command at the front to enquire about the situation. The Japanese reply in all earnestness was: "To tell you frankly, the situation is slightly not so very good".' 'That, Sir, was the case with us also. Our circumstances were slightly not so very good.'[84]

The INA's involvement in the Battle of Imphal and Manipur found mention in a Special Order of the Day issued by Netaji Subhash Chandra Bose on 24 April 1945, as the Fourteenth Army raced towards Rangoon. A part of it is reproduced here:

> It is with a heavy heart that I am leaving Burma – the scene of many heroic battles that you have fought since February 1944 and are still fighting. In Imphal and Burma we have lost the first round of our fight for independence. But it is only the first round. We have many more rounds to fight. I am a born optimist and I shall not admit defeat under any circumstances. Your brave deeds in the battles against the enemy on the plains of Imphal, the hills and jungles of Arakan and the oil-field area and other localities in Burma will live in the history of our struggle for independence for all time.[85]

Perhaps the most interesting hill to explore on the Shenam Saddle today is what the British called Recce Hill. At some 5,200 feet above sea level, it is also the highest on the Shenam Saddle. Recce Hill is a sprawling feature around which the Tamu–Palel Road curls on one side. The remains of another branch of the road that hugged the hill from the other side are still easily discernible; both join up again before Gibraltar/Hill 5185. There is a Manipur Rifles – a local Manipuri security force – post at the southern end of Recce Hill, near Saivom village, and this is the best access point for the hill. It is strongly recommended to take the permission of the Manipur Rifles personnel posted there before climbing the hill; in the experience of the author, the former are usually friendly and permission has always been granted.

As one begins the short hike up to the multiple peaks of Recce Hill, and provided the weather does not play spoilsport, one is greeted by a terrific view of the Imphal Valley to one side. It is again to Hudson we must turn for a perfect summing up of this view:

> On the few occasions when the clouds lifted and the mist drew aside we had panoramic views across The Plain to the distant ring of mountains. We could see remote glints of water, rice paddy, tree-shrouded villages and forests cloaking the slopes. Manipur looked like an Arcadian paradise. In those brief interludes we lifted our eyes from the filth of our lives, imbibed clean air and glimpsed beauty.[86]

His words ring true 70 years on, although the forests he mentions have unfortunately thinned to a large extent today.

Continuing on up and past the Manipur Rifles' living quarters, one comes across the first outlines of old trenches. As one explores further, the remains of an extensive network of trenches, dugouts and bunkers dating back to 1944 that still pockmark this feature are revealed. Indeed, of all the hills of the Shenam Saddle mentioned earlier, it is on Recce Hill where one can still easily retrace and walk along trenches that snake all over (Figure 4.19). These remnants help us to visualise and imagine the conditions in which men lived and fought on the Shenam Saddle as perhaps no spoken or written word can.

Recce Hill also affords panoramic views of the hills along the India–Burma border. From its highest peak, Gibraltar/Hill 5185 and Malta/Yajima Hill are clearly visible, as is the Tamu–Palel Road curving around them. It is when one is taking in these views and that of the Imphal Valley from Recce Hill that the enormity of what happened here on the Shenam Saddle during the Second World War really sinks in – as does the

Figure 4.19 Trenches on Recce Hill
Source: Photo by Hemant Singh Katoch

fact of how the fortunes of the British-Indian and the Japanese sides at the time rested on a razor's edge. Hudson words it best:

> We were locked like two wrestlers, eyeball to eyeball, neither gaining, neither giving. We had very little ground to yield before we would be tumbling downwards down the precipitous slopes to The [Imphal] Plain. They had very little ground to capture to open the doorway to India.[87]

The Ukhrul Road and Shangshak: where Imphal and Kohima met

Historical overview

The Ukhrul Road connects Imphal to the mountain town of Ukhrul in the north-east of Manipur. The road and its environs in Manipur's present-day Ukhrul district saw fighting from the second half of March to July 1944. This was the vast north-east sector of the Battle of Imphal, an area of high hills and jungle. While the Japanese had been expected to approach Imphal in strength from the south-east and the south and south-west in 1944, these hills to the north-east, with no easy passes through, were considered impenetrable for any large force. As a result, this entire sector was relatively ill-defended by the British-Indian forces at Imphal. Yet it was through these same hills around Ukhrul that two entire Japanese divisions, the 31st and the 15th, made their way towards Kohima and Imphal at the start of their U Go offensive in 1944.

It is in the Ukhrul area that the Battles of Imphal and Kohima overlap. The town itself lay in the path and within the area of responsibility of the Japanese 31st Division, commanded by Lieutenant General Kotuku Sato, as it advanced towards Kohima in March 1944. It fell to the Japanese later that month and stayed under their control until the end of July. To the far north of Ukhrul lie the villages of Kharasom and Jessami, both of which fall under Manipur's Ukhrul district today. The two villages are connected more to the Battle of Kohima as it was here that men of the 1st Battalion, the Assam Regiment, had been sent from Kohima to act as the first line of defence against any approaching Japanese. They were both the scene of brief – albeit fierce – battles before they fell to the advancing columns of the Japanese 31st Division.

The Japanese 15th Division passed to the immediate south of Ukhrul on its way to Imphal and the Imphal–Kohima Road. It was also from Ukhrul that men of the 58th Regiment, 31st Division, were sent to battle British-Indian forces in a village to the south that lay in the 15th Division's area of responsibility: Shangshak or Sangshak, as it is known in military accounts. This battle, which embroiled men of both divisions, affected the outcome of the twin battles at Imphal and Kohima. Finally, it was at Ukhrul where the survivors of both the Japanese 31st Division from Kohima and the 15th Division from the north and north-east of Imphal gathered in July 1944 to make their last stand.

This book concerns itself with the fighting on and along the Ukhrul Road in 1944 that is connected to the Battle of Imphal. This involved the Japanese 15th Division's approach towards Imphal from the north-east and, as in the other sectors, the British-Indian response to first halt this advance and then roll it back. Since men of this division also approached Imphal from the north, the fighting here is closely connected to and intertwined with that on the Mapao-Molvom Range and the Iril River Valley, as well as along the Imphal–Kohima Road.

15th Division was commanded by Lieutenant General Yamauchi. The main infantry units under his command included Honda Raiding Unit, commanded by Major Honda, 3/67th Regiment, whose task was to cut the Imphal–Kohima Road at 'Mission' (Kangpokpi). There was an assault column under Colonel Matsumura, 60th Regiment, which was tasked with advancing – via Shangshak – to Karakhul and Kuraopokpi, to the west of Sekmai on the Imphal–Kohima Road. Another column commanded by Colonel Omoto, 51st Regiment, was also ordered to the Sekmai area, passing over Imphal in a northern arc that included the Mapao-Molvom Range. 15th Division Headquarters, with supporting units, followed close behind.

Facing the Japanese in the Ukhrul Road sector were British-Indian formations that were rotated on several occasions. In March 1944, the area fell under the responsibility of 23rd Indian Division that was in reserve at Imphal. Towards the middle of that month, the 50th Indian Parachute Brigade replaced this division's 49th Brigade, only to become immediately involved in the Battle of Shangshak. By the end of March, the 5th Indian Division was rushed up the Ukhrul Road almost as soon as it arrived from the Arakan in Burma. In mid-April, the 23rd Indian Division took over the Ukhrul Road; it in turn was replaced by the 20th Indian Division in mid-May. By the time the British forces mounted a final assault on Ukhrul in early July 1944, this task had been handed over from 4 Corps to 33 Corps.

The Ukhrul Road is the only sector of the Battle of Imphal and area in Manipur where the Chindits played an operational role in 1944. As it had done in the Battle of Kohima, the Chindit 23rd Long Range Penetration Brigade targeted the Japanese lines of communication and cut their escape routes out of Ukhrul to the Burma border to the east.

The INA is also said to have been present in the Ukhrul area in 1944. This included the 2nd and 3rd Battalions of the INA 1st Division's Subhash Brigade. Commanded by Lieutenant Colonel Shah Nawaz Khan, who would later famously stand trial at the Red Fort in New Delhi, these men had earlier been active in the Chin Hills of Burma. They were in Ukhrul in May–June 1944; some of them are believed to have undertaken reconnaissance activities even beyond Ukhrul in the direction of Kohima.[88]

The battlefields today

The Ukhrul Road is a large area to cover from a battlefield perspective. The task is made harder because while a part of the Japanese 15th Division was active along and near the Ukhrul Road in 1944, many of its units advanced against the grain of the country, in an arc crossing east to west towards the north of Imphal. As a result, the battles in that area, especially as the British-Indian forces sought to push them back, took place in locations that are either far from the main road to Ukhrul today or not that easy to access.

This book follows the present-day road to Ukhrul from Imphal, covering those battlefields and places of relevance to the Battle of Imphal that lie on or near the road. At the time of writing, these were the places that were relatively easy and secure to access from Imphal. Another point to be borne in mind is that the present-day road does not follow the war-era alignment, especially in the stretch from Litan to Ukhrul. This has changed since 1944, presumably in favour of gentler gradients as it climbs the hills, much like the case of the Silchar Track around Point 5846.

Heading out from Imphal on the Ukhrul Road, one is confronted with what should by now seem like familiar views on the Imphal Valley: paddy fields on both sides, interspersed with villages and towns. What is different here, however, is the profusion of hills of varying heights, some closer to the road than others; one is at the north-eastern edges of the Imphal Valley, which the road traverses from Sawombung until Yaingangpokpi. From then on, it is a winding climb – with stretches of descent into a couple of valleys – all the way up to Ukhrul in sparsely populated countryside that some visitors say is reminiscent of Scotland.

A passage from a 20th Indian Division intelligence summary captures well the significance of this spoke leading to the hub at Imphal. The passage is produced here:

> Of all rds which lead to Imphal at the present time the Ukhrul Rd offers several advantages for an offensive aimed at Imphal.
>
> (a) Its northern flank is partly covered by Jap posns and to its south there is a very large gap only lightly held by our forces, and offering opportunities for infiltration in strength in a direction which leads straight to the objective via a most dominating feature, Nongmai Ching.
>
> (b) It has a relatively short and not too difficult MT L of C, albeit not all weather, leading to a good forming-up and stocking-up area widely dispersed yet served by MT routes.
>
> (c) It has no dominating key posn comparable to Shenam and held by us.
>
> (d) It has no 'Bishenpur' impractical to bypass in strength.
>
> It is therefore to be expected that in a renewed offensive aimed at capturing Imphal as quickly as possible, an important and possibly large scale thrust will develop from the Ukhrul area.[89]

Of course, this was issued at the end of May 1944, by which time the immediate threat the Japanese had posed to Imphal from this sector at the outset of the battle had long since passed.

The following is a brief sequence of events in this sector in 1944, involving the main battlefields covered in this book:

19–20 March	Point 7378 falls to the Japanese
22–26 March	Battle of Shangshak
26 March	Japanese attack Litan
4–6 April	Battle of Kameng
Mid-April	23rd Indian Division takes over from 5th Indian Division
Mid-May	20th Indian Division takes over from 23rd Indian Division
3 June	20th Indian Division starts attacking east of the Iril River and along the Ukhrul Road
1–8 July	Battle of Ukhrul

KANGLA AIRFIELD

As one heads out of Imphal past Lamlong Bazar, one crosses an open stretch of paddy fields before the Ukhrul Road curves right near the town of Sawombung. It is in the paddy fields east of the road here that the fair-weather airfield the British named Kangla was sited in 1944 (Figure 4.20).

Figure 4.20 The paddy fields that were once the Kangla Airfield along the Ukhrul Road

Source: Photo by Hemant Singh Katoch

As with Wangjing and Sapam in the Tamu–Palel Road sector, the area was reclaimed by the surrounding villages after the Second World War and the old airfield has reverted to its pre-war status as paddy fields.

Looking at the fields today, one is reminded that the conditions for air force personnel stationed at these – especially fair-weather – airfields during the Battle of Imphal were not easy. Norman Franks, in his book *The Air Battle of Imphal*, sums up about the living conditions at airfields during the Burma Campaign in general, but with particular reference to the Imphal airfields such as Kangla:

> Heat, insects, poor food, monsoon rains, humidity, prickly heat, leaking tents, mud, jungle sores, bites, snakes, limited or hard to come-by spares – the list was endless. How the ground crews managed to keep a high rate of aeroplane serviceability in these conditions while working on machines in the open – there were no sturdy, dry hangars on these jungle airstrips – was a miracle in itself.[90]

From this point, one can see in the distance up ahead, to the northwest of the road, part of the feature the British called Nungshigum and the Japanese Hill 3833. Its heights were the scene of a key battle in April 1944; one of the reasons the British counter-attacked the Japanese on the massif with such force was the threat they posed to this very Kangla Airfield.

KAMENG

Continuing on, one crosses the Iril River before approaching a point near Lamlai where the hills on both sides close in, leaving a space of about 1,000 yards through which the Ukhrul Road passes. By early April 1944, a battalion each of 123rd Brigade, 5th Indian Division, had been posted on the hills closest to the road on either side. The 2nd Suffolks were on the hill – Hill 4057 – to the north (left of the road), while the 1st Battalion, the Dogra Regiment (the 1st Dogras), was in the south (right of the road).[91] They had been sent here to try and stop the Japanese 15th Division from advancing towards Imphal down the road.

Amazingly, this entire gap between the hills through which the Ukhrul Road passes had been blocked by barbed wire at the time to prevent a Japanese advance down this way. Anti-personnel mines added to the defences, as did heavy machineguns on either side. The Japanese nevertheless did attack the area in the first week of April 1944, and they chose the hill to the immediate south of the road here (Figure 4.21). Close as it was to a small village called Kameng just off the Ukhrul Road, this clash is sometimes now referred to as the Battle of Kameng.

Figure 4.21 The battlefield of Kameng

Source: Photo by Hemant Singh Katoch

A company of 3/67th Regiment, 15th Division, put in the attack on the night of 4 April. It is believed that its ultimate aim was Kangla Airfield.[92] The Japanese who got onto part of the hill were furiously counter-attacked – by the guns of 28 Field Regiment near Sawombung, the Dogras themselves, as well as tanks of the 3rd Carabiniers, who surrounded the hill and fired at their targets from two sides. The British secured the hill by the morning of 6 April. At least 98 Japanese bodies were found at the position the next day.[93]

It is possible to climb this hill to the south of the Ukhrul Road today. Even a short hike up reveals excellent views of the Ukhrul Road in the Imphal Valley and the surrounding hills. With one's back to the hill at Kameng, in the distance on the left can be clearly seen the hulking, sprawling shape of Nungshigum, while right in front is the hill known to both sides as Hill 4057, which also saw clashes in 1944.

LITAN

From Kameng, the road continues on past Yaingangpokpi, climbs up a saddle – also the scene of clashes in 1944 – before descending down towards the village of Litan. As in 1944, it is up to this village that the road from Imphal is broad and wide; from here on it narrows considerably in width.

At the time of the Battle of Shangshak towards the end of March 1944, Litan was where some of the men of the 50th Indian Parachute Brigade had been left behind, together with some soldiers from the 23rd Indian Division's administrative and supply services.[94] They had formed a defensive position here to try and block any advance by the Japanese 15th Division. They were joined by the 2/1st Punjab of 123rd Brigade, 5th Indian Division. The Japanese put in an attack on its C Company on the night of 26 March 1944, which was fended off after fierce hand-to-hand fighting.

Surrounded as it is by hills on three sides, the village was considered difficult to defend over a long period – one author commented that 'it was patently a deathtrap'[95] – and too isolated. The detachment at Litan was finally withdrawn on March 28, with the main defensive position on the Ukhrul Road then becoming Kameng. Litan and its surroundings were to witness further fighting in the later stages of the Battle of Imphal as the British-Indian forces pushed up the road towards Ukhrul.

FINCH'S CORNER

Continuing on up the road, one comes across a modern marker for Finch's Corner (Figure 4.22). This is where the present-day road forks to Ukhrul on the left, while the village of Shangshak is up the right fork. This is not the original Finch's Corner of Second World War vintage, however. That lies a couple of hundred yards up a track that sharply branches off to the left just short of the new junction. The spot is quite atmospheric as it is where the war-era Ukhrul Road in this area can still be seen – today a dirt track coming in from the direction of Litan and heading north towards Ukhrul. It is then one realises that the track off the main road that one has just climbed to get here was part of the old, war-era route to Shangshak. Before they decided to make their stand at Shangshak, it was near here that the headquarters of the 50th Indian Parachute Brigade had been located.

What truly adds to the sense of history of this place is the original stone marker for Finch's Corner that still stands here, largely intact some 70 years on (Figure 4.22). In the faded inscription on the marker, tribute is paid to a Major Finch, who built this road. One can just about make out part of the inscription that ends with this moving line: 'We hill people never had a dream to have a sight of such a thing near our doors.' The 'thing' is supposed to refer to a motorable road.

Figure 4.22 Old Finch's Corner

Source: Photo by Hemant Singh Katoch

SHANGSHAK (SANGSHAK)

From the new Finch's Corner, one takes a right off the road to head to the village where the defining battle of the Ukhrul Road sector took place: Shangshak, or Sangshak of military memoirs. It was a short battle but one which delayed the Japanese by a few days in the crucial opening stages of their offensive towards Imphal and Kohima. Indeed, the battle in and around this mountain village is today recognised as crucial to the outcome of the overall clash of the British Fourteenth Army and the Japanese Fifteenth Army in 1944.

It occurred in the second half of March, when in the other sectors, such as on the Tiddim Road, Silchar Track and the Tamu–Palel Road, the Japanese push into India had just begun. The main British-Indian force at Shangshak and at Ukhrul further north at the time consisted of the 50th Indian Parachute Brigade, commanded by Brigadier M. Hope-Thompson, which had only recently arrived in Manipur. They had been deployed here, replacing 49th Brigade of the 23rd Indian Division, which had been sent down the Tiddim Road. They were soon to find themselves facing a far superior force in numbers from the Japanese 31st Division bound for Kohima, as

Figure 4.23 Looking on to what was the main British defensive position at Shangshak in March 1944

Source: Photo by Hemant Singh Katoch

well as elements of the Japanese 15th Division bound for Imphal. Hope-Thompson had under his command 152nd Para Battalion (made up of Gurkhas) and 153rd Para Battalion (Indians), as well as reinforcements left behind by the 49th Brigade in the form of the 4/5th Mahratta Light Infantry and two companies of the Kali Bahadur Regiment.

Shangshak became a battlefield in 1944 primarily because of its location in relation to the routes taken by the two Japanese divisions heading towards Imphal and Kohima (Figure 4.23). The village lay within the northern limits of the area of responsibility of the Japanese 15th Division as it advanced towards Imphal; the 31st Division was to pass just north of Shangshak en route to Kohima via Ukhrul. Several jeep tracks passed in the vicinity. In what is considered one of the most fateful – and much debated – moves by the Japanese in 1944, Major General Miyazaki, who was commanding an infantry group of the 31st Division, decided to direct the bulk of its 58th Regiment to attack the small British-Indian force at Shangshak – which lay outside his area of responsibility.

Ferocious fighting between the two sides followed at the village from 22 to 26 March, with wave upon wave of Japanese attacks at the small British-Indian defensive perimeter at Shangshak. In the closing stages of the battle, the 60th Regiment of the Japanese 15th Division also became involved. The battle finally ended with the withdrawal of the British-Indian forces from the village on the night of 26 March. The upper range of estimates of casualties at Shangshak included around a 1,000 Japanese and some 900 men on the British-Indian side killed and wounded.[96]

The importance of the Battle of Shangshak is something that was realised only after the Second World War. Today it is widely acknowledged that the British-Indian defence at Shangshak delayed the Japanese 15th and 31st Divisions in their advance on Imphal and Kohima, respectively. The delay was crucial given that the Japanese were counting on an already tight timetable for the success of their overall offensive. The battle at Shangshak therefore gave just enough time for the British 4 Corps in Imphal to reorganise itself, kept the Imphal–Kohima Road open for a few more vital days and allowed the 5th Indian Division to be flown into Imphal from the Arakan and straight to the defence of this sector and of Kohima. The battle also severely depleted the strength of the 58th Regiment, Japanese 31st Division, which was to play a key role in the Japanese attack on Kohima.

It is possible to visit Shangshak today and appreciate how the battle here had played out in March 1944. Naturally, the village today is far larger than what it was some 70 years ago, and much of the old battlefield consisting of the British-Indian defensive position now falls within its limits. One arrives at Shangshak via the road (then track) from Finch's Corner that passes the village and continues on to Kamjong, close to the Burma border.

To begin with, from certain vantage points in the village, it is possible to spot in the far distance the bare peak the British had named Point 7378. This was a forward position ahead of Shangshak where C Company of 152nd Battalion, 50th Indian Parachute Brigade, had been sent. The hill came under attack on 19 March as it lay in the path of the 3rd Battalion, 58th Regiment, Japanese 31st Division, as it moved towards Ukhrul. Despite a valiant overnight defence of Point 7378 by C Company, the position was overrun and fell to the Japanese by 20 March.[97] As the British-Indian forces in other forward positions retreated westwards, on 22 March it was decided to regroup and make a stand at Shangshak.

The best way to start exploring the old battlefield is to start with the football field that lies just above the road from Finch's Corner that passes the village. Standing on the field with one's back to the road, one can see on the left what British military memoirs call West Hill. On the plateau to the right was the British-Indian defensive position; the part one faces from the football field is its western and south-western perimeter. On West Hill today stands a smart church; on where the defensive position was in 1944 now stand houses and other structures of present-day Shangshak village.

During the battle, men of the 58th Regiment, Japanese 31st Division, encircled the British position from the north and the west, cutting the route back to Finch's Corner and Litan, and hurled attack after attack against it. The 60th Regiment, Japanese 15th Division, seems to have become involved only on the last day of the battle, 26 March, attacking the village from the south.[98] Because the ground north and south of the British-Indian position fell away steeply, and to the east there was woodland with clear ground in front of the forward positions, it was along the western perimeter that the defenders were most vulnerable to Japanese attacks. It was across from here that West Hill stood, separated from the defensive position by a gulley. This was the direction from where many of the Japanese attacks came in March 1944.

At least one such attack involved an infantry charge at night right across the football field one is standing on, where some 20 Japanese bodies were found the next morning.[99] Standing on the football field, it is worth considering the following vivid account from Harry Seaman's *The Battle at Sangshak* about the first Japanese assault from West Hill. It is written from the perspective of the waiting Gurkhas of C Company, 153rd Battalion, on the plateau across. At the end of this attack, which lasted just 10 to 15 minutes, an estimated 90 of the 120 men of the 8th Company, 2nd Battalion, 58th Regiment, lay dead, including the company commander.

> At first two or three Japanese appeared; soon their numbers had swollen to twenty or thirty – and in no time at all about a hundred men were moving fast down the facing slope [of West Hill]. The time to open fire was not to be determined by word of command, but the moment when the leading enemy soldier set foot on the level ground. The moment came, its consequences awesome. For a split second after the first volley of fire, Hobstock, a young officer with C Company, who had focused his binoculars on the hill before him, thought the hill was moving upwards; it was an optical illusion caused by the mass downward movement of some fifty or sixty tumbling Japanese bodies. As they fell, still more enemy soldiers were coming into view over the brow of the hill, silhouetted against the evening sky, to be cut down by rifle fire.[100]

From the football field one can climb up to the church that now stands on West Hill and observe the plateau across to where the British-Indian defensive position was (Figure 4.23). This can be followed up by a short stroll through a part of the village before climbing up to the old defensive position. Just next to the highest point here lies the spot where the war-era church once stood. The church is mentioned in war memoirs as it stood on the north-western corner of the perimeter and overlooked the western defences. This area was the scene of much fighting during the battle.

It was a particular area of focus on the last day of the battle, 26 March 1944. That morning the Japanese managed to capture a part of this position and its vicinity, and the defenders of Shangshak fought back with equal ferocity to recapture it. Some have considered it the worst day by far of the battle, describing it as 'eleven and a half hours of continuous mayhem' that none who participated in it have ever forgotten.[101] A Japanese officer involved has been quoted as saying, 'Hand-to-hand fighting was everywhere and hand grenades flew everywhere. Our comrades encouraged us, the enemy screamed at us. Thus the top of the hill turned to a hell on earth.'[102] The battle ended later that evening as the defenders of Shangshak were ordered to withdraw to Imphal. As noted earlier, one estimate puts the casualty figures at 1,000 for the Japanese and at 900 for the British-Indian forces at Shangshak.[103]

Continuing on, one can walk through the village beyond, along a west to east axis of the old British-Indian position. It is during this walk that the length of the position sinks in: in March 1944, the defenders of the 50th Indian Parachute Brigade were packed into a tiny area some 600 yards wide by 300 yards long. No wonder then – as the memoirs point out – any shells the Japanese fired on the position found a target.[104] And shelling and mortaring there was aplenty: the Japanese infantry charges were supported throughout by mountain and field guns. From one of the vantage points at the eastern end of the village, one can look across at the hamlet of Nungshang, where four Japanese field guns were situated and where Major General Miyazaki was also said to be present during the battle.[105]

The size of the defensive position had also made air drops to the defenders difficult to make, with supplies often floating over to the Japanese. Historians note two other critical points about the position. One was that it had no sources of water. However, this was not unusual in Naga villages that are often perched on mountain tops, with limited water supplies. The second point was the absence of any barbed wire to ring the perimeter. According to Seaman, despite repeated appeals for barbed wire, this was never sent through from Imphal.[106]

At the eastern edge of the present-day village, one can still spot extensive remains of trenches that weave their way in the undergrowth. On clear days, the area also affords glorious views of the hills and countryside of what is today Manipur's Ukhrul district. It is while standing at one of these vantage points, looking north, east and south, that one can orient oneself to the broad directions from where the Japanese 31st and 15th Divisions made their way towards Imphal and Kohima from the Burma border in 1944.

The last stopover here is the Shangshak War Memorial that is up a steep incline at the entrance to the village, just after the Assam Rifles checkpoint. The memorial has been erected and maintained by the Indian

Figure 4.24 Shangshak War Memorial

Source: Photo by Hemant Singh Katoch

Army, which holds a ceremony to mark the battle annually in the month of March. Although the memorial does not stand on the main battlefield, its presence helps one to focus on the events of March 1944 when this remote village became the unlikely setting for a short but significant battle of the Second World War (Figure 4.24).

Next to the memorial is the home of Yangmasho Shishak, who as a young boy worked for the British and the Japanese during the Second World War. He has constructed memorials to both forces in the compound of his house and has converted part of his home into a private museum. In it he proudly displays his collection of war relics and artefacts.

UKHRUL

Heading north again from Finch's Corner, one finally arrives in Ukhrul. Given what happened in this mountain town in 1944, it is surprising to note the absence of any memorials or reminders of the Second World War. Ukhrul fell to the Japanese 31st Division heading to Kohima in the second half of March 1944 and stayed under their control until early July.

The INA under Shah Nawaz Khan was also said to be present here at some point.

Ukhrul came into particular prominence at the end of June/early July 1944 as this was where the survivors of the Japanese 31st Division from the Battle of Kohima and those of the 15th Division from the north and north-east of Imphal congregated to make their last stand. An overwhelming Allied offensive from all directions was planned to recapture Ukhrul in early July.

Slim notes that Ukhrul had been encircled by 1 July and describes how the town fell:

> The 7th Division attacked from the west and north, the 20th Division closed in from the south and south-east, and 23 LRP Brigade repeated its old role of cutting the escape routes to the east. Two days later, after overcoming stubborn resistance on all lines of advance, our troops were fighting in the outskirts of the village. Although these enemy detachments had suffered heavily and stragglers and small parties were daily being mopped all over the area, it was not until 8 July that the whole of Ukhrul itself was finally in our hands.[107]

Today there are spectacular views to be enjoyed from the vantage points around Ukhrul (Figure 4.25). A trip up to the town is worth it just to soak them up. When one is standing at one of these viewpoints, it is sobering to reflect on what happened here during the Second World War: this was where the last remnants of the Japanese 15th and 31st Divisions, who had sought to capture Imphal and Kohima, respectively, as part of the great offensive into India in 1944, were finally defeated. As the Official History of the Indian Armed Forces in the Second World War records: 'The last stage of the battle for defeating the "invade India" army was therefore to clear the Japanese from Ukhrul.'[108]

It is also worth reflecting on the following words from Captain Shosaku Kameyama of the 58th Regiment, Japanese 31st Division, who fought at Shangshak near here. While this is a Japanese point of view, many of the feelings expressed apply equally to all sides who fought at Imphal in 1944:

> My unit came from Niigata prefecture, where Buddhism is widely believed in and almost every house has a small but fine family Buddhist shrine to worship their ancestors. However, those drafted into the regiment were young and unmarried, and could not be ancestors. Their parents had died and in their family

Figure 4.25 View over the eastern side of Ukhrul town. The bare peak in the distance is Point 7378

Source: Photo by Hemant Singh Katoch

there are only uncles whom the younger generation has not met and who are going to be completely forgotten.

Most of those who died in the war were twenty or twenty-two years old. They fought for their country, to save their country in the national emergency. They believed that the country was in a serious situation, on the brink of survival in the face of the foreign invasion. It was natural at that time that the younger generation should go out and fight in such a national emergency. Moreover, when they left their home town, many schoolchildren and local people cheered their departure, singing songs and waving flags. This had greatly impressed the soldiers, who had a strong obligation to families and local folk.

Nobody wants to die, but soldiers dare to fight bravely to pursue their duties and to fulfil the wishes of the people at home. It is not easy to suppress the wish to live, and they charged at the enemy line in trepidation. Nobody dies smiling. Such brave comrades are now almost forgotten. I wish more people know how they lived, how they fought and how they died.[109]

The Iril River Valley and the Mapao-Molvom Range: at the gates of Imphal

Historical overview

The Iril River Valley runs almost parallel to the Imphal–Kohima Road for several miles north of Imphal. There is a range of hills running north to south between the two, with some peaks soaring to over 5,000 feet above sea level. A stretch of this range, between the war-era location of the villages of Mapao and Molvom, was the scene of much fighting during the Battle of Imphal. Of all of the spokes leading to the hub at Imphal, the one through the Iril River Valley was least road-like and was essentially a path. For ease of explanation, this path and its surrounding heights, especially the Mapao-Molvom Range, have been clubbed together and presented here as a sector of fighting in the Battle of Imphal.

As with the other sectors in the vicinity, including the Ukhrul Road to the east and the Imphal–Kohima Road to the west, the Japanese forces active here belonged to the 15th Division, commanded by Lieutenant General Yamauchi. Their objective was to attack Imphal from the north. In what mirrored the fate of the Japanese lines of attack on all of the other points of the compass, this advance was also checked by the British-Indian forces. Soon thereafter, it was they who went on the offensive. It was in the Battle of Nungshigum in the Iril River Valley sector, however, that the Japanese came closest to actually reaching Imphal in 1944. The men of 51st Regiment, Japanese 15th Division, were involved in the battle, following which they were withdrawn to east of the Iril River.

Further up in the Iril River Valley, the British-Indian forces sought to disrupt Japanese supply lines which stretched from the east right up to the Imphal–Kohima Road in the west. This involved aggressive and extensive patrolling, as well as regular skirmishes with groups of Japanese soldiers. The Iril River Valley was also one side from where the British approached the Japanese positions on the Mapao-Molvom Range. It was on the peaks of this sprawling range, on positions such as those the British had named Hump, Twin Peaks, Penhill, Buttertubs and Foston, that the Japanese had dug in in early April 1944 – and where they stayed against all odds through the Battle of Imphal.

Facing off with the Japanese in this sector were men of the 5th Indian Division, commanded by Major General Harold Briggs. This division was not part of the original 4 Corps in Imphal; it had been flown in from the Arakan in Burma in the second half of March to deal with the Japanese offensive. One brigade – the 161st – had been sent to Dimapur to assist in Kohima; this included the battalion of Royal West Kents that would become famous during the Siege of Kohima. The other two brigades – the 9th and the 123rd – were flown to the Imphal airfields. They were joined in early May by the 89th Brigade of the 7th Indian Division that had also been flown in from the Arakan.

Their main task was to stem the Japanese advance towards Imphal from the north, especially via the Imphal–Kohima Road, and to clear them from their positions on the Mapao-Molvom Range.[110] The bulk of the fighting for the Mapao-Molvom Range positions took place from end of April to early June 1944. During this period the battalions of the 5th Indian Division repeatedly attacked the Japanese-held peaks from all possible directions, including from the Iril River Valley. Except for capturing the odd hill, these attacks were largely unsuccessful. Nothing seemed to be able to move the Japanese from these heights.

The frustrating lack of progress eventually prompted the division's commander, Major General Briggs, to focus his main effort on opening the Imphal–Kohima Road. Not only was the latter a much more important objective, but it was felt that the opening of the road would likely force the stubborn defenders on the Mapao-Molvom Range to abandon their positions. As it so happened, this strategy worked. It was only after the Imphal–Kohima Road was opened on 22 June 1944 did the Japanese on the Mapao-Molvom Range leave their positions as part of a general withdrawal eastwards towards Ukhrul.

The battlefields today

Unlike the hills that make up the Shenam Saddle position on the Tamu–Palel Road, the heights of the Mapao-Molvom Range are not easily accessible. There is no motorable road that passes through these high hills that could make it easy to identify the different positions of 1944 and see them up close. One way to at least get visuals of this range and get a sense of its terrain, even if from a distance, is to drive east of them; another is to catch glimpses of these hills from the Imphal–Kohima Road.

This book suggests a short route that gives views of this range from the Imphal Valley and allows one to see parts of the Iril River Valley, as well. It also covers Runaway Hill, the site of an action in early April 1944 for which a Victoria Cross was awarded, and one of the most important battlefields of the entire Battle of Imphal, Nungshigum (Figure 4.26). Though narrow, the country road on this route is tarmac and in fair condition. The terrain en route is, in tune with the sector covered, a mix of villages and paddy fields on the northern fringes of the Imphal Valley, together with bluish-green hills, often on both sides of the road.

Figure 4.26 The sprawling Nungshigum/Hill 3833 in the distance

Source: Photo by Hemant Singh Katoch

The following is a brief sequence of events in this sector in 1944, involving the main battlefields covered in this book:

6 April	Action at Runaway Hill for which Abdul Hafiz is awarded a Victoria Cross
6–14 April	Battle of Nungshigum/Hill 3833
1–30 May	5th Indian Division attacks on the peaks of the Mapao-Molvom Range

RUNAWAY HILL

Getting started, one heads north out of Imphal on what is locally known as the Pangei Road. Skirting the Imphal River, this road initially passes to the west of the Ukhrul Road. Unlike that road, however, the Pangei Road goes straight in a northerly direction. After passing the small town it has been named after, it goes right to the base of Runaway Hill, a small, bare feature (Figure 4.27). One passes the sprawling massif referred to as Nungshigum or Hill 3833 to get to Runaway Hill, but that battlefield is best viewed from its other side and is covered later.

Figure 4.27 Runaway Hill

Source: Photo by Hemant Singh Katoch

On the early morning of 6 April 1944, the Japanese attacked a standing patrol on Runaway Hill and captured the position. Later that morning, Jemadar Abdul Hafiz of the 3/9th Jats was called upon to recapture the hill with two sections from his platoon. Abdul Hafiz led the assault on Runaway Hill with great dash and fearlessness. Charging up the hill, in the face of machine-gun fire and grenade attacks, he killed several Japanese and eventually retook Runaway Hill. According to one account, it was because of the way the Japanese on this hill fled in the face of Abdul Hafiz's attack that it subsequently became known as Runaway Hill.[111]

But Abdul Hafiz was not done. He started pursuing the Japanese who were now firing from a neighbouring feature. He was injured from their machine-gun fire while doing so and died shortly thereafter. For his actions on Runaway Hill, Abdul Hafiz was posthumously conferred the Victoria Cross. He is buried at the Imphal War Cemetery.

THE MAPAO-MOLVOM RANGE

From Runaway Hill an even narrower country road branches off to the west. This goes up almost to the base of the Mapao-Molvom Range, and it is from where that one can catch a good glimpse of it. It is those very peaks in the distance that were so tenaciously defended by men of the 60th Regiment, Japanese 15th Division, from April to June 1944. As with so many of the Japanese-held positions during the Battle of Imphal, they were subjected to everything the British could throw at them: infantry charges, artillery shelling, air strikes.

One of the peaks in the distance is what the British called Hump. Hump was the most fought over peak on the Mapao-Molvom Range; it was also perhaps one of the best demonstrations of Japanese defensive capabilities at Imphal. With little to dwindling supplies, cut off from the support of any larger force, perched up on peaks between 4,000 and 5,000 feet high, under incessant rains and repeated attack – these men still stayed the course.

In May 1944, the 3/14th Punjab repeatedly attacked Hump, all to no avail. The mountainous terrain necessitated days of close-quarter combat with LMGs and grenades. To get a good sense of the fighting, it is worth considering the entries about Hump in the war diary of 9th Indian Brigade – to which the 3/14th Punjab belonged – for the month of May:

- **2 May**: 2230 hrs. 3/14 Punjab using two platoons attacked Hump. Enemy threw grenades and opened up with small arms as own troops were nearing top of feature. Own troops withdrew and heavy mortar and very effective artillery fire was brought down on Hump.
- **4 May**: 0730 hrs. 3/14 Punjab attack on Hump held up 100 yards from top of feature by heavy fire from three platoon positions areas [around Hump] and Hump. Repeated attacks on Hump throughout day unsuccessful. One platoon own troops counter-attacked by platoon enemy when only 10 yards from top of feature.
- 1700 hrs. Own troops Hump area ordered to withdraw. Enemy strength this area estimated three platoons with high percentage of automatics and at least one MMG. Heavy casualties inflicted on enemy.
- **5 May**: 0700 hrs. Air strike on Hump accurate but enemy bunkers undamaged.
- 0710 hrs. 3/14 Punjab company attack on Hump held up 10 yards from top of feature. Attacking troops came under very heavy automatic fire from top of Hump and MMG fire from ridge to west of Hump. Enemy showered grenades on attacking troops who were forced to withdraw. Enemy on Hump are occupying strong Arakan type of bunker positions. Opposition stronger than ever in Hump area. Positions obviously reinforced during night.
- **15 May**: 1200 hrs. Air strike and strafing on Hump excellent.

- **20 May**: 0500 hrs. 3/14 Punjab attacking Hump came under heavy SA fire when they reached enemy wire. One platoon reached top of feature but forced to withdraw when they came under heavy G/D fire from reverse slopes. 0816 hrs. Further attack attempt to capture Hump unsuccessful. Eight Japs killed.
- **21 May**: 1645 hrs. Air strike on Hump fair. Approx. 50% bombs fell on target area. Strafing good.
- **22 May**: 0430 hrs. 'A' Company and two platoons 'D' Company 3/14 Punjab reached top of Hump after killing occupants of at least six pill-boxes. Own troops remained on top of feature for 25 mins lobbing grenades into enemy trenches and bunker positions but eventually they were forced to withdraw owing to strong fusillade of fire and showers of grenades from enemy entrenched positions on reverse slopes of feature. Between 50 and 100 Japs observed moving up from reverse slopes …Another platoon of 'A' Company attacked Hump from the east but were met by concentrated grenade SA fire and were forced to withdraw. Battalion gun from Twin Peaks fired on southern slopes Hump.
- 1100 hrs. Own troops again attacked Hump reaching top of feature but were grenaded off. Contact was made with 1/11 Sikh on top of feature. They had attacked Hump from the northwest.
- 1200hrs. Own troops ordered to withdraw.
- **24 May**: Five times during day own aircraft successfully strafed top of ridge between Hump and Everest – both features included. Artillery harassed enemy positions this area throughout day.
- **28 May**: 3/14 Punjab section observed 8 Japs with W/T sets near bunker west edge of Hump. Own troops fired LMG and rifles into Japs. Rifle fire and grenades were then directed on section from bunker area. Two sections to east of Hump fired on from west edge of feature. Section grenaded 5 Japs observed moving in communication trench towards top of feature. Two sections remaining below Hump will send snipers forward at intervals towards top of feature.
- **29 May**: First light. 3/14 Punjab sniping patrols moved to area Hump.
- **30 May**: First light. 2 platoons 3/14 Punjab raided Hump and reached within 80 yards of top of Hump where they came under G/D fire from Jhund and small arms fire from top of Hump particularly the western edge. Own troops withdrew after killing 10 Japs, own casualties 5 wounded.
- **31 May**: 3/14 Punjab recce patrol to Hump reports position still occupied. Afternoon air strike on Hump. Bombing and strafing good.[112]

Looking at the Mapao-Molvom Range today, one cannot help but be amazed at the sheer determination of the Fifteenth Army's soldiers to hang on in the face of such overwhelming odds (Figure 4.28). Actions of this nature were reported from all of the sectors of fighting in Manipur.

Figure 4.28 The Mapao-Molvom Range in the far distance. Visible are Twin Peaks (right-of-centre) and Hump (to its left)

Source: Photo by Hemant Singh Katoch

UP THE IRIL RIVER VALLEY

Retracing one's steps, one takes the road that passes to the south of Runaway Hill and joins up at a village named Sagolmang, the main road that traverses the Iril River Valley. From there on, one heads north, passing small villages, the road never too far from the Iril River that snakes alongside. This was patrolling country during the Battle of Imphal, where in regular – albeit small-scale – clashes with the Japanese 15th Division the British-Indian forces sought to disrupt its east–west lines of supply and communication.

The history of the 5th Indian Division gives a sense of what it was like here in April 1944:

> Their efforts were directed towards cutting the Japanese supply routes up and down the valleys that skirted the Imphal Valley, and daily our patrols fought engagements with groups of enemy soldiers. When local villagers reported the presence of Japanese looting parties, the Royal Air Force and Gunners bombarded the place. . . . Long reconnaissance patrols were sent out for several days at a time to search for the enemy. Raiding parties attacked

villages from which the enemy was known to take food by night. Ammunition dumps were bombed and mule convoys strafed.[113]

After going northwards for a few kilometres, one takes a U-turn and reaches the junction at Sagolmang again. This time one takes the left fork to head in the direction of the village of Keibi, the village in the Iril River Valley from where one gets the best views of the hill the British called Nungshigum and the Japanese Hill 3833 in 1944 (Figure 4.28).

NUNGSHIGUM/HILL 3833

This sprawling feature was the scene of an iconic encounter between British–Indian and Japanese forces in the first half of April 1944. All accounts of Imphal and the Burma Campaign dwell in some detail on the Battle of Nungshigum, which was the closest the Japanese managed to get to Imphal during the Second World War.[114] Fortunately, Nungshigum remains largely unchanged 70 years on. As with the hills of the Shenam Saddle, it therefore makes it easy to visualise the events that took place on this hill just outside Imphal in 1944.

The battle pitted men of the Japanese 15th Division against those of the 5th Indian Division who had only recently been flown in to Imphal from the Arakan. On the night of 6/7 April, the massif was attacked by the 3rd Battalion, 51st Regiment, of the Japanese 15th Division. The 51st Regiment was commanded by Colonel Omoto. They were able to drive off two platoons of 3/9th Jats of 9th Brigade, 5th Indian Division, from the heights of Nungshigum. The British had christened the two highest points North Bump and South Bump; the latter peak was higher, at around 3,800 feet above sea level. The Japanese used this reference to call the entire feature Hill 3833. The Jats recaptured the hill the next day, only to lose it to the Japanese by 11 April following repeated attacks.[115]

The decisive day of the battle was 13 April 1944. To the British, the Japanese presence on the heights of Nungshigum posed an unacceptable threat: 4 Corps headquarters and the all-weather Imphal Main were less than 5 miles away, while the fair-weather Kangla Airfield and the outskirts of Imphal itself were even closer. It was decided to evict the Japanese with all speed – and force. The men and machines involved in the counter-attack on Nungshigum included the infantry, including two companies of the 1st Dogras; the artillery, including guns of the 5th Indian Division, with another medium artillery regiment in support; armour, including B Squadron of the 3rd Carabiniers; and the air force, including 24 aircraft in two squadrons of Vengeance dive-bombers and one of Hurribombers.

The use of tanks on such a high feature and on the narrow ridgeline that connected North and South Bump was certainly a bold gamble, and one that the Japanese had not expected. Indeed, some historians attribute the defeat of the 15th Division to its inability to deal with British tanks.[116] Standing at the base of Nungshigum today, it is hard to imagine six tanks making their way up this hill and scaling its heights to tackle the Japanese defenders. On the morning of 13 April 1944, Lee-Grants of the 3rd Carabiniers did just that, their ascent preceded by airstrikes on the Japanese positions and a heavy artillery concentration from east and west. The tanks split up into two groups, each accompanied by a company of the Dogras; they made their way up via two spurs on the south-western side of Nungshigum.

An excerpt from the account of Arthur F. Freer, an N.C.O. of the 3rd Carabiniers who was in one of those tanks that day, makes for a riveting read:

> We continued our slow progress northwards with the infantry just behind each tank when all hell was let loose.
>
> The tanks were sprayed with rifle and machine gun fire. Hand grenades rained on us from the shallow slit trenches on either side of our path.
>
> I could see a bunch of huge Japs running up to the left side of the three tanks in front of us. . . .
>
> . . . Without waiting for an order to fire, I put a burst of Browning into them, and because the gun would not traverse, I was only able to spray up and down about six feet from the sides of the tanks. Three of the Japs fell but the leading survivor tried to climb up the side of Corporal Coram's tank which was still moving. He put a foot on to the top part of the track which was moving forward at twice the speed of the vehicle. He lost his balance and fell heavily to the ground.
>
> Paddy followed closely and he went under our tracks [117]

In the hours that followed, all of the British tank and infantry commanders were either killed or wounded. Five of the former had been shot, mainly because they had had to stick their heads out of their tanks' turrets to guide them safely on the narrow and steep ridgeline. It was finally left to two non-commissioned officers, Sergeant-Major Craddock of the 3rd Carabiniers and Subedar Ranbir Singh of the 1st Dogras, to take charge of their tanks and men, respectively, and complete the battle without their officers.[118] They did so successfully and evicted the Japanese from the heights of Nungshigum/Hill 3833. Some 250 Japanese are believed to have died in the fighting that had begun on 6 April.[119]

Several British military honours were won at Nungshigum. Lieutenant Colonel E.J. Woods of the 1st Dogras who planned and organised the main attack was awarded a Distinguished Service Order; Major L.A. Jones, Captain H.W. Alden and Subedar Tiru Ram of the 1st Dogras won the Military Cross; Subedar Ranbir Singh won the Indian Order of Merit; Sergeant-Major Craddock was awarded the Distinguished Conduct Medal; and Sergeant Hamar and Trooper Smith of the 3rd Carabiniers won the Military Medal.[120] These are, of course, in addition to the Victoria Cross posthumously awarded to Subedar Abdul Hafiz for his actions on Runaway Hill.

The memory of this dramatic battle on a hill outside Imphal lives on to this day. A citation continues to be read by the chaplain of the Royal Scots Dragoon Guards, the successor to the 3rd Carabiniers, to the assembled at the 'Nunshigum Parade' on 13 April every year.[121] Louis Allen refers to other sources and informs that B Squadron of the Royal Scots Dragoon Guards does not parade under the command of officers that day. Instead, to commemorate their role in the fighting of 13 April 1944, the tanks are commanded by the Squadron Sergeant-Major and NCOs.[122]

It is worth reflecting on some points relating to terrain and logistics at the Battle of Imphal here. Besides the villages and paddy fields of the Tiddim Road, a lot of the fighting in 1944 took place in hills of varying heights. This terrain had direct bearing on the type of weaponry deployed by the two sides and the related tactics used. This applied in particular to the Japanese, who had had to swiftly travel dozens of miles from the Chindwin River in their approach towards Imphal. It was why mountain and field guns made up the main Japanese weaponry used against 4 Corps in Manipur in 1944. These could often be manhandled for close-range use onto relatively inaccessible positions, where it would be difficult to deploy heavier guns. On their part, of course, the British could take recourse to the full range of weaponry against the Japanese.

Related to terrain was the matter of logistics, another important factor for the choice of firepower. For example, the Japanese were able to use tanks only on the Tamu–Palel Road (Shenam Saddle) and the Tiddim Road. In fact, it was only in the latter that they were able to play any significant role in the fighting. This is at least partly because these were the only two sectors of the Battle of Imphal where the Japanese forces had anything approaching 'motorable' roads behind them, leading all the way back to Burma. This was certainly the case with the Tamu–Palel Road; on the other hand, the main stretch of the Tiddim Road in the hills became a nightmare for heavy transport as the rains progressed. In all of the other sectors, the units were defenceless against British armour. Worse still, since the Japanese 15th Division to the north and north-east of Imphal had not expected to encounter tanks, they were not even equipped with anti-tank weapons – as seen at Nungshigum.

The battles in this sector also underline how the fighting at Imphal varied in intensity and scale. Sometimes it was spread out over a vast area and involved smaller skirmishes (Ukhrul Road sector). In other parts, it was concentrated and intense (Shenam Saddle). On occasion it was incredibly close range, where the fulcrum of fighting for weeks was a small stream/river in a village (Ningthoukhong) or over one small hill (Scraggy/Ito Hill, Hump), or two (Mortar Bluff and Water Piquet). At times it boiled down to the control of a strategically located peak (Point 5846, Nungshigum).

The Imphal–Kohima Road: Manipur's lifeline

Historical overview

The Imphal–Kohima–Dimapur Road was in 1944 – and remains today – Manipur's lifeline and main connection to the outside world. It was through this road that the steady stream of supplies required to maintain the Imphal-based 4 Corps came. The road connects Imphal to Dimapur in present-day Nagaland – the Naga Hills of Assam during the Second World War – which is the closest railhead to Manipur, and beyond. To get there the road climbs up to Kohima at around 5,000 feet above sea level and then descends towards Dimapur. It is a route rich in Second World War history, especially as the canvas against which the great battles at Imphal and Kohima played out in 1944.

This book covers the stretch from along Imphal Main (or Koirengei Airfield) outside Imphal to the bridge over the river just north of Kangpokpi. This is the area of most relevance to the Battle of Imphal. Indeed, it was the cutting off of the Imphal–Kohima Road at the end of March 1944 near Kangpokpi that effectively started what became known as the Siege of Imphal – the encirclement of British-Indian forces by the Japanese in and around the Imphal Valley.

The road was also a battlefield in its own right. On the Japanese side was the 15th Division that had swept through against the grain of the country from the east to reach the Imphal–Kohima Road. This included the Honda Raiding Unit, as well as the assault column commanded by Colonel Matsumura (60th Regiment). They had as their principal objectives cutting the vital Imphal–Kohima Road and invading Imphal from the north. The Japanese reached as far south as Sekmai, before the British-Indian forces began to push back. The bulk of the fighting along the Imphal–Kohima Road involved 60th Regiment.

On the British side, 63rd Brigade of the 17th Indian Division was present on the Imphal–Kohima Road through April 1944. It had been sent there to check the Japanese advance down the road. It was replaced in the first week of May by 89th Brigade of the 7th Indian Division. It was the 5th Indian Division, however, which led the effort to open the road northwards. As we already know, this included its 123rd Brigade, which moved to the Imphal–Kohima Road in the first half of May. It was joined on the road by its fellow 9th Brigade in early June, which switched places with the 7th Indian Division's 89th Brigade.

The fight to open up the Imphal–Kohima Road from Sekmai was a slow, difficult one. The history of the 5th Indian Division outlines the task at hand for the forces pushing north from Sekmai in mid-May 1944:

> The ground was difficult, the jungle thick, and the site of our dumps in Kanglatongbi wired and mined. Astride the road the three battalions took their turn in hammering at the Japanese. The guns of the 28th Field Regiment supported our attacks and Hurricanes of the Royal Air Force bombed and strafed enemy-held positions when called upon to do so. Road-blocks had to be cleared, enemy troops driven from bends in the road, from hillocks that overlooked this road, from stream beds and patches of jungle on the right of the road.[123]

In fact, it was this push northwards from Imphal to the area of Milestone 109 that involved the fiercest fighting on the Imphal–Kohima Road in 1944. The Japanese blocked the road and had taken up positions in the hills overlooking it, each of which had to be prised from them. In comparison, once the Battle of Kohima had ended in early June, the British 2nd Division sweeping southwards from Kohima met with limited – and exhausted – Japanese resistance as they raced down the Imphal–Kohima Road. The fighting up the road continued until the end of June 1944 – on 22 June, the Imphal–Kohima Road was finally opened at Milestone 109 and the Siege of Imphal lifted.

The battlefields today

This book covers about 28 miles (45 km) of the Imphal–Kohima Road heading north from Imphal. This is a tarmac road that is in good condition today, except some parts near Saparmeina (sometimes referred to as

Safarmeina in war memoirs). Once it leaves the Imphal Valley, the road narrows and passes through low-lying hills on both sides, especially to its east, with the Imphal turel flowing alongside most of the way. As it nears the area of the then Milestone 109, the western hills recede into the distance and the road passes through a beautiful open patch dotted with meadows until Keithelmanbi. Beyond Kangpokpi, further north, the road starts climbing rapidly, twisting and turning until it reaches Kohima. Again, the alignment of this stretch of the Imphal–Kohima Road remains unchanged from the Second World War; thus, the route one takes today is the same that was traversed by the British-Indian and Japanese forces in 1944.

The following is a brief sequence of events in this sector in 1944, involving the main battlefields covered in this book:

29/30 March	Honda Unit cuts the Imphal–Kohima Road
4–7 April	Battle of Kanglatongbi
21 May	British retake Kanglatongbi
1–9 June	Fighting for Isaac and Harry on hills along the Imphal–Kohima Road
3 June	5th Indian Division intensifies offensive up the Imphal–Kohima Road
13–21 June	British-Indian units attack Liver along the Imphal–Kohima Road
22 June	British 2nd and 5th Indian Divisions meet at MS 109 on the Imphal–Kohima Road

KOIRENGEI AIRFIELD (IMPHAL MAIN)

Heading out of Imphal, the first place one crosses is the airfield that was known as Imphal Main during the Second World War. It is known locally as Koirengei Airfield, named after the village to its north. Lying parallel and to the east of the Imphal–Kohima Road, this was the most important of the six airfields in the Imphal Valley during the Battle of Imphal. Its importance stemmed from the fact that it was all-weather and, of course, its location. It lay alongside the crucial Imphal–Kohima Road and around it was spread out 4 Corps headquarters – the 'Keep'.

Interestingly, before it became the main airfield in Manipur, the same area around Koirengei housed the largest camp for the refugees fleeing Burma in 1942. It was around here that tens of thousands of desperate men, women and children arrived after their escape from Burma in the first half of 1942. Most of them continued on up the Imphal–Kohima Road to reach deeper into India.

One can today approach the old airfield from either its northern or southern ends. The northern end, in front of the gates of the Manipur Public School, is easily accessible and allows one to get a good view of the rest of the airfield (Figure 4.29). The southern end provides more dramatic views of the hills that form the western rim of the Imphal Valley, beyond which lies Silchar in Assam.

The airfield was abandoned in the years after the Second World War and today its entire length is separated from the Imphal–Kohima Road by a row of tall eucalyptus trees. It is under the control of the present-day Indian Army, a result of which has been (in this case) that, save for some temporary structures of an Indian Territorial Army base in the middle, much of the rest of the runway has not been built upon.

Standing on the old airfield today, it is worth reflecting on the following passage from the Official History of the Indian Armed Forces in the Second World War.

> During the course of the siege [of Imphal], the Allied air forces delivered over 22,000 British tons of supplies to the IV Corps, and poured in over 20,000 combatant troops as reinforcements.

Figure 4.29 Imphal Main or Koirengei Airfield

Source: Photo by Hemant Singh Katoch

Over 10,000 casualties and 35,000 'useless mouths' were evacuated from the plain. This achievement was probably the most important single factor in defeating the Japanese offensive. If it had failed, even partially, Imphal might have fallen to the Japanese and the course of the war would have been different.[124]

Imphal Main or Koirengei Airfield was at the heart of this Air Battle of Imphal.

Much of the attention on the Air Battle of Imphal inevitably – and rightly – focuses on the airlift during the siege and close air support for the infantry. The point of complete Allied air superiority over the Japanese is always made. But this sometimes obscures the fact that the Japanese were also able to mount air attacks on Allied targets and that there was the occasional dogfight in the air – that a true battle in the air did take place in the skies over Manipur in 1944, however one-sided it may have been.

The Japanese mounted several air attacks during the Battle of Imphal. These included one on 17 March 1944, when two Japanese aircraft bombed 4 Corps headquarters around Imphal Main, killing 20 men on the ground.[125] On 17 April, six Sally bombers and 50 Oscars attacked Palel Airfield.[126] On 21 April, 28 Oscars attacked Kangla Airfield, but inflicted little damage.[127] On 22 April, 20 Oscars attacked Tulihal Airfield and destroyed or damaged at least three aircraft on the ground. On 25 April, five Dakotas flying from Silchar to Imphal were destroyed in a Japanese attack. This prompted the establishment of an air corridor between Silchar and the Imphal airfields, where the Dakotas were escorted by Royal Air Force fighters like Spitfires.[128]

According to one estimate, the Royal Air Force lost some 70 aircraft during the Battle of Imphal, including 16 that fell to Japanese fighters, 17 to ground fire and 37 to other reasons such as operational difficulties and, especially, bad weather; some 33 aircraft were damaged.[129] The tally for Japanese losses by the Royal Air Force's 221 Group was 33 aircraft destroyed, 22 probably destroyed and 61 damaged.[130]

The year 1944 saw a range of aircraft flying in the skies of Manipur. On the Allied side were the Hurricanes, Vultee Vengeance dive bombers, Spitfires and Beaufighters, among others, while the Japanese flew their Nakajima Ki 43 (Oscar), Mitsubishi Ki 21 (Sally) and Mitsubishi Ki 46 (Dinah), among others. But it was the ever-reliable transport aircraft the Dakota that perhaps best epitomises the Air Battle of Imphal. It was decisive in winning it for the Allies and was their warhorse. And this airfield was its centre of gravity in Manipur in 1944.

Of course, the Dakota could not have done its job alone. The plane depended entirely on the fighter squadrons for its own safe flight. As the book *Wings of the Phoenix*, the official (British) story of the air war in Burma, put it so well:

> ... the role of the fighter squadrons was an essential one. Possibly it was the most essential of all. No air force had ever had the chance of finer pickings that were now offered to the Japanese, with up to 300 slow, unarmed transports daily flying in view of them; and it was only Allied fighter supremacy, now maintained by the squadrons at Imphal, which prevented calamity. The Army could not fight without the air transports – the decision to stand at Imphal would never have been taken without them – and the air transports could not fly without the protecting Spitfires and Hurricanes.[131]

And so, Imphal Main was a buzzing hive of activity in 1944. It was also the headquarters of the Royal Air Force's 221 Group, which commanded the Air Battle of Imphal. At all times of the day planes of all kinds were landing or taking off: bringing in reinforcements, ammunition and rations; evacuating the injured; flying towards the battlefields of Imphal and Kohima to support infantry operations; dropping off supplies to men cut off or isolated by Japanese forces; and bombing Japanese supply and communication routes to Burma.

Lyman informs: 'At its height in the second half of April, the airlift [to Imphal] employed 404 aircraft from fifteen squadrons.'[132] He further estimates that 17,183 sorties were flown from April to June 1944 just by fighter and dive-bomber aircraft; the total flown, including transport sorties, in support of Imphal and Kohima, was over 30,000 sorties.[133]

The provision of close air support during the Battle of Imphal involved some innovation between air and ground troops. One tactic developed over time which became quite successful was the 'dummy run' by diver-bombers in support of infantry attacks.[134] This entailed a first run by dive-bombers whereby they actually bombed Japanese defensive positions. They would then perform a 'dummy run', approaching and flying over their target again as if they were about to bomb it a second time round. The Japanese would stay in their trenches and bunkers, expecting a repeat performance. Only this time, the approach of the aircraft was intended to give cover to the advancing infantry, something the distracted Japanese would not notice until the infantry were almost upon them.

Besides the bombing runs, dummy or otherwise, it was the evacuation of casualties, which was of great service to the fighting soldier on the ground. As *Wings of the Phoenix* notes, 'The first was as essential for physical success as the second was for morale.'[135] Indeed, within a short period of time, an injured Fourteenth Army soldier could be evacuated – provided there was space for a light aircraft to land – from a battlefield to a hospital at Imphal. Or, from a hospital in Imphal to even better facilities in Assam. Contrast that with what awaited a similarly injured Japanese soldier. After getting basic care at an advanced dressing station or field hospital, he would be extremely lucky to survive the journey back from Manipur to the Chindwin River. The question of being airlifted did not arise.

Imphal Main was also one of the main airfields to which the 5th Indian Division was flown in from the Arakan in March 1944, the first time a division was transported by air from one battlefield to another. These men were airlifted from the fighting in the Arakan and, immediately after landing at Imphal Main and the other airfields, were rushed to shore up the main approaches to Imphal from the north/north-east – the Imphal–Kohima Road, the Iril River Valley and the Ukhrul Road. The operation was timely as it prevented the Japanese from breaking through to Imphal past these weakly defended routes, which was a distinct possibility during the initial days of the Battle of Imphal.

A Royal Air Force officer has been quoted as describing this fly in of the 5th Indian Division as being:

> just like a train service. These Daks were stacked up one behind the other, quarter of a mile apart, touching down and those with troops were simply taxi-ing along and the soldiers rolling out and then the Dak was straight off again. . . . They were literally coming in, rolling along and then taking off again back to Chittagong.[136]

Imphal Main is also associated with several key personalities and events during the Second World War. It was from here that the last flight carrying the man who pioneered the Chindit operations took off on 24 March 1944. British Major General Orde Wingate departed for Assam from Imphal Main that evening aboard a US B-25 Mitchell bomber. It crashed en route near Thilon village in the western hills of Manipur in what is today Tamenglong district. His remains and those of his American co-passengers were disinterred from the Imphal War Cemetery in 1950 and reburied at the Arlington National Cemetery in the United States.

Imphal Main is also where a young Indian man commanded an Indian Air Force squadron during the Battle of Imphal. This man would go on to become the highest-ranked officer of the Indian Air Force in independent India – Air Chief Marshal Arjan Singh. It was again at Imphal Main where General Slim and his three Corps commanders, Lieutenant General Scoones (4 Corps, Imphal), Lieutenant General Stopford (33 Corps,

Kohima) and Lieutenant General Christison (15 Corps, the Arakan), were knighted in December 1944 for their victories over the Japanese that year.

SEKMAI

Moving past Imphal Main, the road skirts some low hills to the west before turning north towards Sekmai. It is from one of the bends in the road looking east that can one see in the distance the Mapao-Molvom Range. The main area of interest in this sector, however, is the low-lying hills that overlook the Imphal–Kohima Road beyond the town of Sekmai, the next major town up the road.

At the beginning of April 1944 the Japanese 15th Division advanced to just north of Sekmai. Their progress was checked by 9th Brigade of the 5th Indian Division. Soon thereafter, 63rd Brigade of the 17th Indian Division was also deployed here for the same purpose. The Japanese attacked this brigade's positions near Sekmai around mid-April but they were repulsed.[137] It was the farthest south they reached on the Imphal–Kohima Road during the Battle of Imphal.

KANGLATONGBI

Continuing on up from Sekmai is Kanglatongbi. In 1944 this then village was home to a large defensive area, which was known as Lion Box. To its immediate north lay one of the largest supply depots in the Imphal Valley. Making their way towards Imphal with only the bare minimum of supplies, this depot near Kanglatongbi made for a natural target for the Japanese 15th Division. As the threat against it increased, its personnel, along with some of its most valuable supplies, were moved into Lion Box at the beginning of April. This defensive area, through which the Imphal–Kohima Road ran, hosted a few thousand support staff and only a handful of fighting troops.[138]

The Japanese attacked the area on the night of 4 April. These attacks continued and increased in intensity over the next three days. The defenders of Lion Box were supported during the day by the 2nd West Yorkshires, together with a squadron of Lee tanks of the 3rd Dragoon Guards, who would come up from Sekmai. On the morning of 7 April, as its defence became untenable in the face of Japanese shelling and infantry charges by 60th Regiment of the Japanese 15th Division, the evacuation of Lion Box into Imphal was ordered. This evacuation of men and supplies was covered by the West Yorkshires and completed later that day.

Figure 4.30 Kanglatongbi War Memorial

Source: Photo by Yaiphaba Kangjam

Today, a war memorial stands just off the Imphal–Kohima Road at Kanglatongbi. The Kanglatongbi War Memorial was inaugurated after the Second World War by the Indian Army Ordnance Corps (Figure 4.30). It commemorates those who lost their lives in the fighting here in April 1944; in particular, it honours the men of the 221 Advanced Ordnance Depot who played a key role in defending the area against the Japanese. Major J.P.M. Boyd, the deputy chief ordnance officer, was awarded the Military Cross and Havildar (Clerk) Basant Singh the Indian Distinguished Service Medal for their actions at the time.[139] The Army Ordnance Corps of the present-day Indian Army currently maintains the Kanglatongbi War Memorial.

After the evacuation of Allied Forces from Kanglatongbi, the Japanese laid roadblocks around the then village. Towards the end of April and the first week of May, these roadblocks and the Japanese positions at Kanglatongbi were targeted by the British-Indian forces at Sekmai. By mid-May, these consisted of 89th Brigade of the 7th Indian Division and 123rd Brigade of 5th Indian Division. It was now that the drive northwards on and along the Imphal–Kohima Road began in full earnest. On 21 May, after a week of operations, Kanglatongbi fell to the British (Figures 4.31 and 4.32).

Figure 4.31 The Imphal–Kohima Road between Kanglatongbi and Saparmeina

Source: Photo by Ranjit Moirangthem

Figure 4.32 The present-day site of the old Milestone 109 on the Imphal–Kohima Road where the British 2nd Division and 5th Indian Division met on 22 June 1944

Source: Photo by Hemant Singh Katoch

At the beginning of June, 9th Brigade replaced 89th Brigade on the Imphal–Kohima Road. From then on, the push up the road became an entirely 5th Indian Division affair. Today, it takes just over 20 minutes to drive the stretch of the Imphal–Kohima Road from Kanglatongbi and Motbung further ahead to the area of Milestone 109 south of Keithel-manbi (Figure 4.31). It is sobering to know that it took the 5th Indian Division almost an entire month of heavy fighting to prise open this same stretch from Japanese control in 1944.

The fighting was centred on Japanese roadblocks and their positions on the low foothills to the east of the Imphal–Kohima Road. The Imphal turel meanders between the road and the hills through this stretch. As was typical of the fighting all over Manipur around this time, each side was not just battling a formidable and determined foe, but also the elements – in particular, the pouring rain once the monsoon broke. The rain made paths and hillsides ever more slippery, kept men wet and damp for days at end and turned the Imphal turel into a raging torrent difficult to cross. Low-lying mist brought further gloom to the troops.[140]

The battalions of 9th Brigade fought to clear the road, while those of 123rd Brigade targeted the ridge of hills to the east. The latter initially focused on two features named Isaac and James near the old location of Modbung (Motbung) village. This was a couple of miles east of the Imphal–Kohima Road in the hills; the present-day location of the village is on the road itself. One can get a good view of these hills from the grounds of Presidency College, which is a short way up a slope to the west of the Imphal–Kohima Road in present-day Motbung.

The fighting at Isaac and James occurred in the first nine days of June and was led by the 2nd Suffolks, supported by tanks of the 3rd Carabiniers which climbed up the ridge to assist the infantry. The operation was over and the positions secured by British-Indian forces by 9 June. The 3/9th Jats now followed a line of advance on the ridgeline.

A report on the capture of Isaac in the war diary of 2nd Suffolks makes some interesting observations on Japanese tactics of camouflage in this sector. These could equally apply to the other sectors of the Battle of Imphal. The report notes:

> It is well known that the Jap is a past master in the art of cam-
> ouflage – and unless one is at a very close range or armed with
> powerful telescopes it will often be impossible to locate all posns
> which might be seen. However it can be safely assumed that if
> some posns are located there will be many others in close so.

It also noted:

> Great attention is always paid to this [camouflage], for he knows
> that if he is observed it will bring an immediate reply from us.
> Very little movement is observed by day, all defence work has to
> be done by night, and camouflage freshened with green newly
> cut branches.[141]

Further up the road, behind Japanese lines, the fighting centred on three
peaks named Pip, Squeak and Wilfred. 3/14th Punjab of 9th Brigade had
arrived here from the west and crossing the road had captured the hill
in the centre, Squeak. It was counter-attacked by the Japanese, who were
on Wilfred, the hill to the north, but these were repulsed. A roadblock
separated the two groups of the 5th Indian Division. This was cleared
on 11 June, allowing them to link up. The 3/9th Jats caught up with the
3/14th Punjab on Squeak and took Wilfred on 13 June. By this time the
road was clear until Saparmeina.

The fighting over the next week revolved around further clearing of
the Imphal–Kohima Road and on capturing the Japanese positions on
hills east of the road near Saparmeina. The struggle for the main hill on
this ridge, Liver, was particularly desperate, a fact well illustrated by the
war diary of the 3/9th Jats who led the assaults on it. There are several
entries in it detailing the multiple attacks on this feature. Consider the
one for 15 June 1944:

> **15 June**: Attack timed for 1100 hrs. Hurribombers strafe at 0900
> hrs. Heavy arty concentration from 2 btys 25 Pdrs – 2 btys 2.7
> How and 1 tp 3″ mortar on Liver and nearby feature preceded
> A Coy's attack. Two routes of advance on spurs leading to enemy
> positions supported by 1 pl C Coy creating diversionary attack
> from S.E. Original attack partially successful. A Coy held up 100
> yds from top of objective. C Coy pl after reaching within 10
> yards of objective heavy M.G. fire forced them to halt and with-
> draw slightly. . . .
> . . . Total casualties for the day A Coy 7 killed, 7 wounded. C
> Coy 6 killed and 8 wounded. Heavy rain all night which made
> conditions uncomfortable for all but particularly for C Coy in
> their forward positions with no cover whatever.[142]

Yet another attack was launched on 21 June, this time involving three
companies of the 3/9th Jats. Hurribombers again strafed the position

before the infantry went in. Major Risal Singh was killed in this operation, among dozens of casualties for the Jats. The Japanese finally left Liver on 22 June.

The 2nd West Yorkshires were facing similar resistance by the Japanese at a low ridge west of the Imphal–Kohima Road. The 3/14th Punjab was then sent on a left hook off to cut the road behind the Japanese and force them to retreat. By 20 June, this ridge had been captured. In the meantime, the 3/2nd Punjab and the 1/17th Dogras had been sent on a wide left hook through the jungle to cut the Imphal–Kohima Road at Milestone 109 near Keithelmanbi, south of Kangpokpi. It was here on the morning of 22 June 1944, at Milestone 109 from Dimapur, that men of the 1/17th Dogras of the 5th Indian Division met with soldiers of the British 2nd Division coming down from Kohima. The Imphal–Kohima Road was finally open.

The area of the old Milestone 109 is breathtakingly beautiful (Figure 4.32). The scenery to the west opens up, giving way to extensive meadows, with a range of hills in the far distance. Taking it all in on this spot today, one recalls the import of what happened here on the morning of 22 June, some 70 years ago. As Slim had commented on the opening of the Imphal–Kohima Road: 'The Imphal–Kohima battle, the first decisive battle of the Burma campaign, was not yet over, but it was won.'[143]

KANGPOKPI BRIDGE

The last stop on the Imphal–Kohima Road covered by this book is, ironically, the one where it all began. On the night of 29/30 March 1944, a reconnaissance force of the Japanese 15th Division, consisting of two companies of 3/67th Regiment, blew up a bridge near Kangpokpi. This action by the Honda Raiding Unit, so called as it was commanded by a Captain Honda, cut the Imphal–Kohima Road and precipitated the Siege of Imphal. The siege was complete once the Silchar–Bishenpur Track was similarly cut on 14/15 April.

Today there is a modern bridge on this spot, where the Imphal–Kohima Road crosses the turel and starts climbing up towards Kohima. However, the remains of the old bridge can still be seen to the east of the present-day structure (Figure 4.33). Captain Honda is said to have been impressed with the military traffic on the road when he arrived there – some 120–130 trucks and jeeps passing through every hour – and what it implied about Allied power and supplies.[144] He then proceeded to blow up the bridge).[145]

151

Figure 4.33 Remains of old bridge on the Imphal–Kohima Road near Kangpokpi

Source: Photo by Hemant Singh Katoch

Notes

1 William J. Slim, *Defeat into Victory*, London: Cassels, 1956, pp. 371–72.
2 Ibid., p. 372-73.
3 Ian Lyall Grant, *Burma: The Turning Point*, Chichester: Zampi Press, 1992, p. 159.
4 Slim, *Defeat into Victory*, p. 386.
5 Ibid., p. 387.
6 Grant, *Burma: The Turning Point*, p. 119.
7 Geoffrey Evans and Antony Brett-James, *Imphal: A Flower on Lofty Heights*, London: Macmillan, 1962, pp. 195–96.
8 Grant, *Burma: The Turning Point*, p. 176.
9 Evans and Brett-James, *Imphal: A Flower on Lofty Heights*, p. 276.
10 Louis Allen, *Burma – The Longest War*, 1941–45, London: Phoenix Giant, 1984, p. 279.
11 Evans and Brett-James, *Imphal: A Flower on Lofty Heights*, p. 251.
12 Allen, *Burma: The Longest War*, p. 240.
13 Grant, *Burma: The Turning Point*, pp. 119–201.
14 Ibid., p. 125.
15 Allen, *Burma: The Longest War*, p. 279.
16 Intelligence Summary No. 6, May 1944, War Diary of 'G' Branch, H.Q. 20 Indian Division, File No. 601/250/WD/Part II-A, History Division, Ministry of Defence, New Delhi.

17 Grant, *Burma: The Turning Point*, p. 126.
18 Ibid.
19 Ibid., p. 163.
20 Evans and Brett-James, *Imphal: A Flower on Lofty Heights*, p. 248.
21 Ibid., p. 247.
22 Grant, *Burma: The Turning Point*, p. 124.
23 Evans and Brett-James, *Imphal: A Flower on Lofty Heights*, p. 249.
24 War Diary, 2/5 Royal Gurkha Rifles, June 1944, File No. 601/5771/WD, History Division, Ministry of Defence, New Delhi.
25 Grant, *Burma: The Turning Point*, p. 207.
26 Ibid., p. 209.
27 Ibid.
28 War Diary, 2/5 Royal Gurkha Rifles, June 1944, File No. 601/5771/WD, History Division, Ministry of Defence, New Delhi.
29 Grant, *Burma: The Turning Point*, p. 209.
30 War Diary, 1/7 Gurkha Rifles, May 1944, File No. 601/330/WD/Vol. III, History Division, Ministry of Defence, New Delhi.
31 War Diary, H.Q. 48 Indian Light Brigade, May 1944, File No. 601/330/WD/Vol. III, History Division, Ministry of Defence, New Delhi.
32 Peter Ward Fay, *The Forgotten Army*, Ann Arbor: University of Michigan Press, 1993, p. 295.
33 *I.N.A. Martyrs' Memorial*, Department of Art and Culture, Government of Manipur, 2009.
34 Grant, *Burma: The Turning Point*, pp. 244–45.
35 Slim, *Defeat into Victory*, p. 377.
36 Terence R. Molloy, *The Silchar Track*, Ely: Melrose Books, 2006, p. 17.
37 Grant, *Burma: The Turning Point*, p. 128.
38 Ibid., p. 185.
39 Ibid.
40 Ibid.
41 Ibid., p. 128.
42 Ibid.
43 War Diary, 32 Indian Infantry Brigade, April 1944, File No. 601/323/WD/Part II, History Division, Ministry of Defence, New Delhi.
44 Molloy, *The Silchar Track*, p. 23.
45 Ibid., p. 25.
46 Ibid., p. 69.
47 Ibid., pp. 67–68.
48 Ibid., p. 112.
49 War Diary, 2/5 Royal Gurkha Rifles, June 1944, File No. 601/5771/WD, History Division, Ministry of Defence, New Delhi.
50 Allen, *Burma The Longest War*, p. 221.
51 A caveat: There has been some talk of a possible deviation in the future Trans Asian Highway that may take an even shorter route from the Imphal Valley to Moreh (thereby bypassing the Shenam Saddle), but this remains speculative.
52 Norman Franks, *The Air Battle of Imphal*, London: William Kimber, 1985, p. 49.
53 Ibid., p. 47.
54 Slim, *Defeat into Victory*, p. 384.
55 Allen, *Burma – The Longest War*, p. 227.
56 Ibid.

57 Hugh Toye, *Subhash Chandra Bose: The Springing Tiger*, Mumbai: Jaico Publishing House, 1991, p. 348.
58 Ibid., p. 349.
59 Ibid., pp. 349–50.
60 Evans and Brett-James, *Imphal: A Flower on Lofty Heights*, p. 25.
61 Slim, *Defeat into Victory*, p. 125.
62 John Hudson, *Sunset in the East*, Barnsley: Pen and Sword, 2002, p. 73.
63 Ibid., p. 71.
64 Evans and Brett-James, *Imphal: A Flower on Lofty Heights*, p. 234.
65 Ibid., p. 235.
66 Ibid., p. 236.
67 Ibid., p. 242.
68 Ibid., p. 291.
69 Ibid.
70 War Diary, 3/10 Gurkha Rifles, May 1944, File No. 601/5785/WD/Part II, History Division, Ministry of Defence, New Delhi.
71 Evans and Brett-James, *Imphal: A Flower on Lofty Heights*, p. 303.
72 Ibid., p. 302.
73 War Diary, 3/3 Gurkha Rifles, June 1944, File No. 601/5779/WD/Part I, History Division, Ministry of Defence, New Delhi.
74 Evans and Brett-James, *Imphal: A Flower on Lofty Heights*, pp. 303–304.
75 War Diary, 3/10 Gurkha Rifles, May 1944, File No. 601/5785/WD/Part II, History Division, Ministry of Defence, New Delhi.
76 Evans and Brett-James, *Imphal: A Flower on Lofty Heights*, p. 290.
77 Hudson, *Sunset in the East*, p. 78.
78 Ibid., p. 72.
79 Intelligence Summary No. 6, May 1944, War Diary of 'G' Branch, H.Q. 20 Indian Division, File No. 601/250/WD/Part II-A, History Division, Ministry of Defence, New Delhi.
80 War Diary, 3/10 Gurkha Rifles, May 1944, File No. 601/5785/WD/Part II, History Division, Ministry of Defence, New Delhi.
81 Ibid.
82 Evans and Brett-James, *Imphal: A Flower on Lofty Heights*, p. 297.
83 Toye, *Subhash Chandra Bose: The Springing Tiger*, p. 184.
84 Abid Hasan Safrani, *The Men from Imphal*, Calcutta: Netaji Research Bureau, 1971, pp. 9–10.
85 Jagat S. Bright, Ed., *Important Speeches and Writings of Subhash Bose*, Lahore: The Indian Printing Works, p. 309.
86 Hudson, *Sunset in the East*, pp. 70–71.
87 Ibid., pp. 72–73.
88 Toye, *Subhash Chandra Bose: The Springing Tiger*, p. 182.
89 Intelligence Summary No. 6, May 1944, War Diary of 'G' Branch, H.Q. 20 Indian Division, File No. 601/250/WD/Part II-A, History Division, Ministry of Defence, New Delhi.
90 Franks, *The Air Battle of Imphal*, p. 125.
91 Evans and Brett-James, *Imphal: A Flower on Lofty Heights*, p. 211.
92 Lyman, *Japan's Last Bid for Victory*, p. 124.
93 Evans and Brett-James, *Imphal: A Flower on Lofty Heights*, p. 214.
94 Harry Seaman, *The Battle at Sangshak*, London: Leo Cooper, 1989, p. 67.
95 Ibid., p. 68.

96 Ibid., p. 131.
97 Ibid., p. 65.
98 Ibid., pp. 98–99.
99 Ibid., pp. 77–78.
100 Ibid., p. 77.
101 Ibid., p. 92.
102 Ibid., p. 96.
103 Ibid., p. 131.
104 Ibid., p. 86.
105 Ibid., p. 87.
106 Ibid., pp. 69–70.
107 Slim, *Defeat into Victory*, p. 400.
108 Bisheshwar Prasad, Ed., *Official History of the Indian Armed Forces in the Second World War 1939–45 – The Reconquest of Burma, Volume II*, New Delhi: Pentagon Press, 2014, p. 18.
109 John Nunnely and Kazuo Tamayama, *Tales by Japanese Soldiers*, London: Cassell & Co, 2000, pp. 156–57.
110 The task was given to 9th Brigade. 123rd Brigade was active further up the Iril River Valley, before being sent to the Imphal-Kohima Road in the first half of May. By early June, 9th Brigade was also sent to the Imphal-Kohima Road. It switched places with 89th Brigade of the 7th Indian Division, which then became responsible for the Mapao-Molvom Range area. Also in June, 80th Brigade of the 20th Indian Division that was covering the Ukhrul Road sector became active farther north in the Iril River Valley (to the east of the river).
111 Evans and Brett-James, *Imphal: A Flower on Lofty Heights*, p. 283.
112 War Diary, HQ 9 Indian Infantry Brigade, May 1944, File No. 601/305/WD/Pt. IV, History Division, Ministry of Defence, New Delhi.
113 Antony Brett-James, *Ball of Fire: The Fifth Indian Division in the Second World War*, Aldershot: Gale & Polden, 1951, p. 325–26.
114 Evans and Brett-James, *Imphal: A Flower on Lofty Heights*, p. 225.
115 Allen, *Burma: The Longest War*, p. 253.
116 Ibid., p. 260.
117 Arthur F. Freer, *Nunshigum*, Durham: The Pentland Press, 1995, pp. 79–80.
118 Evans and Brett-James, *Imphal: A Flower on Lofty Heights*, pp. 223–24.
119 Allen, *Burma: The Longest War*, p. 259.
120 Evans and Brett-James, *Imphal: A Flower on Lofty Heights*, p. 225.
121 Freer, *Nunshigum*, p. xvii.
122 Allen, *Burma: The Longest War*, p. 258.
123 Brett-James, *Ball of Fire: The Fifth Indian Division in the Second World War*, p. 345.
124 Bisheshwar Prasad, Ed., *Official History of the Indian Armed Forces in the Second World War 1939–45 – The Reconquest of Burma, Volume I*, New Delhi: Pentagon Press, 2014, p. 265.
125 Franks, *The Air Battle of Imphal*, p. 42.
126 David Rooney, *Burma Victory*, London: Arms and Armour Press, 1995, p. 66.
127 Franks, *The Air Battle of Imphal*, p. 82.
128 Rooney, *Burma Victory*, p. 63.
129 Franks, *The Air Battle of Imphal*, p. 202.
130 Ibid., p. 200.
131 Air Ministry and the Central Office of Information, *Wings of the Phoenix: The Official Story of the Air War in Burma*, London: His Majesty's Stationery Office, 1949, p. 77.

132 Lyman, *Japan's Last Bid for Victory*, p. 223.
133 Ibid.
134 Air Ministry and the Central Office of Information, *Wings of the Phoenix: The Official Story of the Air War in Burma*, p. 52.
135 Ibid., p. 64.
136 Franks, *The Air Battle of Imphal*, p. 37.
137 Prasad, *Official History of the Indian Armed Forces in the Second World War 1939–45 – The Reconquest of Burma, Volume I*, p. 255.
138 Lyman, *Japan's Last Bid for Victory*, p. 125.
139 *70th Anniversary: The Battle of Kanglatongbi*, Directorate General of Ordnance Services – Indian Army, New Delhi, 2014.
140 Brett-James, *Ball of Fire: The Fifth Indian Division in the Second World War*, pp. 349–50.
141 War Diary, 2nd Battalion, The Suffolk Regiment, June 1944, File No. 601/5244/WD, History Division, Ministry of Defence, New Delhi.
142 War Diary, 3rd Battalion, 9th Jat Regiment, June 1944, File No. 601/5390/WD/Part II, History Division, Ministry of Defence, New Delhi.
143 Slim, *Defeat into Victory*, p. 397.
144 Allen, *Burma: The Longest War*, p. 248.
145 Some accounts note that two bridges were blown up.

5

BATTLEFIELD TOURISM

Ideas for the future

Manipur's Second World War experience, centred on the Battle of Imphal of 1944, makes for a fascinating story, and one which connects the place with many countries around the world. The narrative is made all the more compelling by what is on offer: the battlefields, trenches, bunkers, war memorials and museums; the culture and traditions of its people; together with the scenic beauty of the place; and its agreeable climate. Indeed, Manipur has all the makings of an excellent Second World War battlefield tourism destination, not just for India but also in the wider Asian and international context.

It has a long way to go before it can begin to fulfil its potential, however. The political and security situation remains a concern. Like much of India's North East, Manipur is short on tourist-friendly infrastructure. A visitor also has to contend with a particular bane of Manipur in recent years – the calling of strikes and agitations, often at short notice, by a bewildering array of aggrieved parties, which block off one or all of the highways.

But things have begun to change, slowly but surely. The security situation in Manipur has generally stabilised in the past few years, barring the odd incident. The government of India no longer requires foreign visitors to obtain extra permits to visit Manipur; an Indian tourist visa suffices. Decent hotels have begun to spring up in Imphal. The city is now the second best-connected by air in the North East, after Guwahati in Assam, with daily, multiple flights to Calcutta and New Delhi. Roads have improved. And there is growing buzz about the prospects of more interaction and trade links with that large eastern neighbour that has finally begun to stir after decades of slumber – Burma (Myanmar).

The positive news extends to the realm of Second World War battlefield tourism as well. A good beginning has been made with the commemoration of the 70th anniversary of the Battle of Imphal from March to June 2014. A more modest event was held to mark the 71st anniversary in 2015. Awareness across Manipur, in the national media and abroad, has increased, thanks first to Imphal–Kohima's naming as 'Britain's Greatest Battle' in 2013 and then by the 70th anniversary commemoration. A couple of privately led war museums have opened, and plans are afoot to expand them.

The first-ever battlefield tours on Imphal were launched by this author in 2013 and subsequently extended to Kohima. For the first time, the tours moved beyond the two cemeteries in Imphal to weave a larger narrative encompassing the battlefields of 1944 around Manipur. The Manipur government is also now much more interested in developing battlefield tourism in the state, a move that is supported by the central authorities in New Delhi. The time is therefore right to consider ideas for taking this encouraging progress on battlefield tourism in Manipur forward. The ultimate aim should be to establish Manipur as a premier Second World War battlefield tourism destination, centred on the Battle of Imphal.

Commemorations

First, an effort should be made to hold commemorations of the Battle of Imphal annually. They need not be as grand as that of 2014, but even smaller-scale events – like the one held in 2015 – to mark key dates and events of 1944 will ensure that the interest generated by the 70th anniversary will not be lost. Besides commemorating those who fought or were affected at the time, such events help focus people's attention on the Battle of Imphal. Many are also keen to attend commemorative functions, however modest, and anniversaries provide useful opportunities for them to travel to distant Imphal.

The next major anniversary will be the 75th in 2019, and a much grander event should be organised to mark this. Learning from the 70th, an effort should be made to partner with New Delhi and countries like the United Kingdom and Japan for 2019 well in advance. A central focus should be to reach out to the people of those countries around the world whose soldiers fought in Imphal in 1944 or were present in Manipur during the Second World War. A similar effort must be made across India in the regions where the men who fought in Imphal came from. Moreover, for an event of this nature to be truly meaningful, it must resonate with the locals and ways must be found to engage with and involve the people of Manipur – especially children – in all future commemorations.

War museum(s)

A second area of focus should be on the establishment of a truly world-class war museum in Imphal. It is incredible that given its significance, any visitor to the city is hard-pressed to find that one venue that presents an overall view of the events of 1944 and of what Manipur experienced during the Second World War. Thankfully, the situation was partially remedied in 2014 by the opening of a private museum by local war enthusiasts. This is not nearly enough. Imphal needs to have a proper museum on Manipur and the Second World War, one that is ideally supported by the state and central governments. The aim of such a museum would be to present the perspective of all sides: the Allies, the Japanese, the Indian soldiers serving in the Indian Army and the INA and the people of Manipur. Tie-ups could be explored with the Imperial War Museum and the National Army Museum in the United Kingdom, as well as with similar institutions in Japan. In terms of venues, possibilities to be considered could include Slim Cottage, a beautiful heritage building that has a central location, symbolic value and instant international recognition. Other worthy contenders could be similar colonial-era bungalows in and around the Kangla Fort Complex in Imphal.

It need not end with just one large war museum in Imphal. Manipur can have a network of smaller, private museums in different locations that display the owners' collections of war-related artefacts. Indeed, this has already happened to some extent – besides the museum in Imphal, places such as Shangshak and Palel have also seen such initiatives, albeit on a smaller scale. This locally led process should be encouraged, and expertise should be provided to enhance the visitor's experience at these venues.

The INA Museum

A final point on museums relates to the only established and government-funded war museum in Manipur at the time of writing: the INA War Museum in Moirang. This museum has served Manipur well over the years by, at the very least, keeping alive the memory of its experience of the Second World War and by highlighting the role of the INA. But it can be so much more, and a dramatic improvement can be effected at the museum with minimal cost. Besides better labelling and lighting for the displays, the area most in need of attention is a general narrative on the INA and on the significance of the Battle of Imphal to the INA story.

Consider the former first. In its current form, the museum has no information panels that explain the fascinating history of the INA in the Second World War. The photos of Netaji Subhash Chandra Bose are useful, but their impact would be much more if they were chronologically displayed, with a concise supporting narrative on the actual INA, its structure and evolution during the war years. Perhaps most important, what the museum and any visitor would greatly benefit from is an emphasis on the link between the INA and the Battle of Imphal. For as we know, Imphal was a big moment for the INA, the start of their March to Delhi, with Manipur being the only place where the 1st INA Division was deployed. These points need to be highlighted in Moirang; they would also help differentiate this museum from the one dedicated to Bose in Calcutta (Kolkata). A collaboration in this regard could be sought with the Netaji Research Bureau in that city.

Markers

A third area of work should be the installation of site and road markers near and along some of the major battlefields and roads related to the Battle of Imphal. Presently there is no signage of any kind to indicate a place's link with the fighting in 1944 – barring a temporary hoarding put up below Red Hill by the Manipur Tourism Forum, which has since been replaced with a proper stone marker in May 2015. People currently visiting or passing by these locations may only have a vague idea of what had happened there during the Second World War. Such markers would serve as a concrete source of information and more generally raise awareness about the Battle of Imphal.

Some of the sites where markers or information panels could be installed are Red Hill (now done), Ningthoukhong and Torbung on the Tiddim Road; near Point 5846 and old Ngariyan village on the Silchar Track/Old Cachar Road; near Palel Airfield/Kakching Garrison, Saivom village, under Scraggy/Ito Hill and near Chamol on the Tamu–Palel Road; near old Kangla Airfield, Kameng, Litan, Shangshak and Ukhrul on the Ukhrul Road; Runaway Hill and near Nungshigum for the Iril River Valley, and a location near the hills of the Mapao-Molvom Range; and Imphal Main (Koirengei Airfield), Kanglatongbi, Motbung, Saparmeina, Milestone 109 and the bridge near Kangpokpi on the Imphal–Kohima Road. Similarly, road markers or information panels should be installed at certain points on all of the main roads ('spokes') leading to Imphal; these would note the fighting that had occurred on that respective road in 1944.

Regimental and other memorials

In addition, the different units and regiments of all sides that continue to exist could be approached for the installation of memorials at related sites. One could also explore the commissioning of sculptures to depict different aspects of the Battle of Imphal, for example, near Bishenpur or

Ningthoukhong for the village and paddy field fighting on the Imphal Valley; at Imphal Main (Koirengei Airfield) for the Air Battle of Imphal; near Chamol for the INA; and at the Shenam Saddle on the Tamu–Palel Road for the fighting in the hills. Another idea to consider is re-creating a battlefield of 1944, to give people a feel of what it was like during the Battle of Imphal.

Battlefield preservation

Before any effort at recreating sites however, urgent steps must be taken to at the very least secure, and eventually preserve, any trenches, bunkers, dugouts and other surviving reminders of the Second World War that continue to be discovered across Manipur to this day. These are sites of immeasurable value which help us understand and imagine the fighting and conditions during the Battle of Imphal as perhaps nothing else can. Unless preserved, they could very well disappear in the years to come or be wiped out in developmental works. As required, the assistance of an institution like the In Flanders Fields Museum in Ypres, Belgium, could be sought for suggestions on the preservation of trenches and bunkers.

Trekking routes

A fourth area of work should be to develop Battle of Imphal–themed trekking routes (two were started by Hemant Singh Katoch in 2014). Manipur has good trekking country, and these routes would incorporate some of the hills and ranges where the fighting took place in 1944. Any trekking would naturally be subject to security conditions along the proposed routes. The best-placed organisation to take the lead in developing these treks would be the Manipur Mountaineering and Trekking Association (MMTA), which has excellent contacts with all concerned and a proven track record over the years in the field.

In terms of possible trekking routes, some immediately come to mind. One which the MMTA already offers is from Lamdan northwards along the ridge of the western hills towards Point 5846 and past the old Silchar Track. This could eventually be extended to the old British positions of Mortar Bluff and Water Piquet once they are pinpointed. From Lamdan, the route could also head southwards towards the old location of the village of Mollou. Another route could include Runaway Hill and Nungshigum in the Iril River Valley sector; yet another could be from Recce Hill to Crete East/Ikkenya Hill via Scraggy/Ito Hill along the Tamu–Palel Road. Finally, one could be developed along the Mapao-Molvom Range, as could another encompassing the low-lying hills east of the

Imphal–Kohima Road from Kanglatongbi to Saparmeina. As noted earlier, since many of these are remote locations and off the beaten track, any trekking considered here should be subject to security conditions and, ideally, in collaboration with the MMTA.

Academic research

A fifth area of focus should be in the realm of academic research. Most available accounts of the Battle of Imphal are written by Western – mainly British – authors, several of whom were veterans. These naturally present their own viewpoints and version of events, a lot of which is well documented and archived in the United Kingdom. Thankfully, some military historians, such as Louis Allen, have also done extensive research of Japanese source materials. For the most part, however, one has little information about the Japanese version of events at Imphal. There seems to be little that has been translated and made available in English, especially referring to 1944. This is a gap that should sought to be filled, perhaps as a collaboration between Manipur University and a similar academic institution in Japan. Only then will we have a full picture of the Battle of Imphal.

On a related note, what is even less documented is Manipur's version of events. The only well-researched paper in English that takes an overall perspective of Manipur's experience of the Second World War is the one by Prof. N. Lokendra Singh mentioned earlier. Another useful resource is the paper by Jangkhomang Guite, although it is more narrowly focused on the Kuki community's role in the war. Parts of Nimaicharan Singh's memoirs are also wonderfully personal and revealing. But this is all woefully inadequate for a place that was completely transformed by its Second World War experience and whose people were involved in so many direct and indirect ways in the events of 1942–45. This chapter of Manipur's history deserves better, deeper treatment, and it is hoped that local academics will take up the challenge.

A regional approach to battlefield tourism

A sixth area of focus should be to take a regional approach to developing Second World War tourism. To begin with, this should comprise of a core circuit of Imphal–Kohima–Dimapur, the canvas against which the events of 1944 unfolded. This should then be extended to include Dibrugarh, Digboi and Ledo in Upper Assam, as well as Jairampur and the India–Burma (Myanmar) border at Arunachal Pradesh. Besides the Battles of Imphal and Kohima, such a North East-wide circuit would cover the

Stilwell Road (Ledo onwards), flying the Hump (airfields in the Dibru-garh area and Ledo), Second World War cemeteries (Commonwealth one at Digboi; Chinese one at Jairampur) and the North East Frontier Rail-way line (last abandoned stop at Lekhapani near Ledo). Guwahati, with its Commonwealth cemetery, could also be included.

A final addition for India could be Calcutta (now Kolkata), given that it was a major military transit camp for the Allies during the war and a rest and recuperation city for soldiers fighting at Imphal-Kohima and in Burma.

It should not end with India; indeed, it is with Burma that a wider Second World War tourism circuit must be sought to be established. For Imphal–Kohima is seen as the turning point of the Burma Campaign, and the history of North East India from 1942 to 1945 is intertwined with that of Burma. The trend of visiting Second World War–related sites in Burma either before or after a visit to Imphal and Kohima has already begun. This currently involves long detours, such as a transit in Bangkok.

As transport links between India and Burma intensify in future, includ-ing the much-awaited opening of the land border between Moreh and Tamu, it should become much easier to combine visits to the two coun-tries. To capitalise on this opportunity, an effort must begin to be made to establish cross-border contacts to offer a seamless tour of the Second World War sites. One should then be able to take in Imphal–Kohima, together with the Chindit sites at Indaw or Mandalay and Meiktila or Rakhine State (the Arakan) or Rangoon/Yangon. Only this will allow the interested to get a more complete picture of the Burma Campaign.

And so among other issues of bilateral concern, India – and Manipur at the state level – could work with Burma (Myanmar) to look at how to jointly develop a regional circuit of Second World War battlefield tour-ism. This is a new, niche sector for both countries, and they would do well to learn from each other. They could also look at how the Second World War affected their respective peoples; in India's context, the special focus could be on North East India.

Reaching out to the rest of the world

Finally, a focused effort could also be made to target all of those nations that have a Second World War connection with Manipur. For it was the Battle of Imphal and the Second World War that brought people from many foreign lands and different parts of India to Manipur for the first time. In a way it was also for the last time that the state saw such a diverse gathering of nationalities and people from around the world. After the end of the battle, and eventually of the Second World War in 1945,

Manipur went back to being a quiet part of the world, with few foreigners visiting Imphal and its environs.

It is worth briefly considering who was in Manipur during the war. There were, of course, the British, Japanese and Indian soldiers from other parts of the country at Imphal in 1944. There were then the hundreds of thousands of Allied soldiers who passed through Manipur both before and after the Battle of Imphal. Some of the different nationalities are mentioned here, mostly with a specific reference to the Battle of Imphal.

United States of America

American involvement in the Battle of Imphal was mainly through pilots of the United States Army Air Force. These men flew in and out of the airfields scattered around the Imphal Valley – bringing in reinforcements and evacuating casualties, among other things.

A lesser-known fact is that members of the American Field Service were active throughout the Battle of Imphal. Their ambulances were in operation on the front lines and they evacuated casualties from, among others, the Silchar Track, the Tamu–Palel Road, the Tiddim Road and around Imphal.

Canada

Canada's participation was in the form of dozens of pilots of the Royal Canadian Air Force who flew in the squadrons based in and around the Imphal Valley. These men transported reinforcements into the valley, flew reconnaissance missions into Burma and supported troops on the ground during the Battle of Imphal and Kohima. Canadian pilots were also actively involved in supporting the advance of the Fourteenth Army from Imphal into Burma in the latter half of 1944. Twelve Canadians are buried in the Imphal War Cemetery, including eleven members of the Royal Canadian Air Force and one soldier.

Australia and New Zealand

Like their Canadian counterparts, dozens of Australians and New Zealanders of the Royal Australian Air Force and the Royal New Zealand Air Force, respectively, took part in the Battle of Imphal. These men gave close support to the Fourteenth Army during the fighting on the ground, helped relieve the Siege of Imphal and bombed Japanese supply lines. Five members of the Royal Australian Air Force, two of the Royal New

Zealand Air Force and one of the New Zealand Infantry are buried in the Imphal War Cemetery.

East Africa

Men from then British-ruled Kenya, Uganda, Tanganyika (now Tanzania) and Nyasaland (now Malawi) were also in Manipur during the Second World War. They made up the 11th East African Division that came under 33 Corps in Imphal at the end of July 1944. While the 11th East African Division did not participate directly in the Battle of Imphal, it passed through Manipur and entered Burma through Tamu en route to the Kabaw Valley. It fought in the Kabaw Valley from August to December 1944 and reached as far as the Irrawaddy River.

Manipur is thus linked to perhaps one of the least-known, yet interesting, aspects of the war – that of the participation of Africans as part of the Allied forces in the Burma Campaign. Today there are some 40 African graves in the Imphal War Cemetery.

Southeast Asia

The Indian communities settled in South East Asia formed the bedrock of support for Netaji Subhash Chandra Bose and the INA. Besides providing material support, many Indians from South East Asian countries volunteered to fight for the INA. Although exact numbers are hard to find, some of them took part in the Battle of Imphal as part of the INA's 1st Division that was deployed off the Tamu–Palel Road.

Nepal

The Gurkhas played a major role in the Battle of Imphal as part of the Indian Army. Of the 49 or so infantry battalions who fought in Manipur, a third were Gurkha.

Pakistan and Bangladesh

While Pakistan and Bangladesh did not exist as independent countries in 1944, there is nevertheless a connection between both countries and the Battle of Imphal. This is because many of the soldiers who fought in Manipur as members of the then Indian Army subsequently found themselves to be citizens of Pakistan (in 1947) and of Bangladesh (in 1971). Interestingly, of the over 600 Muslim soldiers buried in the Imphal Indian

Army War Cemetery in Hatta, some 400 are from present-day Pakistan (the overwhelming majority) and from Bangladesh.

Chinese

At least 5,000 Chinese soldiers were said to be among the thousands of Allied soldiers that retreated into Manipur after the Japanese took over Burma in 1942.

The range of possibilities to explore with these nations in relation to the Battle of Imphal is endless. With Japan, the focus could be on academic partnerships to study the Japanese experience of 1944 and making this available in English, as well as encouraging visitors to Manipur. The latter, and increasing awareness about what some consider 'Britain's Greatest Battle', could be action points with the West.

With the Indian diaspora of South East Asia, especially Malaysia and Singapore, the emphasis could be on the INA. With East and West African countries, attention could be directed at bonds formed in the Fourteenth Army and the comradeship that came with fighting the Japanese during the Burma Campaign. For instance, there are some 40 graves of East African soldiers at the Imphal War Cemetery. As a small gesture of ensuring that they are not forgotten, perhaps India could consider sponsoring a visit to Imphal by military attachés of the embassies of the concerned countries in New Delhi, or similarly invite representatives of their defence ministries to come to Manipur to pay their respects. These are just some possible activities; there are many others that could be jointly conceived.

CONCLUSION

The 'greatest' battle

The word 'great' has been used to describe the clash between the Japanese Fifteenth Army and the British Fourteenth Army at Imphal in 1944. One historian has called Imphal 'one of the greatest Allied victories of the war'.[1] Some have described the battle as 'the greatest defeat on land ever suffered by the Japanese in the course of their history'.[2] Another has written that Imphal/Kohima was the 'greatest Japanese military disaster of all time'[3] and 'one of the four great turning-point battles in the Second World War'.[4] And then there is, of course, the naming of Imphal/Kohima as 'Britain's Greatest Battle' by the United Kingdom's National Army Museum in April 2013.

These are not entirely careless descriptions of the Battle of Imphal (or Imphal–Kohima together). For what happened in Manipur during the Second World War was no minor skirmish. Although it is hard to be too precise with numbers, more than 200,000 Britons, Japanese, Indians, Gurkhas and men of several other countries clashed in the hills and valley of this land on the India–Burma border from March to July 1944. They fought in some of the harshest conditions and terrain on earth, often in pouring rain and at heights of over 5,000 feet above sea level.

This book has deliberately sought to concentrate only on the Battle of Imphal and on Manipur's experience of the Second World War. For far too long have too many either not known enough about this battle or, more likely, been unaware about it ever having taken place. Far too little has been written about Imphal 1944, and even less so exclusively; the Manipur part of the story is for all practical purposes unknown. This needs to change. The battle well merits much greater awareness about it, both in India and abroad.

The relative lack of attention towards this encounter between the British Fourteenth Army and Japanese Fifteenth Army is a little surprising. For the overarching objective of the Japanese offensive of 1944, in the way it was both authorised and executed, was Imphal. While General Mutaguchi may have harboured personal ambitions to make a dash for Dimapur, it was to capture Imphal that the bulk of his Fifteenth Army, including two entire divisions and reinforcements, was committed. Kohima was to be secured to isolate Imphal and to prevent British-Indian reinforcements from reaching Manipur's capital by blocking the all-important Imphal–Kohima–Dimapur Road.

Here one would tend to agree with a concluding point from a 20th Indian Division intelligence summary of end-May 1944 about Japanese intentions and the importance they placed on Imphal's capture:

> The main objective of the enemy's offensive is Imphal. All other objectives, no matter how important, are secondary to the capture of Imphal, which besides its significance from the dual points of view of morale and propaganda, is essential to his future plans. The Jap has attained his secondary objectives of cutting the rd Imphal–Kohima and at least for a time, the track Silchar–Bishenpur. But it is not in the Jap character to be satisfied with secondary objectives. His main objective remains Imphal. Even if he can reach Imphal with a token force only, he will fight to the last to do so.[5]

For the British as well, it was at Imphal and the India–Burma border around Manipur where most of their troops had been concentrated, in the form of three infantry divisions. Consequently, it was around Imphal that most of the fighting took place, with Manipur serving as the main canvas against which the British Fourteenth and Japanese Fifteenth Armies clashed in 1944. The vast majority of the casualties suffered by both sides was also in the Battle of Imphal.

Perhaps the neglect of Imphal has to do with the messiness of the battle. Its course is not the easiest to explain or chart, and it lacks a dramatic fulcrum such as the Siege of Kohima or an iconic battlefield like the tennis court. As Slim described it, the fighting on the Imphal front in 1944 was as bitter as at Kohima but it was more – and this is the operative word – diffuse.[6] So while the Japanese 33rd Division and 17th Indian Division were fighting around Bishenpur, the Japanese 15th Division and the 5th Indian Division were clashing on the Imphal–Kohima Road, even as Yamamoto Force was trying to push past the British-Indian defences on the Shenam Saddle, and fighting continued off the Ukhrul Road and around the Iril River Valley. Thanks to Slim's hub and spoke analogy that one can make more sense of how the Battle of Imphal unfolded.

Maybe Imphal has been of less interest abroad, especially in the United Kingdom, because it had far less British involvement than at Kohima.

Indeed, the British 2nd Division had a limited role to play at Imphal, except in the opening of the Imphal–Kohima Road from the north on 22 June 1944. Thus, that division's units, including the Royal Scots, Camerons, Berkshires, Dorsets and Royal Welch Fusiliers, were absent from the main fighting in Manipur during the Battle of Imphal.

The fact remains, however, that Imphal was the great strategic prize for both sides on the India–Burma border in 1944. Geography dictated then, as it does today, that the easiest route between India and Burma lay through the Imphal Valley and whichever side controlled it controlled access between the two countries. Moreover, to the Japanese the 1st Chindit expedition in 1943 had shown that the mountainous frontier was not impossible to penetrate by a large military force – and so Imphal was within their reach from Burma. Any shortages of supplies could, in theory, be made up by capturing the supply depots that came to dot the Imphal Valley. What only enhanced Imphal's attractiveness and importance as a target was the network of six all- and fair-weather airfields that were constructed as the Second World War progressed.

And so a lot was at stake at Imphal in 1944. A Japanese capture of the town would have blocked the main land-based route from India into Burma for the Allies. This was the route through which the Fourteenth Army poured into the country after July that year, racing all the way down to Rangoon/Yangon by mid-1945. Japanese victory at Imphal would have ensured that the Imphal Valley and the Tamu–Palel Road would no longer have been available for this great dash through central and southern Burma for hundreds of thousands of Allied soldiers. The Burma Campaign may not have ended as rapidly and dramatically as it did had the Japanese taken Imphal.

Moreover, as long as the Japanese had Imphal, even their defeat at Kohima could not have prevented them from consolidating their hold over Manipur, the main entry/exit point to Burma. The captured depots could have supplied the Japanese, and control over airfields such as Imphal Main and Palel could only have served to strengthen their position. At the very least, after the months of hard fighting, the Japanese Fifteenth Army at Imphal would have found the space to regain its strength, address its supply situation and prepare itself for any Allied force that might have made its way down the Imphal–Kohima–Dimapur Road. The Japanese Fifteenth Army could also perhaps have planned a more aggressive thrust onwards into India, not just aimed at the railway line to Ledo that passed through Dimapur, but beyond.

A crucial variable that would have come into play in the event of a Japanese victory at Imphal would have been the INA. It had been, at best, a junior partner during Operation U Go, its strength about a tenth that of the Japanese Fifteenth Army in Manipur. But its true value and allure among the people of India would have been tested only after the Japanese had captured Imphal. For here would have been the opportunity for Netaji Subhash Chandra Bose to cross the India–Burma border and set foot on Indian soil after a defeat of the British. He would have had the perfect platform to address the Indian people from within India's borders – a powerful, symbolic action, of which word would have started to get around in the country, regardless of British efforts to prevent this.

More of the thousands of INA soldiers in Burma could then have been assembled at Imphal, including the women's Rani Jhansi Regiment. An offensive aimed at Assam and perhaps even Bengal could have been contemplated by the INA, with Bose at its helm. What such an operation might have achieved is hard to speculate about today. At the very least, the presence of an enigmatic leader like Bose leading an Indian army of liberation in India could have complicated matters for the British. It may have fired the imagination of the masses, especially in Bengal, and tested the loyalty of at least some Indians in the Indian Army, however fanciful some consider this today.

In the end, of course, none of this happened, and the Japanese suffered their largest defeat on land in their history in 1944. Some might argue that given overall Allied superiority in numbers, supplies, logistics and air support, this was a foregone outcome at Imphal. Be that as it may, it was certainly a close shave for the British, especially in the opening stages of the battle. Had the clash at Shangshak not happened and delayed the Japanese; had it not been possible to airlift the men of the 5th Indian Division from the Arakan and send them straight into battle at Imphal; had the British-Indian defences in any of the sectors, especially the Tiddim Road, given way to allow the Japanese to take 4 Corps headquarters – had any number of such things not gone the way of the British at Imphal, the results in 1944 may very well have been different. These will remain, of course, as some of the great 'what ifs' of history.

What is not in the realm of speculation is the impact of the Battle of Imphal and the Second World War on Manipur. In so many ways, it was a transformative experience for the place and its people. Whether socially, economically or politically, the Manipur that emerged at the end of 1945 was not the one that had existed prior to 1942. Like many such places around the world, its people had played no role in bringing about the Second World War nor were they much able to affect its outcome; and yet, it had changed them and their homeland forever.

Coming to the present, this fascinating historical narrative – at the local, national and international levels – is reflected today in Manipur's rich Second World War heritage. To start with, there are the battlefields.

The previous sections highlighted the sheer range of landscapes across Manipur that saw fighting in 1944. There were the villages and paddy fields of the Imphal Valley (Potsangbam, Ningthoukhong). Other villages, albeit up in the hills, were also battlefields (Shangshak). There were individual, stand-alone hills (Nungshigum/Hill 3833, Red Hill/Point 2926) and then there were mountain ranges that formed interconnected battlefields. Some of these were at an altitude of around 5,000 feet and had a major road running through them (Shenam Saddle), while others of similar height were far less accessible (Mapao-Molvom Range). Lower ranges along key roads were also fought over (between Kanglatongbi and Saparmeina), as were individual jungle pickets (Silchar Track). At times, the road itself was a battlefield (Torbung Roadblock, Imphal–Kohima Road).

As we have seen, many of the battlefields in the hills and valley survive to this day. Some of the old battlefields are remarkably unchanged after over seven decades, and trenches and bunkers dating back to the war continue to be discovered on a regular basis. There are the two Commonwealth War Graves Commission–maintained war cemeteries in Imphal, as well as a number of memorials linked to the British, Japanese, Indian and even local Manipuri participation in the war. More recent additions to this legacy are the private museums, with their displays of military artefacts and remnants of war.

Taken together, this is quite a considerable – and growing – collection of assets for Manipur, underpinned by what is surely one of the most interesting episodes of the Second World War. The challenge then is on how to make this heritage and historical narrative more relevant today and in the future. Chapter 5 on ideas for battlefield tourism addressed this question to some extent.

But there is a broader, final point to be made here than simply promoting battlefield tourism. The fact is that the Second World War in Manipur – centred on the Battle of Imphal in 1944 – is a shared historical experience. It uniquely connects this little-known place with many different parts of India and the world in a personal and emotional way. From 1942 to 1945, hundreds of thousands of people from around the world found themselves in Manipur. Many thousands died here, in a place far away from home, whose own residents had little say in the devastating events they and their land were witness to.

Looking to the future then, both Manipur at the state level and India more generally should look at this shared past to further and deepen their relations with the outside world. What is important is to chart a way forward in a spirit of drawing on the shared experience of the Battle of Imphal and the war as another pillar of collaboration among Manipur,

India and the rest of the world. There could perhaps be no more fitting a tribute to all those who were a part of this great chapter of the Second World War.

Notes

1 Peter Heehs, 'India's Divided Loyalties?', *History Today*, July 1995, 45(7): 16–23.
2 Geoffrey Evans and Antony Brett-James, *Imphal: A Flower on Lofty Heights*, London: Macmillan, 1962, p. xi.
3 Robert Lyman, *Japan's Last Bid for Victory*, Barnsley: Praetorian Press, 2011, p. 254.
4 Ibid., p. 262.
5 Intelligence Summary No. 6, May 1944, War Diary of 'G' Branch, H.Q. 20 Indian Division, File No. 601/250/WD/Part II-A, History Division, Ministry of Defence, New Delhi.
6 William J. Slim, *Defeat into Victory*, London: Cassels, 1956, p. 371.

APPENDIX

March 1944

7/8 March	Japanese 33rd Division attacks Tiddim and the road to Imphal
15 March	Japanese 15th and 31st Divisions begin crossing Chindwin River
18–29 March	Fly in of 5th Indian Division from Arakan to Imphal airfields
19–20 March	Point 7378 falls to the Japanese
22–26 March	Battle of Shangshak
24 March	General Orde Wingate dies in a plane crash
26 March	Japanese attack Litan
29/30 March	Honda Unit cuts the Imphal–Kohima Road

April 1944

1–16 April	Fight for Nippon Hill/Maejima on the Shenam Saddle
4–7 April	Battle of Kanglatongbi
4–6 April	Battle of Kameng
5 April	17th Indian Division arrives safely in the Imphal Valley
6 April	Action at Runaway Hill for which Abdul Hafiz is awarded a Victoria Cross
6–14 April	Battle of Nungshigum/Hill 3833
13–26 April	Fight for Point 5846, Wooded Hill/Mori and Wireless Hill/Antenna on the Silchar Track
14 April	INA flag hoisted at Moirang
14/15 April	Japanese blow up bridge on the Silchar Track
Mid-April	23rd Indian Division takes over from 5th Indian Division on the Ukhrul Road
16 April–9 May	Yamamoto Force captures positions on the Shenam Saddle, including Crete East/Ikkenya Hill and Crete West/Kawamichi Hill
29 April	Japanese move into Potsangbam on the Tiddim Road

May 1944

1–30 May	5th Indian Division attacks on the peaks of the Mapao-Molvom Range
2/3 May	INA attack on Palel Airfield
7 May	89th Brigade of 7th Indian Division flies into Imphal from the Arakan
10–11 May	Japanese attack and occupy part of Scraggy/Ito Hill
10–15 May	Fighting for the bridge at Potsangbam on the Tiddim Road
Mid-May	20th Indian Division and 23rd Indian Division switch places on the Ukhrul Road and Tamu–Palel Road
17–24 May	Battle of Torbung Roadblock
20–29 May	Battle of Red Hill/Point 2926 (Maibam–Lotpaching)
20–26 May	Japanese attack junction of the Silchar Track and Tiddim Road at Bishenpur
21 May	British retake Kanglatongbi
23–24 May	Battle for Gibraltar/Hill 5185 on the Shenam Saddle

June 1944

1–9 June	Fighting for Isaac and Harry on hills along Imphal–Kohima Road
3 June	20th Indian Division starts attacking east of the Iril River and along the Ukhrul Road
3 June	5th Indian Division intensifies offensive up the Imphal–Kohima Road
6–7 June	Japanese attacks on Potsangbam and Ningthoukhong Action at Ningthoukhong for which Hanson Victor Turner is awarded a Victoria Cross
9–10 June	Japanese take crest of Scraggy/Ito Hill on the Shenam Saddle
10 June	32nd Brigade's first attack on Dome south of the Silchar Track
12 June	Japanese attack on Ningthoukhong Action at Ningthoukhong for which Ganju Lama is awarded a Victoria Cross
13/14 June	32nd Brigade's second attack on Dome south of the Silchar Track
13–21 June	British-Indian units attack Liver along the Imphal–Kohima Road

21–26 June	Fighting rages for the picquets along the Silchar Track
22 June	British 2nd and 5th Indian Divisions meet at MS 109 on the Imphal–Kohima Road
26 June	Action at Mortar Bluff for which Netrabahadur Thapa is awarded a Victoria Cross
	Action at Mortar Bluff and Water Picquet for which Agan Singh Rai is awarded a Victoria Cross

July 1944

1–8 July	Battle of Ukhrul
3/4 July	Japanese destroy eight aircraft on Palel Airfield
16/17 July	Ningthoukhong Kha Khunou on the Tiddim Road cleared of Japanese forces
24 July	Assault begins to clear Japanese positions on the Shenam Saddle
31 July	33 Corps takes over from 4 Corps

BIBLIOGRAPHY

L. Achung Kom, Upper Kom Keirap, Manipur, January 2015. Personal interview.

Air Ministry and the Central Office of Information, *Wings of the Phoenix, The Official Story of the Air War in Burma*, London: His Majesty's Stationery Office, 1949.

Louis Allen, *Burma: The Longest War, 1941–45*, London: Phoenix Giant, 1984.

A. S. Arthur, Imphal, Manipur, November 2014. Personal interview.

Christopher Bayly and Tim Harper, *Forgotten Armies: Britain's Asian Empire and the War with Japan*, London: Penguin Books, 2005.

H. Bhuban Singh, *The Merger of Manipur*, Imphal: Pritam Haobam, 1988.

M. K. Binodini Devi, 'The Late Yengkhom Ongbi Hemabati', Imasi: The M.K. Binodini Devi Foundation, Imphal (original interview in Meiteilon transliterated by Pradip Phanjoubam).

Pukhrambam Birachandra, Ningthoukhong, Manipur, January 2015. Personal interview.

Antony Brett-James, *Ball of Fire: The Fifth Indian Division in the Second World War*, Aldershot: Gale & Polden, 1951.

Antony Brett-James and Geoffrey Evans, *Imphal: A Flower on Lofty Heights*, London: Macmillan, 1962.

Jagat S. Bright, Ed., *Important Speeches and Writings of Subhash Bose*, Lahore: The Indian Printing Works, p. 309.

Burma Operations Record: 15th Army Operations in Imphal Area and Withdrawal to Northern Burma, Headquarters, United States Army, Japan, Revised Edition, 1957.

Lal Dena, 'Indo-Japanese Soldiers in the Khuga Valley of Churachandpur', *Hueiyen Lanpao*, Imphal, 28 March 2014.

Peter Ward Fay, *The Forgotten Army*, Ann Arbor: University of Michigan Press, 1993.

Norman Franks, *The Air Battle of Imphal*, London: William Kimber, 1985.

Arthur F. Freer, *Nunshigum*, Durham: The Pentland Press, 1995.

Jangkhomang Guite, 'Representing Local Participation in INA-Japanese Imphal Campaign: The Case of the Kukis in Manipur, 1943–45', *Indian Historical Review*, 2010, 37(2): 291–301.

Peter Heehs, 'India's Divided Loyalties?', *History Today*, July 1995, 45(7): 16–23.

John Hudson, *Sunset in the East*, Barnsley: Pen and Sword, 2002.

I.N.A. Martyrs' Memorial, Department of Art and Culture, Government of Manipur, 2009.

Intelligence Summary I.6554, H.Q. 20 Indian Division, File No. 601/250/WD/Part II-A, Historical Division, Ministry of Defence, New Delhi.

Intelligence Summary No. 5, April 1944, H.Q. 20 Indian Division, File No. 601/250/ WD/Part II-A, Historical Division, Ministry of Defence, New Delhi.

Intelligence Summary No. 6, May 1944, H.Q. 20 Indian Division, File No. 601/250/ WD/Part II-A, Historical Division, Ministry of Defence, New Delhi.

Intelligence Summary No. 140, April 1944, H.Q. 5 Indian Division, File No. 601/221/ WD/Part IX-B, Historical Division, Ministry of Defence, New Delhi.

John Latimer, *Burma: The Forgotten War*, London: John Murray, 2004.

Letter to Dr N.L. Bor from C. Gimson, 23 February 1945, in Rehabilitation of the Dispossessed Population of Manipur State and Naga Hills, Assam, File No. Progs., Nos. 5(50)-P.A., 1951, National Archives of India, New Delhi.

N. Lokendra Singh, *Manipur during World War II (1941–45): Socio-Economic Change and Local Responses*, Imphal: Manipur State Archives, 1993.

N. Luikham, *Transformed Headhunters: The Pioneers of Tangkhul Education*, Ukhrul: El Shaddai Resource Centre, 2011.

N. Luikham, Ukhrul, Manipur, November 2014. Personal interview.

Ian Lyall Grant, *Burma: The Turning Point*, Chichester: Zampi Press, 1992.

E.F. Lydall, *Administration Report for the Manipur State for the Year 1943–44*, Imphal: State Printing Press, 1945, Manipur State Archives, Imphal.

Robert Lyman, *Japan's Last Bid for Victory*, Barnsley: Praetorian Press, 2011.

Ningthoukhongjam Moirangningthou, Keibi, Manipur, February 2015. Personal interview.

Terence R. Molloy, *The Silchar Track*, Ely: Melrose Books, 2006.

Khuraijam Nimaicharan Singh, *The Second World War in Manipur and My Childhood*, Imphal: Kh. Ratankumar Singh, 2012.

John Nunnely and Kazuo Tamayama, *Tales by Japanese Soldiers*, London: Cassell & Co, 2000.

John Parratt, *Wounded Land*, New Delhi: Mittal Publications, 2005.

F.F. Pearson, *Administration Report for the Manipur State for the Year 1944–45*, Imphal: State Printing Press, 1946, Manipur State Archives, Imphal.

Bisheshwar Prasad, Ed., *Official History of the Indian Armed Forces in the Second World War 1939–45: The Reconquest of Burma, Volumes I and II*, New Delhi: Pentagon Press, 2014.

Question in Parliament by Shri Sidhva Regarding Arms and Ammunition Left Over by the Allied Armies in Manipur Hills after the Termination of World War II and the Steps Taken to Recover Unlicensed Arms and Ammunition in the State, File No. Progs., Nos. 5(50)-P.A., 1951, National Archives of India, New Delhi.

David Rooney, *Burma Victory*, London: Arms and Armour Press, 1995.

Abid Hasan Safrani, *The Men from Imphal*, Calcutta: Netaji Research Bureau, 1971.

Harry Seaman, *The Battle at Sangshak*, London: Leo Cooper, 1989.

70th Anniversary: The Battle of Kanglatongbi, Directorate General of Ordnance Services – Indian Army, New Delhi, 2014.

Y. Shyam Singh, 'Japan Laan and the People of Tulihal', *Poknapham*, Imphal, 15 October 2014 (translated from original Meiteilon edition by Yaiphaba Kangjam).

Asem Tomchou Singh, Maibam Chingmang, Manipur, January 2015. Personal interview.

Sitrep I.6803, May 1944, H.Q. 20 Indian Division, File No. 601/250/WD/Part II-A, Historical Division, Ministry of Defence, New Delhi.

Sitrep I.7119, May 1944, H.Q. 20 Indian Division, File No. 601/250/WD/Part II-A, Historical Division, Ministry of Defence, New Delhi.

Sitrep I.7864, May 1944, H.Q. 20 Indian Division, File No. 601/250/WD/Part II-A, Historical Division, Ministry of Defence, New Delhi.

William J. Slim, *Defeat into Victory*, London: Cassels, 1956.

Special Sitrep, I.8672, May 1944, H.Q. 20 Indian Division, File No. 601/250/WD/ Part II-A, Historical Division, Ministry of Defence, New Delhi.

Julian Thompson, *Forgotten Voices of Burma*, London: Ebury Press, 2009.

Hugh Toye, *Subhash Chandra Bose: The Springing Tiger*, Mumbai: Jaico Publishing House, 1991.

Shankazip Varu, Shangshak, Manipur, January 2014. Personal interview.

War Diary, 1/7 Gurkha Rifles, May 1944, File No. 601/330/WD/Vol. III, Historical Division, Ministry of Defence, New Delhi.

War Diary, 2nd Battalion, The Suffolk Regiment, June 1944, File No. 601/5244/WD, Historical Division, Ministry of Defence, New Delhi.

War Diary, 3rd Battalion, 9th Jat Regiment, June 1944, File No. 601/5390/WD/Part II, Historical Division, Ministry of Defence, New Delhi.

War Diary, 2/5 Royal Gurkha Rifles, June 1944, File No. 601/5771/WD, Historical Division, Ministry of Defence, New Delhi.

War Diary, 3/3 Gurkha Rifles, June 1944, File No. 601/5779/WD/Part I, Historical Division, Ministry of Defence, New Delhi.

War Diary, 3/10 Gurkha Rifles, May 1944, File No. 601/5785/WD/Part II, Historical Division, Ministry of Defence, New Delhi.

War Diary, HQ 9 Indian Infantry Brigade, May 1944, File No. 601/305/WD/Part IV, Historical Division, Ministry of Defence, New Delhi.

War Diary, 32 Indian Infantry Brigade, April 1944, File No. 601/323/WD/Part II, Historical Division, Ministry of Defence, New Delhi.

War Diary, H.Q. 48 Indian Light Brigade, May 1944, File No. 601/330/WD/Vol. III, Historical Division, Ministry of Defence, New Delhi.

INDEX

Anglo-Manipuri War 12–13, 61
Assam 5–7, 14–15, 40, 44, 48, 53–4, 58,
    70, 83, 102, 139, 142, 144–5,
    157, 162, 170
Assam Rifles 14, 17, 35, 43, 98,
    103–4, 125

battlefields 57–152
  Imphal 57–60
  The Imphal–Kohima Road 139–52
  The Iril River Valley and the
    Mapao-Molvom Range
    129–39
  The Silchar–Bishenpur Track 82–95
  The Tamu–Palel Road and the
    Shenam Saddle 95–113
  The Tiddim Road 61–82
  The Ukhrul Road and Shangshak
    113–28
battlefield tourism 3, 157–66, 171
  academic research 162
  Australia 164–5
  Bangladesh 165–6
  Canada 164
  Chinese 166
  commemorations of 158
  East Africa 165
  INA museum 159–60
  Nepal/Gurkhas 165
  New Zealand 164–5
  Pakistan 165–6
  preservation 161
  regimental and memorials 160–1
  regional approach to 162–3
  site and road markers 160

South East Asia 165
  trekking routes 161–2
  United States of America 164
  war museum(s) 158–9
Bishenpur 23, 29, 38–40, 63–4, 66–8,
    70–1, 73, 78, 80, 82–5, 87,
    89–91, 93–4, 160, 168
Bose, Netaji Subhash Chandra 9–10, 34,
    36, 80–1, 100, 110–11
Briggs, Major General Harold 50, 129–30
Britain's Greatest Battle 55, 158, 166–7
British Fourteenth Army 2–3, 50–5,
    57–8, 122, 144, 164, 166–70
British-Indian Formations and Units
  4 Corps 8, 15, 20, 50, 53–4, 58, 62, 83,
    99, 115, 123, 129, 136, 138–9,
    141–2, 170
  5th Indian Division 36, 50, 54, 115,
    119–20, 123, 129, 130, 135–6,
    140, 144, 146–51, 168, 170
  9th Brigade 136, 140, 146–7,
    149–50, 155
  2nd West Yorkshire Regiment 51,
    147, 150
  3/9th Jat Regiment 131, 136,
    149–50
  3/14th Punjab Regiment
    133–4, 150
  123rd Brigade 119–20, 130, 140,
    147, 149, 155
  1/17th Dogra Regiment 119,
    136–8, 151
  2nd Suffolk Regiment 51,
    119, 149
  2/1st Punjab Regiment 120, 151

179

7th Indian Division 50, 54, 130, 140,
147, 155
89th Brigade 130, 140, 147, 155
1/11th Sikh Regiment 134
17th Indian Division 23, 50–1, 54,
61–2, 67, 70, 72, 78, 83, 87, 104,
140, 146, 168
48th Brigade 78, 80
1/7th Gurkha Rifles 75, 78–9
2/5th Royal Gurkha Rifles 74, 76,
78, 93
63rd Brigade 72, 78, 80, 140, 146
1/3rd Gurkha Rifles 72
1/4th Gurkha Rifles 68
1/10th Gurkha Rifles 72
others
1st West Yorkshire Regiment 74
7/10th Baluch Regiment 67–8
20th Indian Division 33, 38–9, 50, 54,
62, 68, 70, 83, 95, 104–5, 108,
115–6, 168
32nd Brigade 62, 68, 70–1, 78, 83,
87–9, 95, 104
1st Northamptonshire Regiment
51, 87–91, 93
3/8th Gurkha Rifles 87–9
9/14th Punjab Regiment 71
80th Brigade 104, 155
1st Devonshire Regiment 104
3/1st Gurkha Rifles 68, 105
9/12th Frontier Force
Regiment 68
100th Brigade 104
2nd Border Regiment 104
4/10th Gurkha Rifles 104
23rd Indian Division 50, 62, 95,
105–6, 115, 120, 122
37th Brigade 106
3/3rd Gurkha Rifles 106
3/5th Gurkha Rifles 106, 109
3/10th Gurkha Rifles 106–9
49th Brigade 115, 122
4/5th Mahratta Light Infantry
122
5/6th Rajputana Rifles 108–9
6/5th Mahratta Light Infantry 68
others
1st Assam Regiment 33, 114
50th Indian Parachute Brigade 50,
115, 119–20, 122–3, 125

152nd Indian Parachute Battalion
122–3
153rd Gurkha Parachute Battalion
122, 124
254th Indian Tank Brigade 51
3rd Carabiniers 51, 68, 72, 119,
137–8, 149
7th Light Cavalry 51, 68
Chindits 8, 50, 115
Operation Longcloth 8–10
Operation Thursday 65
Royal Air Force 52, 97, 124, 126,
135, 140, 143, 163–4
V Force 17, 27, 32–3, 35, 50
Burma Campaign 2, 49, 55, 117, 135,
151, 163, 165–6, 169
Burma Road 4–6
Burton, Brigadier Guy 72

Cameron, Brigadier Ronnie 78
Chindwin River 4–5, 13, 15, 50, 54–5,
62, 138, 144
Churachandpur 26, 64, 76
Cowan, Major General D.T. 'Punch' 50,
61, 67, 72
Crete East/Ikkenya Hill 102, 105, 161
Crete West/Kawamichi Hill 102–3, 105

Dimapur 6–7, 10, 14, 83, 129, 139, 168–9
Dome 87–8, 92

Finch's Corner 120, 123, 126

Gibraltar/Hill 5185 101–3, 105,
108–9, 112
Gracey, Major General Douglas 50, 95

Hafiz (VC), Jemadar Abdul 131
Hope-Thompson, Brigadier M. 122
Hump 129, 133–4, 136, 139
Hump, Flying the 6, 54, 163

Imphal 14–18
attack 13, 129
1944, battle 53–5
and Kohima, battles of 2, 8, 114, 162, 164
post-battle of 39–42, 82
siege of 54, 99, 139–40, 152, 164
see also Manipur
Imphal Indian Army War Cemetery 58

Imphal–Kohima Road 3, 12–13, 40, 57, 83, 114–15, 123, 129–30, 139–52, 160, 162, 168–9, 171
Imphal Main/Koirengei Airfield 13, 54, 58, 65, 98–9, 136, 139, 141–5, 160–1, 169
Imphal Valley 7–8, 12–13, 54, 61–4, 72–3, 87–8, 95–7, 99, 112–13, 116, 130, 141–2, 164, 169
Imphal War Cemetery 58, 74, 131, 145, 164–6
Indian National Army (INA) 1, 9–10, 34–6, 39, 42, 52–3, 80–3, 96, 99–100, 109–10, 115, 127, 159–61, 165–6, 169–70
Memorial Complex 80–1
museum 159–60
Indian National Army (INA) Formations and Units
1st Division 52, 80, 96, 99, 109–10, 115, 160, 165
Azad Brigade 52, 96, 110
Gandhi Brigade 52, 96, 99, 109–10
Subhash Brigade 52, 115
Special Groups 52, 80–1
India Peace Memorial 65, 69
Japanese war memorial 65, 69
Iril River Valley 29, 40, 89, 114, 129–39, 144, 160–1, 168

Japanese Fifteenth Army 2–3, 9–10, 42, 48–50, 52–3, 55, 58, 104, 122, 134, 167–70
Japanese Formations and Units
15th Division 25, 48, 53, 95, 114–15, 119–20, 122–3, 127, 129, 131, 135–7, 139, 146–7, 152
51st Regiment 115, 129
60th Regiment 114, 122–3, 131, 139–40, 147
Honda Raiding Unit 114, 139, 152
31st Division 33, 36, 53, 114, 122–3, 126–8
58th Regiment 114, 122–4, 128
33rd Division 25, 48, 53, 55, 61–3, 67, 70, 74, 76, 78, 81, 83–4, 87, 93, 95, 168
213th Regiment 62, 83
214th Regiment 62, 67, 70, 83, 87–8, 94

215th Regiment 62, 83, 87
Yamamoto Force 48, 53, 95–6, 104–6, 110, 168
others
67th Regiment 62, 74, 83, 114, 119, 152
151st Regiment 62, 83
154th Regiment 62, 83
Japanese Army Air Force 48, 54, 57, 70
Jessami 33, 114

Kameng 119–20, 160
Kangla Airfield 20, 29, 54, 117–9, 136, 142, 160
Kanglatongbi 57, 140, 146–9, 160, 162, 171
Kangpokpi 24, 40, 114, 139, 141, 151–2, 160
Khan, Colonel Shah Nawaz 99, 115, 127
Kharasom 17, 33, 114
Khathing, Captain (later Major) Ralengnao (Bob) 32–3
Kiani, Colonel Mohammad Zaman 109
Kiani, Lieutenant Colonel Inayat Jan 99–100
Kukis 8, 32, 34–7, 39
Japan gal la 37–8

Lama (VC), Rifleman Ganju 75, 79
Ledo 6, 10, 162–3, 169
Litan 116, 119–20, 123, 160
Liver 150
Loktak Lake 7, 24, 63–4, 70, 78, 80–1, 86, 88, 97

Mackenzie, Brigadier D.A.L. 78, 83
Maibam Lotpaching 57, 65–6, 69
village 67–8
Malik, Colonel S.A. 81
Malta/Yajima Hill 101–3, 105–6, 108–9, 113
Manipur 7–8
aerial bombing of 14–15
forward supply base 15–18
impact of the Second World War 42–5
voices on the Second World War 18–31
warring sides, local support 31–7

Manipur Mountaineering and Trekking
    Association (MMTA) 85, 161–2
Mapao-Molvom Range 114–15,
    129–39, 146, 160–1, 171
Matsumura, Colonel 114, 139
Meiteis 7–8, 34
Milestone 109 140–1, 147–9, 151, 160
Miyazaki, Major General 122, 125
Moirang 23, 28, 30, 34, 38–40, 63, 80–2,
    96, 159–60
Mortar Bluff 93–4, 139, 161
Motbung 147, 149, 160

Naga Hills 6–7, 44, 48, 53, 58, 81, 139
Nagas 8, 32, 34–5, 45
Tangkhul 25, 34, 41
Ningthoukhong 12, 23–4, 30, 63, 71–6,
    79, 85, 93–4, 139, 160–1, 171
Ningthoukhong Kha Khunou 76
Nippon Hill/Maejima Hill 102–6,
    108, 111
Nungshigum/Hill 3833 29, 57, 82, 89,
    117, 119, 129–31, 135–9
    military honours 138, 160–1

Omoto, Colonel 115, 136

Palel Airfield 98–100, 110, 142, 160
Point 5846 73, 82–95
Potsangbam 57, 63–4, 71–3, 76, 78, 171

Rai (VC), Naik Agan Singh 94
Recce Hill 102–3, 105, 112–13, 161
Red Hill/Point 2926 30–1, 57, 65–8,
    70, 81, 87, 160, 171
Renya, General Mutaguchi 8–10, 48,
    50, 53, 55, 167
Roberts, Major General Ouvry 50, 95
Runaway Hill 130–2, 135, 138, 160

Sakuma, Colonel 62, 83
Sapam Airfield 54, 97–8, 117
Saparmeina 12, 140, 148, 150, 160,
    162, 171
Sasahara, Colonel 62, 83
Sato, Lieutenant General Kotuku 48, 114
Scoones, Lieutenant General Geoffrey
    50, 58, 145
Scraggy/Ito Hill 102, 103, 105–9, 111,
    160–1

Sekmai 24, 115, 140, 146–7
Shangshak 12, 24, 82, 113–28, 117,
    119–23, 125, 128, 159–60, 170–1
Shenam Saddle 95–113, 135, 138–9,
    161, 168, 171
Silchar 7, 14, 70, 84, 142–3
Silchar–Bishenpur Track (Silchar Track)
    12–13, 16, 25, 63, 70, 76, 82–95,
    152, 161, 164, 171
Singh, Maharaja Bodhchandra 13, 17,
    31–2
Singh, Maharaja Churachand 17, 31
Slim, Lieutenant General (later Field
    Marshal) William J. 50–1, 54,
    57–8, 61, 145, 168

Tamu–Palel road 25, 95–113
    see also Shenam Saddle
Tanaka, Lieutenant General 48, 61
Tengnoupal 12, 96, 103–4, 109
Thapa (VC), Subadar Netrabahadur
    93, 94
Tiddim Road 3, 16, 17, 20, 23, 25, 30,
    40, 61–85, 87, 90, 93, 95–7, 122,
    138–9
Torbung Roadblock 64, 78–9, 171
Tulihal Airfield 7, 20–1, 54, 64–5, 142
Turner (VC), Sergeant Hanson
    Victor 74
Twin Peaks 129, 134, 136

Ukhrul 14, 16–17, 25, 34–5, 38, 40–1,
    44, 51, 53, 113–17, 120, 122–3,
    126–8, 130, 160
Ukhrul Road 20, 24, 40, 113–29, 131,
    139, 144, 160, 168

Wangjing Airfield 54, 97–8, 117
Water Picquet 93–4, 139, 161
Wingate, Major General Orde 5, 8–9,
    97, 145
Wireless Hill/Antenna 85, 87–9, 92
Wooded Ridge/Mori 85, 88–9, 92
Woods, Brigadier (formerly Lieutenant
    Colonel) E.J. 68, 138

Yamamoto, Major General 48, 55, 95
Yamauchi, Lieutenant General 48,
    114, 129
Yanagida, Lieutenant General 48, 61